Controversies in Contextual Theology Series

Controversies in Body Theology

Edited by

Marcella Maria Althaus-Reid
and
Lisa Isherwood

scm press

© Marcella Maria Althaus-Reid and Lisa Isherwood 2008

The Editors have asserted their right under the Copyright, Designs and
Patents Act, 1988, to be identified as the Editors of this Work

British Library Cataloguing in Publication data

A catalogue record for this book is available
from the British Library

978 0 334 04157 3

First published in 2008 by SCM Press
13–17 Long Lane,
London EC1A 9PN

www.scm-canterburypress.co.uk

SCM Press is a division of
SCM-Canterbury Press Ltd

Typeset by Regent Typesetting, London
Printed and bound in Great Britain by
William Clowes Ltd, Beccles, Suffolk

Contents

Controversies in Contextual Theology

Contextual theologies such as Liberation, Black or Feminist theologies have been the object of critical studies in the past. Such critiques, especially when mounted by western academics, have tended to adopt an essentialist approach to these distinct theologies, assuming homogeneity in their development. In reality, on closer inspection, they display profound differences of both content and method. Controversies in Contextual Theology is the first series to highlight and examine these divisions. Each volume brings together protagonists from within one form of contextual theology. The issues which divide them are openly addressed. Arguments are developed and positions clarified, but there is no guarantee that reconciliation can be achieved.

Marcella Althaus-Reid
Lisa Isherwood
Series editors

List of Contributors

Marcella Althaus-Reid is Professor in Contextual Theology at the University of Edinburgh, Scotland, UK.

Elizabeth Baxter is Director of the Holy Rood House Centre for Health and Pastoral Care in Yorkshire, UK.

Inga Bryden is Associate Dean in the Faculty of Arts Research at the University of Winchester, UK.

Beverley Clack is a Reader in Philosophy of Religion at Oxford Brookes University, Oxford, UK.

Lisa Isherwood is Professor of Feminist Liberation Theologies and Director of Theology and Religious Studies at the University of Winchester, UK.

Martin Hugo Córdova Quero, originally from Argentina, now serves in ministry in Hawaii. He studied at the ISEDET School of Theology in Buenos Aires before pursuing additional graduate studies at the Church Divinity School of the Pacific in Berkeley, California.

Paul Reid-Bowen is a Lecturer in Study of Religions at Bath Spa University, Bath, UK.

Victoria Rollins is freelance scholar.

Janet Wootton is Director of Studies for the Congregational Federation in the United Kingdom, Nottingham, UK.

Introduction

Slicing Women's Bodies:
Christianity and the Cut, Mutilated and
Cosmetically Altered Believers

MARCELLA ALTHAUS-REID AND
LISA ISHERWOOD

'Slicing Women's Bodies . . .' Recent press reports state that in June 2007 a 44-year-old woman from Norfolk, UK, committed suicide by lying down in front of a train because she feared her wrinkles . . .[1] During the last economic crisis, which literally sent thousands of people to live in the streets, paradoxically, Argentina suffered a shortage of silicone used for breast implants due to the popularity of the procedure . . .[2] A 21-year-old anorexic Brazilian model died weighing only 88 pounds . . .[3]

We have been asked why we would choose a title (and a theme) for this book that may sound aggressive and destructive towards women. And we have chosen this title and this theme to create a reflective body theology in order to value and love women's bodies: the cut, mutilated, battered, drugged and cosmetically altered bodies of women are a reality and Christianity has never been neutral in this carnage. The fact is that the slicing of women's bodies has been both a violent hermeneutical clue but also a pervading theological praxis with direct consequences for women's bodies and lives.

---

1 'Woman Commits Suicide after becoming Depressed with her Wrinkles', *The Daily Mail*, 8/6/07.

2 'Depressed Argentines put their Faith in a Pretty Face', *The Guardian*, 6/9/02.

3 'Brazil Model who Battled Anorexia Dies', *The Washington Post*, 16/11/06.

What we have witnessed and experienced is a Christian culture that does indeed continue to slice the bodies of women through acts of theological dismemberment that begin with the fundamental split of mind from body that is the insidious and deadly weapon of dualism which sustains patriarchal ideologies. These acts have been repeated over generations and so have in a sense disappeared under the radar of the construction of the normal. They have raised very little interest in theological reflections except from moral responses: either there is nothing that can be done because everything is natural or more worryingly there is an acknowledgement that things could be different but the moral weakness of the individual prevents change from occurring. As liberation theologians we no longer accept either the responsibility of the victims for their own sufferings or the naturalization of violence against women's bodies in a world where theological ideologies still influence social perceptions. Instead, we prefer to ask questions about structures of religious violence, the construction of women's bodies and their implications in the everyday lives of women.

We are all by now familiar with the debates about how even the construction of sexuality places women on the back foot, and the arena is opening for a more profound understanding and questioning of gender. We have even come as far as seeing that the way in which we are all forced into a very narrow performance of one gender is indeed a fundamental way of slicing women physically and spiritually since it literally cuts us off from a more abundant life. The fundamental rupture that occurs with the words 'It's a girl' has implications far beyond those simple words. It sets in place a performance. She will become a girl by being moulded into a feminine gender performance and if she learns well will take over the internal lack of permission that is required in order that the moulding, shaping and slicing is kept as a reality that affects her whole life for all of her life. If she does not learn well she will be reminded at every turn through comments about her body, her appearance and ultimately her femininity and following from that her moral standing. This in turn will affect her access to her location in the society in which she lives and will, despite rhetoric to the contrary, limit the life she is able to choose with dignity to live. Sex and gender then are foundation cuts/slices in the human psyche which under patriarchy slice deeper into the flesh of women than they do at present into the flesh of men.

This book aims to expose some of the hidden and taken for granted ways in which women are sliced in our society and in so doing asks what forms of action we are called to engage in. It will become obvious that the ways in which women slice their own bodies are often more nuanced than at first we appreciate and that no single and uniform response to these actions can do justice to the depth of feeling and awareness that the actions themselves signify. We will be reminded throughout that religion and theology are no innocent bystanders in this moulding of women and so we are asked to ponder on whether either has enough resources to even appreciate the issues, let alone offer creative and abundant counter realities.

Body theology has challenged traditional theology to look again at the way in which the human person is understood and to overcome the dualism that carries within it a large dose of negativity about the way in which we express our humanness through our flesh. This book continues the challenge and indeed challenges body theology itself to deal with some of the harsher realities of the body and the way in which it manifests and reacts in the world and most importantly to the world. We are not suggesting that body theology has never dealt with matters of abuse and the way in which women are turned against their own flesh but we do believe that in this book we have uncovered some of the deeper and more disturbing questions for this new discourse. Through it all we wish to keep faith with the flesh because even when it is getting sliced or slicing itself we believe that profound truths are being revealed about what it is to be human, the pain and the pleasure of this divine/human reality in which we all dance and at times scream our becoming.

The issues covered

This book highlights some controversial issues concerning the cuttings and bruising of women's bodies and many of these questions have not been raised in any sustained theological enquiry before – we have then hardly had time to develop controversies.

Beverley Clack takes us on a challenging journey with the Marquis de Sade and his portrayal of the murder of mothers. Of course he is not alone in this ambivalence to the maternal and Clack suggests that what he highlights so graphically is indeed a reality of the world in which we live – a reality that affects all women but is so deeply embedded that it seems almost to be a myth. The horror of the vagina, that hole that gave us life and can also consume, is played out through a libertine desire to control and to kill unruly nature through the death of the mother. Clack asks us to consider whether the world of de Sade is indeed so alien to us; it is a world in which the maternal and nature are feared, controlled and destroyed, and if we only look around what is it we see?

Inga Bryden presents the reader with questions about the penetration of the skin and the way in which this problematizes the borders between inside and outside. She observes that men cut open the bodies of women to substitute for self-knowledge and that under this scheme purification is through reduction; when there is nothing left to take away we have the perfect female. Bryden puts before us the reality of women as freaks in culture and reminds us that we are all sliced in this way under patriarchy.

Elizabeth Baxter reminds us that our scars are our stories since our bodies are the maps on which we make our meaning. She has found in her work with young women who self-harm that what is carved into their bodies is nothing short of an image of society in a world that denies them power in their lives, and they need to have witnesses to this pain if they are to find the internal power to reconnect and move ahead.

Marcella Althaus-Reid makes a hermeneutic out of mutilation and restoration since these are ways in which we are able to overcome the narrow boundaries of the self and society. She reminds us that from the beginning Christianity has had within its ranks those who change their identity once they become Christian, who are seemingly required to undergo extreme body restoration. However, as there is no original to be restored to then the outcomes are revolutionary. She reminds us too that sexual identities can only ever be grounded on earthquakes.

Martín Hugo Córdova Quero takes us on an incarnational journey accompanied by those in transgender and intersex bodies – what, he asks, does this do to the notion of incarnation? Incarnation, he says, is a cosmic event that embraces multiplicity rather than serves hetero-patriarchy, and for this reason he has questions about the way in which medicine deals with intersex and transgender people. Where is the multiplicity of incarnation if they have operations that in a sense restore the status quo of gender division and neat categories?

Victoria Rollins boldly asserts that the abuse of women is akin in magnitude and psychological motivation to that of the Holocaust against the Jews. This is a bold assertion and although the mass genocide of the Jews was an event that has no parallels in history, Rollins wishes us to realize and remember that there are structures of violence and motivating factors behind the Holocaust that do exist today taking place in many violent homes. The Holocaust event functions here as a hermeneutical clue to understand the historical epidemic proportion of domestic crimes against women worldwide and the frequent silence of the churches.

Janet Wootton reminds us that the slicing of women has biblical prece-dent and indeed there may be links between the way in which women are treated in the contemporary world and the way in which we have received our founding stories. Wootton takes us on a biblical journey that is disturbing and is one that has been sanitized through hermeneutics over the centuries. It is time we saw it for how it is, as this too will be another way to see more clearly and then to be able to act more directly in relation to the horrors that we take for granted.

Lisa Isherwood expresses her disquiet at the Protestant 'Slim for Him' programmes that are making billions of dollars at the same time as making fat women feel unworthy and sinful. She attacks the advanced capitalist agenda that lurks behind a racist and misogynist programme, and she offers women an alternative way to live abundantly in their skins.

Paul Reid-Bowen is concerned with the world of women body-builders and the way in which, even in the world of the strong, women need to be feminized and made safe. He does acknowledge that all this slicing and shaping raises many questions for feminist thinkers, but he wonders if the world may need these strong and powerful women if they could only shake off the regulation of their flesh that occurs in the competitive world of the bodybuilders.

This volume highlights some of the important current themes in the discussion of a body theology pertinent for the twenty-first century. It is our hope that with this book, a new dialogue will be developed on some of the hard issues of women's bodies, the theological, political and social implications of which we are just starting to unravel.

1

Slicing Mothers: Violence and the Maternal in the Marquis de Sade

BEVERLEY CLACK

Introduction

I decree that into my pretty Mama's body will be driven a thousand
wicks coated in pure sulphur; I shall personally set them alight, one by
one.

(Sade, [1795] 1995, p. 150)

The writings of Donatien-Alfonse-François, the Marquis de Sade (1740–
1814) usher the reader into a terrifying universe of unbridled sexuality
and violence. At turns titillating and sickening, his is a complex canon
that defies any easy categorization. One aspect of his writings stands out
as particularly disturbing: in a world where ultimate sexual pleasure is
derived from destruction of the Other, Sade glories in describing the
suffering of mothers, often at the hands of their own children. My intention is to offer one possible reading of this disturbing feature of Sade's
universe: a reading that seeks less to isolate him from the broader swathe
of humanity, and more to explore the possible connections between his
experience and ours. Through applying psychoanalytic theory to his
description of the torture and murder of mothers, an exploration is made
possible not just of the forces that shape the peculiarities of sadistic
personalities, but, moreover, of the connections between the early psychic experiences of such individuals and those of the broader majority.
Read psychoanalytically, Sade's stories offer the reader entrance into the
repressed desires of the child's earliest years. In particular, his stories

7

suggest something of the ambivalence surrounding the figure of the mother in the developing psyche of the child: an ambivalence which may, in turn, suggest something of the deep-rooted fears that inform negative attitudes to the female and all that she seems to represent.

The Sadeian universe

At the outset, it is worth setting the scene for the violent treatment meted out to mothers in Sade's literary universe. Sade's world is one of stark brutality, where pleasure is invariably linked with sexual acts that almost always involve some kind of violence, often death. His 'libertines' are committed to an ideal of total freedom, and they pursue their desires to the extreme, regardless of the number of victims left in their wake. An inevitable escalation of violence occurs in Sade's writings, and each of the major novels culminates in some hideous scenario of death.[1]

Placing Sade's novels within a specific genre is fraught with difficulties, for a simple description of them as 'pornographic' fails to engage sufficiently with the variety of writing that they contain. Alongside the graphic description of sexual acts and the mind-numbing violence, there are long debates, running to tens of pages, concerning points of theology and morality that seem at odds with any straightforward designation of Sade as a pornographer, or, to use Andrea Dworkin's evocative phrase, as 'the consummate literary snuff artist' (Dworkin, 1981, p. 92). While the works written in prison can be read as the masturbatory fantasies of a lonely man, Sade, at least overtly, viewed his enterprise rather differently. He saw himself as a philosopher whose works provided a dramatic rendition of that philosophy (Airaksinen, 1995, pp. 5–6). And perhaps these views are not at odds, for, as Robert Stoller has suggested, pornography may provide 'a special tool' (Stoller, [1975] 1986, p. 83) through which one can explore the deepest (and darkest?) desires and fears of the

---

1 For example, the fourth part of *The 120 Days of Sodom* is subtitled: 'the 150 murderous passions', and details the torture and murder of the libertines' captives (Sade, [1785] 1990a, pp. 625–72).

human psyche. (It is this claim, in part, that informs my approach to Sade's texts.)

What, then, characterizes Sade's philosophy? At its heart lies the rejection of any kind of transcendent moral order in favour of the rule of Nature. This means that the transcendent God is rejected, or at best used as an entity against which to transgress. So, for the depraved monks of St-Mary-in-the-Wood, pleasure is derived in large part from committing sacrilege.[2] At the same time, Sade rejects any morality based upon a high view of what it is to be human in contradistinction to the rest of the animal world. In Sade's universe, there is no justice, only the 'natural' law of survival of the fittest, which, in practice, means survival of the strongest.[3] This suggests that the 'Nature' Sade advocates emulating is not the idyllic and harmonious Nature of a Wordsworth. Sade's Nature is severe, brutal and destructive, resonating with Hume's description of 'a blind nature, impregnated by a great and vivifying principle, and pouring forth from her lap, without discernment or parental care, her maimed and abortive children' (Hume, [1779] 1947, p. 211). Sade, in similar vein, understands Nature's 'purpose' to be entropic, for 'her' ultimate goal is destruction, even if, through that destruction, new things are created. As one of Sade's characters, Bressac, puts it, 'Of what concern is it to Nature, endlessly creating, if a mound of flesh which today has the shape of a woman, should reproduce itself tomorrow as countless insects of different types?' (Sade, [1787] 1992, p. 40). To kill is thus to accept and replicate one of Nature's most basic laws.

This is not to say, however, that Nature is always portrayed as the friend of the libertine. Their relationship is categorized by both amity and enmity. Nature is friend insofar as she provides a rationale for the libertine's actions. She is enemy, in the sense that she has the ability to crush even the libertine. As I shall argue, it is possible to discern a similar ambivalence behind Sade's account of the mother: while she provides a

---

2 See Sade, [1791] 1990b, pp. 612–13.

3 Hence Dolmancé's attack on the poor: 'Destroy mercilessly, raze to the ground those revolting hovels where you billet the progeny of the poor's lechery . . . What purpose, I ask, can there be in so carefully preserving these monsters?' (Sade, [1795] 1995, p. 40).

possible (all-encompassing) source of nourishment and possible partner for the child, she also threatens the child with annihilation. Identifying this ambivalence offers a possible way of reading Sade that goes some way to explaining the deliberate violence perpetrated against the maternal in his writings, and that connects his behaviour and attitudes with more general trends in human psychic development.

Psychoanalysing Sade

Given the complexity of Sade's writing, it is not surprising that his work can be read in a variety of ways. For theorists like Roland Barthes, Sade is the master of transgression whose rejection of bourgeois values and morality enables a new, liberated existence. In order to support such a reading, Barthes has to maintain a sense of the 'irrealism' of Sade's descriptions of horrifying sexual violence, as exemplified in this comment:

> If some group conceived the desire to realise literally one of the orgies Sade describes . . . the Sadian [sic] scene would quickly be seen to be utterly unreal: the complexity of the combinations, the partners' contortions, the potency of ejaculations, and the victims' endurance all surpass human nature: one would need several arms, several skins, the body of an acrobat, and the ability to achieve orgasm *ad infinitum*. (Barthes, 1977, p. 136)

This is one way to read Sade: ignore the extent to which he could be read as offering exaggerated forms of the kind of abuse to be found in actual human relationships. The *ideas* behind Sade's images are what matters; Sade is not providing a torturers' manifesto, whatever readers like Moors Murderer Ian Brady might have believed.[4] Not surprisingly, many feminists, myself included, have been disturbed by the implications of

---

4 See Deborah Cameron and Elizabeth Frazer, 1987, pp. 138–44, for discussion of the role Sade's texts appear to have played in shaping Brady's actions and his self-designation as 'an intellectual'.

making such a distinction between fantasy and fact, imagination and reality. Elsewhere, I have argued against the kind of uncritical dualism that informs Barthes' approach.[5] What Barthes and others like him do, in practice, is to make an almost absolute distinction between 'the idea' and the way in which one acts in the world.[6] To make such a distinction is to ignore the complex way in which action is informed by ideas and the imagination.

To challenge readings of Sade that do not engage with the lived experience of sexual violence does not mean that when faced with his writings we should burn them as dangerous texts leading, inevitably, to destructive actions.[7] Neither does it mean accepting a view of Sade as a hero who challenges social mores: despite the claims of his supporters, there is little evidence in the novels of Sade – or indeed in his life – to suggest that he advocated a society where gender hierarchies or class distinctions no longer existed. Instead, a rather more neutral but perhaps more challenging method can be employed, where Sade is viewed as offering a way into the realm of unconscious, repressed desire that may resonate, uncomfortably, with our own earliest psychic experiences.

To introduce the idea of the unconscious is to suggest something of the extent to which my reading is dependent upon an acceptance of the broad thrust of psychoanalytic theory.[8] Approaching Sade in this way is not new in itself: feminists such as Angela Carter and Jane Gallop have

---

5 See Clack, 2002, pp. 96–9; also Clack, 2001, pp. 262–75.

6 See also Camille Paglia's comment that: 'these are ideas, not acts' (Paglia, 1991, p. 242). While this may be the case, there are clearly connections between Sade's fictional accounts of sexual torture and events that happen in this world. To seek to remove any blame from Sade by this strategy is misguided, for it makes impossible any complex engagement with the relationship between phantasy and reality: a relationship that is considered below.

7 Simone de Beauvoir's introduction to *The 120 Days of Sodom* addresses precisely this conclusion: 'Must we burn Sade?' (Sade, [1785] 1990a, pp. 3–64).

8 For those who do not accept the validity of psychoanalytic theory, what follows will probably provoke disbelief and irritation in equal measure. I suspect that one's response to psychoanalysis is not dissimilar to the leap required by religious faith: when confronted with the idea of the unconscious and its proposed significance for understanding behaviour, this theory will either make sense of one's experience or it will not.

used psychoanalytic ideas to interrogate what might lie beneath Sade's terrifying images and scenarios.[9] While building upon aspects of their respective approaches, my approach is defined by considering the complex relationship between ideas and the way they are shaped by the child's earliest experience of the external world, which, in turn, shapes the way in which the developing child comes to understand the nature of that reality. In psychoanalytic terms, sexuality is never simply a matter of biology but is always informed by the imagination, and thus *phantasies* – both conscious and unconscious – are understood to shape one's psychosexual development.[10]

The notion of *unconscious* phantasy is controversial, even in psychoanalytic circles, and it was Melanie Klein's advocacy of this idea that divided her and her followers from Anna Freud and her supporters in the years following Sigmund Freud's death.[11] Yet the idea that the phantasies of earliest childhood, now repressed and forgotten, inform the way in which the world is viewed and experienced seems central to Freud's own theorizing. In 'Formulations on the Two Principles of Mental Functioning' (1911), Freud argues that the most basic mental function relates to the unconscious and the phantasies that babies create when first encountering the external world. He views such phantasies as attempts at maximizing pleasure: so the child hallucinates the presence of the absent breast (evidenced through the motion of sucking when the breast is withdrawn) in order to limit the pain of the absent mother (Freud, 1911, p. 219 note 4). Such hallucinations, however, do not bring satisfaction, and it is this disappointment that contributes to the development of a second mental principle concerned with reality: phantasies need to be checked against the experience of the external world.

If Freud focused on the maximizing of pleasure in early phantasy, Klein shifted the discussion to explore the possibility that the child's

---

9 See Carter, 1979; Gallop, 1982 and 1995.

10 The reader will note the spelling of 'phantasy' here: this is deliberate, for it is this term that is used in the literature to highlight the *unconscious* phantasies that, it is claimed, shape our engagement with the world.

11 For discussion of the 'Controversial Discussions' of the 1940s, see King and Steiner, 1990.

experience was shaped by a range of phantasies that describe the good *and bad* aspects of the child's encounter with reality (Klein, 1936). Moreover, she understood all forms of thought – rational and irrational – to rest upon such infantile and now unconscious phantasies (Klein, 1921). Later analysts such as Jean Laplanche and J. B. Pontalis extended this view, refusing to accept that a simple division could be made between phantasy and reality. In particular, they rejected the idea that any clear distinction might be made between 'unconscious phantasy' and 'conscious fantasy'. 'Unconscious phantasy' refers to the child's earliest phantasies about the world and its relation to it – including its relationship to its parents – of which the adult now has no memory, while 'conscious fantasy' refers to activities such as daydreaming, and is, as the definition suggests, a conscious and active process. Laplanche and Pontalis resisted this distinction, arguing that there is a connection between both types of phantasy: one's earliest phantasies inform one's later (conscious) wishes. Their concern was that in making such distinctions the complex connections that exist between the unconscious and conscious worlds of our experience are effectively ignored (Laplanche and Pontalis, 1964). And it is in the world of the imagination that one can begin to explore the unconscious phantasies that are at play, and that, in their turn, inform the way in which we engage with our world.[12]

It is this perceived interconnection between conscious and unconscious phantasy that informs my discussion of Sade and his portrayal of violence against the mother. My reading of Sade suggests a writer whose sexual scenarios, while revealing something of the vicissitudes of his own psychosexual development, more significantly enable a wider exploration of more general human experiences. His descriptions of violence against the mother might be read as illustrations of common early childhood psychic experiences, now rendered inaccessible by the processes of repression. In the process of repression, 'unacceptable feelings and thoughts are pushed from consciousness' (Milton *et al.*, 2004, p. 20). But what is repressed is not dead, and it is my contention that Sade's writings can be read as examples of 'the return of the repressed' (see Freud, 1919,

---

12 See Segal, 1991 for further development of this point.

p. 249). In part, this would account for the disturbing experience of reading Sade, for he both fascinates and repels. This 'uncanny' experience suggests that something unacceptable is being brought to consciousness,[13] something that might now be analysed and explored.

Psychopathology and normality: Sade and ourselves

For the psychoanalyst, human sexuality is never simply biological and reproductive, but is constructed by the realities and vagaries of the human mind, itself the product of early childhood experiences. This developmental view of the human psyche, distinguished by the identification of specific overlapping stages (or positions) through which the child passes, suggests something of the complexity of the achievement of human individuality. The child moves from total dependence on the mother to becoming an individual. The classical formulation of the process sees the child moving through stages of mental development associated with the experience of particular parts of the body. The pleasures of sucking (the oral stage), bowel control (the anal stage), and the sexual organs (the phallic stage) are particularly significant in this process. Negotiating the pleasures and terrors of each stage in order to achieve individuality is a complex process whose very complexity means that there is considerable scope for things to go wrong. If Freud's early drive theory focused on the internal forces shaping the child's development, later object relations theory focused on the child's relationship with its mother, and the ways in which the child's *experience* of the mother affected the way in which it responded to the world. Psychoanalytic work in the area of psychopathology has extended this work to consider the implications of a disrupted relationship between mother and child.[14]

Against this theoretical backdrop, Sade's litany of abuse against the

13 As Freud describes it, 'the uncanny is that class of the frightening that leads back to what is known of old and long familiar' (Freud, 1919, p. 220).

14 To highlight problems resulting from a disrupted relationship between mother and child can seem problematic, particularly if analysis of this relationship is used to attribute blame. See Gerhardt, 2004, pp. 21–5 for sensitive engagement with this issue.

mother might be read as revealing something of his problematic relationship with his parents (particularly his mother) and the impact that this had upon shaping his sexuality. As a child, Sade witnessed the abuse of his mother at the hands of his father, a man who in many ways resembles the libertine characters that Sade would later create. When he reached the age of five, his mother left the family home, and he was sent to live with his uncle, the Abbé de Sade, who was jailed in 1762 for debauchery. By his early twenties, Sade had acquired a reputation as a libertine, and it is perhaps not surprising that his relationship with his mother-in-law, Mme de Montreuil, a mother whose overwhelming presence seems the reverse of his experience of a largely absent mother, should have been fraught with difficulties. The Testard affair, when a young woman complained that Sade had sought to flagellate her and to have anal sex with her, led to his imprisonment. Released into the custody of his mother-in-law, the stage was set for a relationship between Sade and Montreuil of extreme animosity, during which time Sade was repeatedly jailed for sexual crimes where beatings and anal sex took place.[15]

Sade's literature, then, seems to reveal something of his own psychosexual development. The kidnappings, beatings, and aggressive sexual practices that define his actual sexual practices as well as the phantasies presented in his writings, suggest that he provides a fitting case study for an exploration of sadistic sexual behaviour. In such behaviour, Robert Stoller notes the 'essential interplay between hostility and sexual desire' (Stoller, [1975] 1986, p. xi). In particular, he draws attention to an inadequate establishment of one's gender identity: so, a weak sense of one's masculinity has to be continually addressed and affirmed by one's sexual activity and phantasies. This problematic sense of identity is, Stoller suggests, constructed out of 'a triad of hostility: *rage* at giving up one's earliest bliss and identification with the mother, *fear* of not succeeding in escaping out of her orbit, and a need for *revenge* for her putting one in this predicament' (Stoller, [1975] 1986, p. 99).[16] That Sade might represent

---

15 For further details see Gear, 1963.

16 See also Glasser, 1979 for a similar understanding of what he calls 'the core complex' for understanding sadistic behaviour: namely, a desire for merging with the mother accompanied by the fear of being consumed by her.

an example of just such a correlation of experiences does not seem an odd conclusion to make. The abuse dealt out to the mother in his novels can be read as revealing the desire to effect revenge upon the mother for her absence. In phantasy 'one's tormentors in turn will be one's victims' (Stoller, [1975] 1986, p. 106).

Fascinating as such an exploration may be, it is not my intention to offer a psychoanalytic biography of Sade based upon an analysis of the phantasies he presents. As Stoller says, while distinctive types of pornographic literature may tell us much about the idiosyncrasies of the individual psychosexual development of the author, they also illuminate the experiences that create and shape human sexuality more generally (Stoller, [1975] 1986, p. 83). In this sense, the fact that Sade's writing both repels and fascinates suggests that there *is* some connection between our own, long-forgotten phantasies, and those that are presented to us in Sade's writing.

To suggest that there may be some common core to Sade's tales of violence that links him, however tenuously, with our own psychosexual development is a disturbing and potentially alienating claim to make. To distance the Sadeian universe from our own is tempting: not least when we consider the murderous attitude taken towards the mother.[17] Yet one of the great insights of Freudian theory is its disturbance of any straight-forward distinction between 'normal' and 'abnormal' behaviour. For Freud, 'every normal person, in fact, is only normal on the average. His ego approximates to that of the psychotic in some part or other and to a greater or lesser extent' (Freud, 1937, p. 235). Psychopathology and normality are not so far apart, and that is not so surprising given that all have to negotiate the different stages that shape our growing individuality and independence. Read against this background, Sade might be seen as enabling through his stories access to the horrors that lie within the psyche. As the psychotherapist Thomas Moore notes: '[Sade] speaks for hidden and repressed mystery over against known and tested mores of civilisation' (Moore, 1990, p. 10).

---

17 And in psychoanalytic theory one of the key ways in which the developing child protects itself from what is felt to be bad is to project that badness onto others, a defence that can be repeated through life.

One of the most interesting aspects of Sade's work, read in the way Moore suggests, revolves around the relationship between mother and child. Sade challenges the romantic account of the mother–child relationship, and confronts its ambivalent nature. Julia Kristeva has written extensively on this ambivalence: the mother is all-encompassing, and in order for language and the entrance into society to be effected, the father has to break the symbiotic relationship between her and her baby.[18] The importance of the father in Kristeva's theorizing has been dismissed as reinforcing patriarchal norms (see Jantzen, 1998, p. 51), but this claim misses Kristeva's point. Her concern is to detail both the significance *and* the potential danger the mother poses to the child's developing individuality. The mother who provides everything I need is also the mother who threatens to subsume/consume me. To consider the ambivalence, then, of the way in which the child perceives the mother is to open up a possible way of reading Sade. He presents a world where the unconscious phantasies of violence towards this all-powerful figure are brought out into the open. What is unconscious is made conscious in his writing.

Violence against the mother

The mother is most obviously present in Sade's universe when she is being violated and murdered. Violence against her is used to represent a range of possibilities and positions that are to be rejected or embraced by Sade's libertines. The mother is habitually connected with the processes of Nature, representing its overwhelming fecundity. Her creativity, however, is not celebrated, and the reproductive woman is particularly despised in Sade's novels. This response suggests something of the ambivalence felt towards the natural world by the libertine. Pregnant women, linked with Nature's fertility, enter the narrative in order to be

18 See Kristeva, 1977 for a powerful description of the symbiotic connection between mother and child; also Kristeva, 2001, pp. 115–18 for her criticism of Klein's over-valuation of the role of the mother that clarifies Kristeva's own views on the role of the father.

mistreated and murdered. Grand Duke Leopold, for example, notes that he knows 'no greater satisfaction than causing a woman I have ingravidated to miscarry' (Sade, [1797] 1968, p. 618), and he proceeds to bring about this end for four women in a range of ingeniously cruel ways (Sade, [1797] 1968, pp. 618–22). In similar fashion, pregnancy is treated as a crime under the ordinances of the libertines of *The 120 Days of Sodom*. Constance, having heard stories of the butchering of pregnant women, is then tortured and murdered by Curval, who rips her child from her womb (Sade, [1785] 1990a, p. 670).

Ripping a foetus from the womb is seen as a pleasurable, liberating act. Birthing, on the other hand, is viewed as something repellent. The Comte de Belmor uses the image of a woman giving birth as a way of undermining any affection that a lover might feel for her: 'Picture her giving birth, this treasure of your heart; behold that shapeless mass of flesh squirm sticky and festering from the cavity where you believe felicity is to be found' (Sade, [1797] 1968, p. 510). Drawing attention to the vagina – shunned by Sade's libertines in favour of the anus – suggests something of the horror felt towards the female reproductive organs. In language reminiscent of the existentialist philosopher Jean-Paul Sartre,[19] Sade describes the female sex organs as 'that hole' (Sade, [1791] 1990b, p. 631). There is something potentially destructive and terrifying about reproduction, associated with the (dark) place from whence we came but also with the grave (that other hole) that is our inevitable destiny. The overt powerlessness of the mother in the hands of the libertines thus seems to mask another reality: the womb that is shunned is all-powerful, and represents the possibility of annihilation.

It is not just the process of reproduction, represented by the female, which is abused: actual mothers, mothers-in-relationship, are also mistreated. The novels reveal a number of examples of matricide. In *The Misfortunes of Virtue* (1787), Bressac offers a justification for the murder of his own mother that is almost absurdly Aristotelian: his life is dependent upon his father's seed; his mother contributed nothing to his

---

19 See Sartre, [1943] 1985, p. 612 for a similar image of the feminine as 'the gluey, the sticky, the hazy, . . . holes in the sand and in the earth, caves'.

creation.[20] Moreover, she undoubtedly enjoyed the act that led to his creation, so he has no obligation towards her (Sade, [1787] 1992, p. 41). This account of the mother who provides 'nothing' resonates with the previous representation of feminine sexuality as a hole. This language suggests that the despised female represents something that is to be feared in terms of its absence. This is symbolized by the female sex organs, but also by what the mother does – or does not – provide. The violence against the mother seems to originate in the recognition of the nothing that lies beneath the something of existence.

A similar fear of maternal power pervades the ordeal of Madame de Mistival in *Philosophy in the Boudoir* (1795). Come to rescue her daughter Eugenie from the clutches of the libertines Dolmancé and Madame de Saint-Ange, she becomes her daughter's victim. Eugenie, now thoroughly schooled in libertinage, takes a needle threaded with red cotton and stitches up her mother's vagina and anus. Of all the horrific images that bombard Sade's reader, this is particularly memorable. Perhaps it is because in this act we arrive at the central place that abuse of the mother takes in the Sadeian universe. The mother is such a problematic figure that she has to be sealed up, eradicated as a potential source of life. The 'hole' from whence one came is so terrifying that it must be plugged. This underlying terror can be explained in a variety of ways. Angela Carter suggests that this act plays out the fears and desires of the Oedipus complex: for the mother, the daughter is a rival, and for the daughter, the mother is a warning of her own destiny (Carter, 1979, p. 123). At the same time, the child's jealousy of future rivals is given concrete form in the act that makes intercourse impossible and that therefore renders the mother sterile (Carter, 1979, p. 135).[21] At the heart of this act, however, seems to be a connection between rage against life itself and the playing out of this rage on the body of the mother. The sterile mother comes to represent both the desire to be the centre of a universe that

---

20 See Aristotle, *On the Generation of Animals* 1.21 (730a). In fact, even Aristotle does not go as far as Sade, for while he defines the male as the animating principle for life, he allows that the female contributes the material elements.

21 See also Mitchell, 2003 for discussion of sibling rivalry.

is constantly changing, and the desire to halt the cycle of life that will, eventually, lead to one's own destruction.

Sade's images are so astounding that it is difficult to know quite what conclusions one is to draw if one wishes to take them seriously. The rejection of the procreative woman suggests something of the libertine's relationship with Nature. We have already noted the ambivalence of this relationship: Nature both nurtures libertine desire and threatens it with the inevitable destruction that is the lot of all things. Indeed, the acts against the mother suggest that a kind of revenge against Nature is being enacted. The procreation of Nature is eschewed in favour of appropriating her destructive trends. More than that, there seems to be a realization of and a resistance to the destruction that lies at the heart of creation. As Simone de Beauvoir notes, 'Wherever life is in the making – germination, fermentation – it arouses disgust because it is made only in being destroyed' (Beauvoir, [1949] 1972, p. 178). By taking revenge against the creativity of Nature, represented by the mother, the libertine attempts to enact a sense of control over the unruliness and unpredictability of life. Death is anticipated and enacted on the bodies of the procreative feminine that brought us into being in the first place.

The ambivalence and hostility towards life and Nature is replicated in a further feature of the violence shown to the mother. The mother is never just subjected to physical violence: she is invariably the object of some kind of incestuous sexual attack. The mother is desired, as well as annihilated. The events that precede the stitching up of Mme de Mistival's genitals by her daughter Eugenie suggest something of this ambivalence. Eugenie's new identity as libertine is revealed through an incestuous action. She offers 'Mama dearest' her buttocks to kiss, covered as they are in the dried blood and spunk of the orgies in which she has been participating (Sade, [1795] 1995, p. 143). As the scene develops, Eugenie shows a growing fascination with her mother's sexuality. Strapping on a dildo with which she proceeds to sodomize her mother, she exclaims: 'Come, lovely Mama dearest, come, let me serve you as a husband . . . Ah, dear Mother, how beautifully you scream when your daughter fucks you! . . . Wait, dearest Mama; I believe you are discharging . . . look at her eyes, Dolmancé – she is coming, is she not?' (Sade, [1795] 1995, p. 147).

How to read this shocking connection of hostility and desire? The ability of the repressed to return has already been noted, and Janine Chasseguet-Smirgel suggests such a return to pervade Sade's writings. His works, she argues, represent a 'regression to the anal-sadistic phase' (Chasseguet-Smirgel, 1985, p. 2). At this time, around the age of two, the child's developing bowel control makes it aware that it can both give and withhold, and so notions of ownership accompany this stage. I become aware of what I have, and also what others possess. In the process, I come to envy what others have (see Rosenberger, 2005, pp. 481–7). In noting Sade's attempt 'to reduce the universe to faeces, or rather to annihilate the universe of differences' (Chasseguet-Smirgel, 1985, p. 4), Chasseguet-Smirgel identifies the connection of envy with destruction. I envy what is yours, and seek to possess it even if that means that, in the process, I destroy it. In sadism proper, this feeling is not abated by other mitigating experiences. Destroying not just the presence of the mother but also the very idea that she *is* one's mother is part of the attempt to undermine all difference and to possess everything. So *all* bodies are simply to be fucked. The incestuous desire for the mother thus goes hand-in-hand with the attempt to annihilate her. The absent mother, the uncontrollable mother, becomes in sadism the mother who is now controlled through controlling the current partner/victim.[22]

That Sade portrays a regression to an earlier stage of childhood development opens up an interesting way of reading his world of desire and death. And if we accept the view of staged child development, this is a phase that we, too, have negotiated. We have had to negotiate similar fears and desires regarding the figure of the mother. Consider, then, the not dissimilar images that Klein presents when describing the development of the child's psychic world.[23] For Klein, the mother is never simply a figure of love and plenty for the child. The breast which is present, which nourishes, is also the breast which is withdrawn and absent (see

---

22 See Glasser, 1979.

23 Rosenberger notes Klein's 'brilliant, radical, and, admittedly, somewhat misdirected drama regarding her observations of infants, even in the first months of life, as they lusted for and raged against their mothers' breasts' (Rosenberger, 2005, p. 468).

Klein, 1926; [1932] 1997). The breast that gives life can also be felt as the breast that can destroy. Adopting Klein's theory allows for a reading of Sade to emerge that necessitates engaging not only with the mother who is destroyed, but also with the mother who can destroy. It is a reading that suggests that there may be more common ground between 'normal' psychic development and Sade than we might like to admit.

The annihilating mother

Given the many examples of violence meted out to mothers, the presence of the annihilating mother can easily be overlooked. In a universe where family ties exist only to be broken, the murderous mother constitutes a particularly terrifying figure. The dynamic of desire and death identified above similarly permeates this version of the mother–child relationship. Consider Olympia's confession to Juliette that she is 'guilty of child-murder' (Sade, [1797] 1968, p. 711). This murder takes place after Olympia has taken her daughter Agnes as her lover. Satiated with this incestuous relationship, Olympia quickly becomes bored. Sexual pleasure can now only be affected by contemplating her daughter's death: 'only the thought of her destruction moistened my cunt' (Sade, [1797] 1968, p. 711). She has Agnes incarcerated, and proceeds to torture and murder her. Olympia's description of this process suggests something of the mother's overwhelming power: 'after three hours of the most various tortures, the most hideous and merciless, I restored to the elements an inert mass which had received life in my womb only in order to become the toy of my rage and my viciousness' (Sade, [1797] 1968, p. 714). Juliette eventually emulates her friend, and is party to her daughter's rape, torture and immolation at the hands of Noirceuil (Sade, [1797] 1968, pp. 1186–7).

These horrific acts, which fly in the face of everything that is commonly assumed about the mother–child relationship, almost defy interpretation. At the same time, some mothers *do* abuse, torture and murder their children. The phantasies that Sade spins are not outside the bounds of possibility. And if one considers less extreme, day-to-day examples, some mothers describe having deeply ambivalent feelings about their children.[24] My contention is not that we are all therefore Sades/sadists, but that there is common ground between our earliest phantasies. And read against Klein's theories, Sade's tales of the murderous mother suggest a possible explanation for the prevalence of stories that have violence against the mother at their centre. Klein focuses her attention upon the relationship between mother and child in the first three months of life, and specifically upon the phantasies that the child constructs in response to finding itself in a strange and potentially hostile world. This description of what is happening in the child's mind at such an early stage in development can provoke considerable scepticism.[25] At the same time, there is something about her account that rings true if we attempt to enter imaginatively into the child's world, or if we consider the inconsolable crying of a baby. According to Klein, the child has to find ways of managing the potentially overwhelming anxiety of finding itself outside of the protective womb. Two basic psychic mechanisms are employed to manage this anxiety: the 'paranoid-schizoid' position and the 'depressive' position. It is the first position that offers a possible framework for understanding the hostility expressed towards the mother in Sade's work, and which itself connects with his descriptions of the annihilating

---

24 For example, Adrienne Rich's reflections on motherhood: 'The bad and good moments are inseparable for me. I recall the times when, suckling each of my children, I saw his eyes open full to mine, and realised each of us was fastened to the other, not only by mouth and breast, but through our mutual gaze . . . I recall the physical pleasure of having my full breast suckled at a time when I had no other physical pleasure in the world except the guilt-ridden pleasure of addictive eating . . . I remember being uprooted from already meagre sleep to answer a childish nightmare, pull up a blanket, warm a consoling bottle, lead a half-asleep child to the toilet. I remember going back to bed starkly awake, brittle with anger, knowing that my broken sleep would make next day a hell, that there would be more nightmares, more need for consolation, because out of my weariness I would rage at those children for no reason they could understand. I remember thinking I would never dream again' (Rich, 1977, pp. 31; quoted in Gerhardt, 2004, pp. 16–7).

25 As Rosenberger notes, 'Klein's rendition [of these phantasies] can only be a fantasy/project (by her, of course, given the infant's cognitive capacity at that age)' (Rosenberger, 2005, p. 476).

mother. Confronted with this frightening world, the child is gripped by phantasies of annihilation from which it must protect itself, and it does so by keeping what is felt to be good separate from what is felt to be bad. The child thus keeps the phantasy of the 'good' breast that is loving, feeding and creative, separate from the phantasy of the 'bad' breast that is felt as biting, hurtful, and terrifying. Through this process of splitting, the baby learns to distinguish between love and cruelty. The mother's ability to contain the child's hostility enables anxiety to be managed. Eventually, the child needs to recognize that the mother contains both good and bad, weakness and power: a unifying process that denotes the work of the depressive position (see Klein, 1935; 1946).

Klein's theory suggests a complex mother–child relationship. The child feels the mother to be both loving *and* hostile, and thus ambivalence surrounds the figure of the mother. Moreover, her ability to feed the child, to give her all that she needs, is not just met with gratitude, but also with envy. The mother contains everything, the child (apparently) nothing. Behind the hostility of the child lies a realization of the power of the mother, for the mother who gives all, like the mother who offers nothing, suggests a mother who can annihilate.[26] The graphic description of Klein's conception of the unconscious as 'somewhere where you fry your parents' kidneys' (Phillips and Stonebridge, 1998, p. 3) resonates with the brutality of Sade's images and suggests something of their source. In the image of the tortured and torturing mother, Sade provides a literary rendition of the unconscious fears and desires experienced by the child who is totally dependent upon the mother as the source of all things. The mother who can give is also the mother who can withhold; the mother who is loved is also envied. To hold together these views is a psychic achievement of the depressive position. Sade's life suggests a problematic resolution of these different maternal qualities, yet the anxieties surrounding the mother with which he struggled are, if we take Klein seriously, common to us all.

---

26 If one dislikes the drama of Klein's formulation, Sue Gerhardt's description of what constitutes stress for babies might prove more palatable, but arguably the point is the same: 'Babies' resources are so limited that they cannot keep themselves alive . . . Without the parent's help, they could in fact die' (Gerhardt, 2004, p. 70).

Read thus, there is considerably more connection between the images of the tortured and torturing mother than might initially seem to be the case. Sade presents us with a journey into the (repressed) imagination of the child's hostility towards its mother that is itself based upon fear of and desire for her. He offers up a mirror in which to see graphic representations of early emotional experiences, and read against Klein's framework some of the disturbing images that he presents are rendered explicable.

Conclusion

I have suggested, then, that reading Sade allows access to aspects of the unconscious. The complex mix of emotions stirred up when reading Sade suggests what Freud calls the presence of the uncanny: that which seems to be frightening because it is unfamiliar turns out to be all-too-familiar (Freud, 1919, p. 241). The violence, the incestuous desires, the fears of annihilation, can be read as the return of unacceptable desires and fears that have been repressed. In this sense, it is not just that Sade provides an insight into the phantasies that shape and express the desires of the sadistic personality. His writing might indeed suggest something of the psychic experiences that shape such psychosexual pathologies, but it does more than that, for it corresponds with the phantasies of early childhood psychosexual development that may have been more successfully negotiated by the reader. Sade's work becomes accessible because his is not a psychic world completely alien from our own.

To read Sade is to journey into some of the deepest and darkest recesses of our own psychosexual development. Thomas Moore accepts that Sade is dangerous and repellent, but he also argues that through engaging with the Sadeian universe access is granted to the dark underbelly of human identity. In order to become integrated individuals who do not simply project our own internal darkness on to others, it is important to engage with the horrors within our own hearts. An exploration of Sade's graphic descriptions of violence against the mother can, then, be read as revealing something of the earliest childhood fears and desires. These fears of the powerful mother might go some way to explaining violence perpetrated against women as representatives of dangerous natural processes. They might also explain the common derogation and casual misogyny of much speech and behaviour. Interrogating our phantasies through those that Sade presents enables discussion and reflection on such attitudes. In confronting Sade, we confront ourselves.

References

Airaksinen, T. (1995), *The Philosophy of the Marquis de Sade*, London: Routledge.

Barthes, R. (1977), *Sade, Fourier, Loyola*, trans. R. Miller, London: Jonathan Cape.

Beauvoir, S. de ([1949] 1972), *The Second Sex*, trans. H. M. Parshley, Harmondsworth: Penguin.

Cameron, D. and E. Frazer (1987), *The Lust to Kill*, New York: New York University Press.

Carter, A. (1979), *The Sadeian Woman*, London: Virago.

Chasseguet-Smirgel, J. (1985), *Creativity and Perversion*, London: Free Association Books.

Clack, B. (2001) 'Sade: Forgiveness and Truth in a Desacralised Universe', *Literature and Theology* 15.3, pp. 262–75.

Clack, B. (2002), *Sex and Death: A Reappraisal of Human Mortality*, Cambridge: Polity Press.

Dworkin, A. (1981), *Pornography: Men Possessing Women*, London: Women's Press.

Erikson, E. (1968), *Identity: Youth in Crisis*, London: Faber & Faber.

Freud, S. (1905), 'Three Essays on Sexuality', in *Standard Edition of the Works of Sigmund Freud* (hereafter, *SE*), vol. 7, trans. J. Strachey, London: Vintage, pp. 125–245.

Freud, S. (1911), 'Formulations on the Two Principles of Mental Functioning', *SE* 12, trans. J. Strachey, London: Vintage, pp. 213–38.

Freud, S. (1919), 'The "Uncanny"', *SE* 17, trans. J. Strachey, London: Vintage, pp. 218–56.

Freud, S. (1937), 'Analysis Terminable and Interminable', *SE* 23, pp. 216–53.

Gallop, J. (1982), *Feminism and Psychoanalysis*, Basingstoke: Macmillan.

Gallop, J. (1995), 'Sade, Mother and Other Women', in *Sade and the Narra-*

tive of Transgression, ed. D. B. Allison, M. S. Roberts and A. S. Weiss, Cambridge: Cambridge University Press, pp. 122–41.

Gear, N. (1963), *The Divine Demon: A Portrait of the Marquis de Sade*, London: Frederick Muller.

Gerhardt, S. (2004), *Why Love Matters: How Affection Shapes a Baby's Brain*, London: Routledge.

Glasser, M. (1979), 'Some Aspects of the Role of Aggression in the Perversions', in *Sexual Deviations*, ed. I. Rosen, Oxford: Oxford University Press, pp. 278–305.

Hume, D. ([1779] 1947), *Dialogues Concerning Natural Religion*, Indianapolis: Bobbs-Merrill.

Jantzen, G. (1998), *Becoming Divine: Towards a Feminist Philosophy of Religion*, Manchester: Manchester University Press.

King, P. and R. Steiner, eds (1990), *The Freud–Klein Controversies 1941–45*, London: Routledge.

Klein, M. (1921), 'The Development of a Child', in *The Writings of Melanie Klein*, vol. 1: *Love, Guilt and Reparation*, London: Hogarth Press, 1975, pp. 4–13.

Klein, M. (1926), 'Infant Analysis', *International Journal of Psycho-Analysis* 7, pp. 31–63.

Klein, M. ([1932] 1997), *The Psycho-Analysis of Children*, London: Vintage.

Klein, M. (1935), 'A Contribution to the Psychogenesis of Manic-Depressive States', in *The Writings of Melanie Klein*, vol. 1: *Love, Guilt and Reparation*, London: Hogarth Press, 1975, pp. 236–89.

Klein, M. (1936), 'Weaning', in *The Writings of Melanie Klein*, vol. 1: *Love, Guilt and Reparation*, London: Hogarth Press, 1975, pp. 290–305.

Klein, M. (1946), 'Notes on Some Schizoid Mechanisms', in *The Writings of Melanie Klein*, vol. 3: *Envy and Gratitude and Other Works*, London: Hogarth Press, pp. 292–320.

Kristeva, J. (1977), 'Stabat Mater', in M. Joy, K. O'Grady and J. L. Poxon, eds, *French Feminists on Religion: A Reader*, London: Routledge, 2002, pp. 112–38.

Kristeva, J. (2001), *Melanie Klein*, trans. R. Guberman, New York: Columbia University Press.

Lacan, J. and the École Freudienne (1982), *Feminine Sexuality*, ed. J. Mitchell and J. Rose, trans. J. Rose, London: Macmillan.

Laplanche, J. and J. B. Pontalis (1964), 'Fantasy and the Origins of Sexuality', in R. Steiner, ed., *Unconscious Phantasy*, London: Karnac Books, 2003, pp. 107–43.

Milton, J., C. Polmear and J. Fabricius (2004), *A Short Introduction to Psychoanalysis*, London: Sage.

Mitchell, J. (2003), *Siblings*, Cambridge: Polity Press.

Moore, T. (1990), *Dark Eros: The Imagination of Sadism*, Connecticut: Spring.

Paglia, C. (1991), *Sexual Personae*, Harmondsworth: Penguin.

Phillips, J. and L. Stonebridge (1998), *Reading Melanie Klein*, London: Routledge.

Rich, A. (1977), *Of Woman Born*, London: Virago.

Rosenberger, J. (2005), 'Envy, Shame and Sadism', *Journal of the American Academy of Psychoanalysis and Dynamic Psychiatry* 33.3, pp. 465–89.

Sade, D.-A.-F., Marquis de ([1785] 1990a), *The 120 Days of Sodom*, trans. A. Wainhouse and R. Seaver, London: Arrow Books.

Sade, D.-A.-F., Marquis de ([1787] 1992), *The Misfortunes of Virtue and Other Early Tales*, trans. D. Coward, Oxford: Oxford University Press.

Sade, D.-A.-F., Marquis de ([1791] 1990b), *Justine, Or Good Conduct Well Chastised*, in *Justine, Philosophy in the Bedroom, and Other Writings*, New York: Grove Press.

Sade, D.-A.-F., Marquis de ([1795] 1995), *Philosophy in the Boudoir*, trans. Meredith X, London: Creation Books.

Sade, D.-A.-F., Marquis de ([1797] 1968), *Juliette*, trans. A. Wainhouse, New York: Grove Press.

Sartre, J.-P. ([1943] 1985), *Being and Nothingness*, trans. H. E. Barnes, London: Methuen.

Segal, H. (1991), 'Imagination, Play and Art', in R. Steiner, ed., *Unconscious Phantasy*, London: Karnac Books, 2003.

Stoller, R. ([1975] 1986), *Perversion: The Erotic Form of Hatred*, London: Karnac Books.

2

'Cut 'n' Slash': Remodelling the 'Freakish' Female Form

INGA BRYDEN

This chapter discusses a nexus of cultural and theological concerns surrounding what happens if the human body is 'cut', that is, if the skin as border between inside and outside is penetrated so as to problematize that binary. Relatedly, if the body's borders are threatened or attacked (whether self-willed or by an external agent), this necessarily brings into play questions of scale, size, and the relation of the body to space, through the alteration of form. To facilitate discussion I am focusing on two literary texts – Fay Weldon's *The Life and Loves of a She Devil* (1983) and Jenefer Shute's *Life-Size* (1992) – in the contexts of late-twentieth-century cultural and feminist discourses about beauty, femininity and the representation of the female form. Both novels deal with contrasting ways in which women's bodies are altered, through the protagonists' quests to change shape in pursuit of perfection: in the former, by undergoing cosmetic surgery and in the latter, by starving.

In pre-seventeenth-century western culture, the body (or matter) was considered inessential, while the being (or form) was essential; the being viewed as one flesh, or as an 'open body'. Consequently, the body was placed at the bottom of the Chain of Being and moreover, women were aligned with the 'chaos of the body'. In the modern era the distinction lessened and matter and form became the subjects of more 'uniform relations' (Colebrook, 2003, p. 16). Nonetheless, feminist critics have highlighted the gendered notion of the 'chaotic', liminal, unstable body, arguing that the male subject attempts to define a stable self against the perceived 'thingness' of the female body (Hurley, 1996, pp. 123–4). As

Elaine Showalter argues, 'men do not think of themselves as cases to be opened up. Instead, they open up a woman as a substitute for self-knowledge' (Showalter, 1990, p. 134).

Weldon's and Shute's texts are examples of cultural representations which investigate the 'otherness' of women, or more particularly, the 'otherness' of women as 'freaks' of culture, rather than of nature, as famously articulated by Simone de Beauvoir. The misshapen forms of the female body (both prior to, and following, intervention from the surgeon's knife, the nurse's needles and tubes, or the refusal to eat) are seen to embody western culture's (gendered) fears and to articulate anxieties about, in Leslie Fiedler's words, our 'secret selves' (Fiedler, 1978, p. 314).

The freak in this sense challenges conventional boundaries 'between male and female, sexed and sexless, animal and human, large and small, self and other, and consequently between reality and illusion, experience and fantasy, fact and myth' (Fiedler, 1978, p. 24). The literary narratives discussed here can thus be read within the popular cultural tradition of the freak symbolizing the overturning of hierarchies – from medieval street entertainment to the spectacle of Victorian freak shows.

Both texts are primarily interested in the process of reconstructing the human form, specifically via techniques which violate women's bodies. Employing the image of the freak allows a variety of cultural myths to be destabilized. In *The Life and Loves of a She Devil*, Ruth Patchett's transformation (narrated partially by her) from suburban 'angel in the house' to avenging she-devil is an inversion of the romantic myth or fairy-tale which legitimates marriage as a happy ending for women (embodied in the 'goddess' of romantic fiction, Mary Fisher, with whom Ruth's husband goes to live). While Weldon exposes 'otherness' as an illusion, she also asserts the power of the 'other' woman within culture, testing the boundaries of feminist ideology in the 1980s.

Shute's first-person fictionalized account, narrated by Josie, of being 'treated' for anorexia in hospital and of the conditions which led to this, is also an exposé of the pressures of cultural myths which depend on con-formity to idealized models (and which continue to sustain the cosmetic surgery industry and the 'glossies', the women's magazine market).

Pertinently, *Life-Size* was published a year after Naomi Wolf's polemical *The Beauty Myth* and can be read as a response to the very ideologies which Wolf sought to undermine. 'Beauty', as a currency system, is determined by politics, and its ideals change. Wolf argued that the 'beauty myth' is not based on 'evolution, sex, gender, aesthetics or God', but rather, is composed of 'emotional distance, politics, finance and sexual repression' (Wolf, 1991, p. 13). The ideology of beauty is also underpinned by the link between body and soul, and the presumption that moral goodness is expressed through beauty of form – it is this which is at stake when the form is punctured, marked or sliced.[1]

What is hidden beneath the 'beauty of form' or the ideal is the matter of these novels. Both texts highlight the 'grotto-esque' – the 'hidden, earthly, dark, material, immanent [and] visceral' (Russo, 1994, p. 1). In this sense it can be argued that the bodies of Ruth and Josie – as they are reconfigured and as metaphorically described – have wider cultural resonances of the 'grotesque'. The grotesque body, with its emphasis on orifices and bulging body parts, is an aspect of Mikhail Bakhtin's theory of the carnivalesque. Bakhtin argues that the monstrous image in popular culture is related to primordial fears that Calvinists saw in the soul, but that it induces laughter rather than guilt. Both protagonists are preoccupied with the notion of 'excess' of form and how to cut back or reduce it, although the texts' focus, on the 'gruesome' detail of food, sex and the body being turned inside-out, undermines this: 'the very material bodily lower stratum of the grotesque image (food, wine, the genital force, the organs of the body) bears a deeply positive character' (Bakhtin, 1984, p. 62). The grotesque body is one in the act of becoming and a body of parts (the texts are process, where the final, stabilized body is always out of reach). Yet the *spectacle* of the grotesque involves a distancing and aestheticization of the body/object (and thus an avoidance of contamination). As Susan Stewart suggests, 'the history of the aberrations of the

---

1 The tradition of seeing the body as microcosm (where the body and the universe are variously projected upon each other) involves an establishing of correspondences which 'tends toward theology and the promulgation of a "grand design"' (Stewart, 1993, p. 128).

physical body cannot be separated from this structure of the spectacle' (Stewart, 1993, p. 108).

In articulating the processes by which the boundaries of the body are breached, Weldon's and Shute's texts highlight the paradoxical status of the body as container and contained. This raises broader questions concerning what happens to notions of the self and to definitions of privacy. Cultural and religious taboos, together with regularization of the body, work to reinforce divisions of public and private space. If, as Mary Douglas has argued, pollution is 'matter out of place' (boundary violation) then the spatial order of public and private becomes a means of controlling sensual 'appetites' and protection against (other people's) odour, noise and dirt. The body as a threat to the purity of space (Poovey, 1995) is central to this: the concept of the body as a house with an interior and openings which need constant surveillance was first mentioned in a fourteenth-century treatise by Henri De Mondeville (Wigley, 1992, p. 358). If the body is seen as 'enclosed space' then it creates a dialectic 'between inside and outside . . . private and public property . . . the space of the subject and the space of the social. Trespass, contamination, and the erasure of materiality are the threats presented to the enclosed world' (Stewart, 1993, p. 68).

The moment at which the skin is cut (described by Weldon and Shute) focuses attention on the limits of the body (seen from the exterior, the body as object; from the interior, the body's extension into space) and particularly on products which cross these boundaries. Moreover, where the body's surface is marked by cuts and gaps becomes culturally sensitive territory, or what Jacques Lacan has termed 'erotogenic' zones (Lacan, 1977, pp. 314-5). These zones heighten the sense of 'edge' and require cultural policing (and relatedly, anything which is both inside and outside the body has an ambiguous status).

Questioning preconceived notions of the possibilities, limitations and definition of the human body has an increased urgency in the current western context of developments in science and new surgical technologies which penetrate and restructure the inner and outer spaces of the body. A further word ought to be added at this stage. In investigating cultural representations, it is

necessary to stress the fundamental difference between real violence
done to a physical body and any 'imagined' one . . . to collapse the two
levels on which signification works might also mean not doing justice
to the uniquely horrible violence that occurs when a body is used quite
literally as the site for an inscription by another. (Bronfen, 1992,
pp. 59–60)

In Weldon's and Shute's texts the protagonists elect to reshape their
own bodies, although this is shown to be informed by socio-cultural and
religious discourses. Any violence done to a body, Laura Tanner points
out, 'not only has the capacity to destroy the form of the victim's body,
but the familiar forms of understanding through which that victim constructs him- or herself as subject' (Tanner, 1994, p. 4).

In Weldon's *The Life and Loves of a She Devil*, 'wifedom and motherhood' is seen to involve reciting the Litany of the Good Wife (pp. 29–30),
shackles which the dark, 'immeasurably large' Ruth decides to throw off,
along with the romantic myth that 'a knight in shining armour will gallop
by, and see through to the beauty of the soul' (p. 62). The 'giantess' Ruth
embodies the 'fury of a woman scorned' as she seeks revenge against
her husband, Bobbo, who has left her to live with the petite romantic
novelist Mary Fisher. Negating the soul in favour of the body, the socially
ostracized Ruth embarks on a process of self-transformation: 'I have no
place, so I must make my own, and since I cannot change the world, I
will change myself' (p. 62). The process involves assuming different
identities, making money and having extreme cosmetic surgery (which
the surname 'Patchett' ironizes).

Remodelling: cosmetic surgery

Life and Loves articulates a variety of competing cultural discourses
about cosmetic surgery: it is regarded as both solution and problem; as
empowerment and oppression, and more contentiously, perhaps, as
feminist utopia. Cosmetic surgery, for Ruth, is a process of purification,
transforming ugliness into beauty and thus transforming the human

body, the 'shell of the soul'. The irony is that she is remodelled to look like *a picture* of Mary Fisher, looking 'as if she had a hotline to God' (p. 215). Religious imagery is appropriated throughout the text: the male cosmetic surgeon (in his own eyes) becomes sanctified as the divine mother (p. 229). The surgeon as 'Maker' is also likened to Pygmalion, symbol of the romantic lover who created his ideal female beauty as a statue (visualized, for example, in Sir John Tenniel's watercolour *Pygmalion and the Statue* (1878)). Yet Ruth is no passive victim: 'he was her Pygmalion, but she would not depend on him or admire him, or be grateful' (pp. 230–1).

Indeed, the model of the body as the classical nude is violated, as is any spiritual dimension of the transformative experience, by the drawn-out procedures of cosmetic surgery itself. The secularized 'rebirth' is 'reduced' to the isolation and fetishization of each 'exaggerated' part: the body is only one of parts. 'When Miss Hunter's eyes had healed, they broke her cheekbones and flattened them out: and when the bruising had abated somewhat they trimmed and altered the line of the jaw bone' (p. 231).

That June they started on her torso. They fined down and abbreviated the shoulderblades. They made the breasts smaller. They removed flesh from the upper arms and drew the loose skin up into the armpits . . . the gestalt of her system was under threat. (p. 234)

During the process of shape-altering the 'patient' is subject to both miniaturization and infantilization. 'Now the nose loomed large, hooked and horrific in Miss Hunter's sweet face. The head seemed small in proportion to the body' (p. 232). 'Her eyes suddenly became wide, candid and innocent, and large in proportion to her head: they were enchanting, as kitten's eyes are enchanting, or indeed the eyes of the young of any species – even of the crocodile' (p. 231).

After the process is complete, the new Ruth (a substitute for Mary) inhabits the uncertain realm of the freak: whereas Dr Black compares her to Venus, newly arisen from her conch-shell (p. 238), Mrs Black sees her as 'an insult to womanhood' and the doctors not as doctors or artists, but as 'reductionists' (p. 239).

Transfiguration

The transformation Ruth undergoes is conceptualized within a framework of theological references. In one sense it is an heretical (re)creation: 'I will mould a new image for myself out of the earth of my creation. I will defy my Maker, and remake myself' (p. 170) and in another, a female Second Coming:

> I wouldn't be surprised if I wasn't the second coming, this time in female form; what the world has been waiting for. Perhaps as Jesus did in his day for men, so I do now, for women. He offered the stony path to heaven: I offer the motorway to hell. (p. 174)

For Ruth, radically altering her body shape by submitting to the cosmetic surgeon's instruments is about purification: 'all I am asking you to do is take unnecessary stuff away' (p. 216). However, an alternative view of the relation between body and soul, or outer and inner, is hinted at: 'though you can change the body you cannot change the person. And little by little – this may sound mystical, but it is our experience – the body reshapes itself to fit the personality' (p. 216). The cosmetic surgeons 'work from the *inside out* [my italics] as much as possible . . . We can reshape the body quite dramatically' (p. 215). The irony is that Ruth imagines her pre-surgery body as already a form of the grotesque, with its emphasis on orifices and protrusions which offer little protection from 'knowing too much': 'I was born, I sometimes think, with nerve endings not *inside but outside* [my italics] my skin: they shivered and twanged. I grew lumpish and brutish in the attempt to seal them over, not to know too much' (p. 13). An essential phase of the grotesque body in the act of becoming is, in Bakhtin's formulation, the death of the old. In Weldon's text the image of self-inflicted pain through perforation of the skin is used to convey the repression of the past and painful memories. The point of impact *is* the moment of 'transfiguration':

> A she devil is supremely happy: she is inoculated against the pain of memory. At the moment of her transfiguration, from woman to non-

woman, she performs the act herself. She thrusts the long, sharp needle of recollection through the living flesh into the heart, burning it out. (p. 171)

Resurrection

Indeed, both *Life and Loves* and *Life-Size* can be read as resurrection narratives: Ruth risks death, emerges from it, but at the cost of the death of her past and her self as a woman; Josie, the end of the novel suggests, has chosen to live: 'what a novel idea!' (p. 229). In focusing on the theme of revivification, I would argue that the texts materialize earlier aesthetic versions of a confluence between femininity and death, particularly the trope of the dying or sick woman popular in nineteenth-century culture. In the course of surgery Ruth's body is killed and returns as an embodiment of Mary Fisher, the cliché of feminine beauty (enacting an exchange between social death and rebirth). As Fisher's body deteriorates physically, through disease, Ruth's body is being resubstantiated. As Elisabeth Bronfen highlights, 'what is being reanimated are doubly dead body parts – her killed body and the imitation of the dead Mary Fisher' (Bronfen, 1992, p. 414). Furthermore, the 'resurrection' can happen only because 'Ruth literally cuts her body up' (p. 412) and excessively confirms the cultural discourses that underpin it. Death is represented as a transition, as a liminal stage. 'Ruth hovered, moaning, drifting, on the edge of life and death' – until an electrical storm stimulates her into life. She is referred to as Frankenstein's monster, 'something that needed lightning to animate it and get it moving' (p. 250). Above all, it is purification through pain which characterizes the whole process: 'pain, she knew, was the healing agent. It marked the transition from her old life to her new one. She must endure it now, to be free of it hereafter' (pp. 247–8).

In the new life, Ruth is seen to extend the remapping of her body by inscribing her self on hard-won territory (Mary Fisher's tower and land): 'some people say I've ruined it, with artificial copses and granite-fountained fish ponds and the rest, but I like it. Nature gets away with far too much. It needs controlling' (p. 256). Here, the text can be interpreted within a wider cultural matrix where the aestheticization of a woman's [dead] body acts to repress the 'destructive' force of nature.

Through appropriation and embodiment of the artificial, Ruth wishes to become 'ordinary', although paradoxically, behind this lies the assumption that 'normal' means a bland perfection. The transformation is regarded as being beyond gender; not a matter of male or female, but of power. However, Weldon destabilizes this gender-neutral position by drawing a parallel with Hans Christian Andersen's *The Little Mermaid* which highlights the 'mutilating influence of cultural myths, especially on women' (Thomson, 1996, p. 296). The mermaid is a hybrid of beast and human and she also endures pain to acquire new legs, significant in the fetishization of female sexuality. With Ruth's every step, 'it was as if she trod on knives' (p. 254). Meanwhile, Bobbo suffers from the absence of Mary Fisher, 'or that part of her he remembers most clearly, the bit where the legs split off from the body' (p. 169).

Rituals as techniques of self-transformation

Fashion

Splits and scars on the body's surface can be hidden by techniques of adornment such as fashion or make-up. When Ruth is first reintroduced into society at a party, attention is drawn to her figure-hugging gold lamé dress, fur bolero and gold straps which serve 'to cover scars, but only those in the know would have realised that' (p. 239). Both Weldon's and Shute's texts are informed by, reflect and expose popular cultural ideologies surrounding beauty and the female form, particularly those derived from the fashion system and modelling from the 1980s onwards. Indeed, I would argue that aspects of the nature of fashion and modelling, and the ways in which they are represented (contemporary with the texts discussed here), have much to say about the symbolic nature of 'the cut'. Like cosmetic surgery, the fashion system is based on technologies of self-formation, only using techniques of 'dress, decoration and gesture which attempt to regulate tensions, conflict and ambiguity' (Craik, 1994, p. 204). Both, then, are about disciplining the body. The protagonists of

Life and Loves and *Life-Size* discipline and recreate their bodies, but in the context of narratives about the 'act of becoming' in a much broader sense. This ambivalence about the 'constantly-to-be-recreated self' is also what 'gives fashion its dynamic character' (Hollander, 1993, p. 126).

Arguably, like the bodies of Ruth and (to a lesser extent) Josie, clothes/fashion must also be 'cut up' so as to acquire meaning. In *The Fashion System* Roland Barthes asks his readers to imagine a woman dressed in an 'endless garment'. In order for it to signify, it must be 'cut up and divided into significant units' (themselves operations of transformation and division) (Barthes, [1967] 1990, p. 43). At times fashion collections have emphasized, or ironically hinted at, a link between the cut of the fabric and slashes to the skin (for example, the British designer Vivienne Westwood's 'Cut N Slash' collection, shown at the Pitti Palace, Florence, in July 1990) (Ash and Wilson, 1992, p. 168).

The cutting or dividing of the female form is further emblematized in the pages of magazines, with the double-page fashion spread. Discussing the work of the photographer Guy Bourdin, Rosetta Brookes notes that:

> To turn the page is not only to open and close the spectacle of the fashion spread, but is also to cut up the figure with which we are spatially identified – to open and close her legs. The model is completely engulfed in the vertical divide . . . leaving the two legs isolated on facing pages. (Brookes, 1992, p. 21)

Such images might provoke the question of whether boundaries between fashion photography, art and pornography are increasingly being blurred. This issue was highlighted in the 1990s with, for example, a photograph by Donna Trope in *Dazed & Confused* (issue 14, 1997). The photograph shows, in side-profile, a naked (although body-painted) model licking the edge of a meat cleaver which looks like it is streaked with 'blood'. A metaphor for how women are objectified in fashion, or something leaving a bad taste?

Modelling

The dissolution of the distinction between catwalk and photographic models increasingly requires models to maintain 'a disciplined regime of body rituals' (Craik, 1994, p. 87). Modelling places an emphasis on self-formation through the body, which itself can be a form of addiction whereby identity is also legitimated by the gaze of others. Jennifer Craik quotes a model who notes that when others stop looking at her, there is nothing left (Craik, 1994, p. 91).

The secularized rituals of body worship dominate Shute's narrative. The anorexic Josie, narrating from the confines of a hospital room, is addicted to a daily ritual of naming the parts and tracing the map of her body, feeling the bruises, hollows, scars and bones. Paradoxically, this procedure legitimates her identity – she cannot bear to be looked at. In an inversion of the process of constructing the ideal technical body, Josie develops positions for her wasted body to adopt which will display each part, 'like an inverse bodybuilder' (p. 43). Shute uses striking imagery to underscore the notion of a second skin and to blur the boundary between inside the body and outside it: Josie's vertebrae are like a row of buttons 'as if they held this body together, as if I could unbutton it and step out' (p. 10). This contrasts with Josie's imagining of a previous second skin: in her past, studying at graduate school, she wore the same clothes every day (drawstring-waist sweatpants and an oversized man's shirt), like the second skin of a 'livid, oily monster' (p. 208). Skin markings, or the appearance of them, become charged with symbolic value, signifying not only the health of the body but a sense of self. Josie has effected a transformation from being 'a mutant monster from the sewers' (p. 175) to wearing a hospital-issue robe which, ironically, makes her skin 'look even more cyanotic' (p. 13).

Shute's text, with its confessional mode, is a forerunner of recent auto/biographies on anorexia and eating disorders. It can also be read within the context of 1990s cultural preoccupations with eating, morality and the female body which focus on a 'split identity'. In numerous magazine articles, interviewees adopt a dualistic model of good and evil, thus 'cutting' themselves in two: being an 'angel' and eating healthily (discipline and denial) or being a 'devil' and eating badly (food itself is personified as a devil). Similarly, models 'divide' themselves, separating their '"professional" bodies from their "lived-in" ones, regarding them as alien' (Craik, 1994, p. 88).

In a series of flashbacks which puncture the narrative, Josie recalls how following the (contradictory) rules of the diet books and studying the magazines' instructions became a form of religion, although she 'still failed to transform' herself (p. 65). The quest for the Holy Grail of a perfect, flawless face is undermined in the text through a series of juxtaposed images: lying in the hospital bed, Josie puts a copy of *Vogue* over her face, so that superimposed on her fragile, pin-pricked skin is the face of the magazine cover, 'each eyelash alert, each tooth a dazzling, chunky Chiclet, the skin a sealed and poreless stretch of pink, and the ripe, shiny lips curved into a radiant smirk' (p. 15).

Beauty rituals are a means of controlling the body; in Shute's text they are also techniques for defining self, although the need to outline the limits of being is questioned. The narrator imagines using make-up to inscribe a self, 'paint on a porcelain skin, pencil in some eyes, brush contour into these cheeks' (p. 59) but decides, 'I don't need a crayon to define the edges of my being' (p. 213). Boundaries are needed, though, to prevent seepage of inner into outer: 'I would have to start over, drawing the bounds again, etching the skeletal self again from that blurred mass bleeding at the edges' (p. 217).

Strategies for dealing with Barbie

Whereas the grotesque body erupts into gaps, orifices and erotogenic zones, the doll 'presents a pure, inpenetrable [*sic*] surface' (Stewart, 1993, p. 112), a plastic embodiment of perfect form and flawless skin. Josie recalls owning a Barbie doll and imagining a future in parallel with careers Barbie might have. Barbie, symmetrical and unmarked,

> lived in an elegant black vanity case, shiny plastic . . . where you inhab-
> ited a modest cubicle (coffin-shaped, now that I think of it) surround-

ed by your sumptuous wardrobe . . . that collection of fantasies for which your hard little form was merely a pretext. (p. 57)

In incorporating an American icon, Shute's novel belongs to a range of texts and practices preoccupied with exploring Barbie's cultural legacy and significance. The majority of these texts, as with the extract from *Life-Size*, see Barbie as symbolic of the intertwining of notions of beauty, the female form, violence and death. In Patricia Storace's 1987 poem 'Barbie Doll', the doll is a vampiric monster, a violent affront, a knife capable of cutting human flesh:

Her perfection is a violence.
Fling her to the soil;
she stands upright and
quivers, a thrown knife.
Grasp her carelessly,
her feet and hands
can damage, the flesh
laddered suddenly with blood.
One of the small things
that cause consequences;
a slap, a razor,
a pinch of cyanide.
One of the things
whose smallness is a honing;
a piranha,
the switchblade of the ocean.
(Ebersole and Peabody, 1993, pp. 46-7)

The perfect body, or an artificial version of it, is an 'impenetrable capsule' which can only be destroyed by dismemberment. There is an interesting analogy here with cosmetic surgery, or more specifically, the process Ruth experiences in *Life and Loves*. In a neat reversal of who is wielding the knife, A. M. Homes's 1990 short story 'A Real Doll' describes the inevitable decline of Barbie to victim status. The narrator discovers that his sister has been mutilating Barbie: the doll has scratches on its chest and stomach, 'deep, like slices' and later, burnt-out breasts, a 'reduction'. The pressures of the 'beauty myth' which might, it is suggested, lead to such a reaction, are exposed in Marge Piercy's darkly satiric 'Barbie Doll' (1982). In this poem a teenager teased for her looks and advised to 'diet and smile' eventually 'cuts off her nose and legs'. The 'ending' replaces the Barbie in the coffin (in Shute's text) with the real girl. It thus reinforces the idea of resurrection ('consummation') as a 'doubling' of the image of the beautiful dead or dying woman:

> In the casket displayed on satin she lay
> with the undertaker's cosmetics painted on,
> a turned-up putty nose,
> dressed in a pink and white nightie.
> Doesn't she look pretty? everyone said.
> Consummation at last.
> To every woman a happy ending.
> (Ebersole and Peabody, 1993, p. 1)

Body to space: interior/exterior

The title of Shute's novel highlights its central preoccupation with questions of scale, morphology and how bodies are perceived and constructed in relation to space. As with Weldon's text the process of shape-changing involves miniaturization and infantilization: for Josie, the world has shrunk while food has become gigantic (eating 'big green branches of broccoli' would be 'like munching on a tree' (p. 2)) and Satanic. Childlike, Josie's only remaining right is to try to determine what goes into her body.

Appalled by the way in which her mother occupied space, 'so crassly exceeding bounds' (p. 123), Josie's quest is simply to occupy space, 'perfecting emptiness' (p. 19). Paradoxically, through reducing or 'redesigning' the body by starving, 'the less I found' and 'the more space it claimed' (p. 230). In presenting the body in this way, the text engages with phenomenological discourse: one knows one's surroundings not through thought alone, but through one's 'bodily situation', that is, one is conscious through the body's position in space (Merleau-Ponty, 1964, p. 5). Josie's body is an object 'both here and there at the same time' (p. 218) and, as such, is imagined in the process of being force-fed: shackled, swollen and penetrated by a tangle of tubes and needles (p. 25).

The probing of the body by needles releases, I would argue, an increasing anxiety that interior and exterior will blend; that boundary violation will occur and privacy disappear in the 'displaying' of 'veins and nerves and guts' (p. 173). The fear also manifests in the anthropomorphism of food and a desire to, surgeon-like, break the item open. The narrator wants to take a spoon to a boiled egg 'and smash its shell and smash again and watch it crack and then stab it with the point of the spoon until its membrane that holds it together ruptures once and for all' (p. 17). Baked potatoes have skins to be slit (p. 126); a slice of orange mutates 'out of the realm of the edible' to resemble 'a section from the dissecting room' (p. 147), and tomatoes require dissecting into equal pieces, with 'no oozing' (p. 23).

At several points in the narrative, glass causes the 'inside' (blood) to escape, in actuality (when Josie folds her fist over a palmful of shards of broken glass) and in fantasy: 'I'm eating ground glass from a silver spoon: it's as delicate as spun sugar or shaved ice . . . my lips turn vivid red from the inside out, my skin chalk-pale (with my dark hair, I'm Snow White, I'm an image floating up from a Pre-Raphaelite lake)' (p. 21).

The references to Snow White and, it is implied, Ophelia (particularly John Everett Millais's 1852 painting) are particularly significant: in nineteenth-century culture these images epitomized the beautiful, 'seemingly' dead woman, preserved and exhibited for the gratification of viewers in, respectively, a glass coffin and a framed work of art. These images of a pure, immutable body are also reminiscent of the popular wax anatomical models created to give medical students a more sanitized access to the human body (Bronfen, 1992, p. 99, cites the collection in La Specola, Florence). The wax models were modelled directly from cadavers in a technique, Bronfen notes, that was also used to recreate the relics of martyrs and saints. Any insides 'caught' coming out of the body are thus controlled, as is death.

Epiphany

'In the body, as in art, perfection is attained not when there's nothing left to add, but when there's nothing left to take away', observes Josie (p. 117). Weldon's and Shute's protagonists share a desire to be purified through a process of reduction. Indeed, Shute's text works towards what could be termed an epiphanic moment, when the narrator experiences a quasi-spiritual awakening: 'walking home from classes one dazzling blue day, I was overwhelmed by the brightness, which, inhaled, expanded like helium in the head. My brain became a radiant blur, my limbs very long and light' (p. 222). It is as if the body is immaterial, whereas the consciousness can expand into the universe. For Josie, the quest is crystallized: 'one day I will be pure consciousness, travelling unmuffled through the world; one day I will refine myself to the bare wiring, the irreducible circuitry that keeps mind alive' (p. 7). The means to achieve this goal is starvation; enlightenment through denial. 'Starvation is fulfilling, at first anyway. That is why, I suppose, mystics go in for it. Colors become clearer, sounds sharper, as if some kind of fuzz had been scraped off perception' (p. 117). To achieve clarity of perception, flesh must be stripped away; in a sense the narrator is fashioning herself as a relic ahead of death. 'Just the bones, no disfiguring flesh, just the pure, clear shape of me. Bones. That is what we are, after all, what we're made of, and everything else is storage, deposit, waste. Strip it away, use it up, no deposit, no return' (p. 9). In a particularly striking image, Josie's body 'is here, crucified on this cold metal chair – even the arms, all edges, cut into my bones – but I am not' (p. 70). This is in a sense a double inversion: of the scene of the cross in Christian iconography and as a secular replacement of Christ's body with the 'virginal, innocent' woman who triumphs over death through the spectacle of suffering (Bronfen, 1992, p. 89).

Conclusion

There is always an impasse in dealing with the notion of 'outside': for example, the grotesque or the inappropriated is an impasse to the extent that it remains inaccessible. In order to be brought into discourse it must be internalized or framed.

The 'freak' or the 'monstrous' body importantly transgresses boundaries, especially the boundary that internalizes the body in its own skin.

In Louise Welsh's crime novel *The Cutting Room* (2002) the detective is unable to tell from a photograph whether a beautiful, mutilated young woman is 'dead' or not. The aestheticized body masks any lethal cuts, even as images themselves are 'cut' in the editing suite, or news of horrific or violent events read in a cutting from a newspaper.

Cutting is also a means of propagation (compromised through self-transformation for the protagonists of Weldon's and Shute's texts); something 'cut' with another substance is adulterated; in fashion 'cutting-edge' is a virtue.

Cutting the body leaves scars which can mark out pleasure and pain as territory; map the body's memory; be a stigma or sign of disgrace. If the scar is a memory, it has a direct link to the past, to the 'old pattern' or the body prior to remodelling. In *Life and Loves*, Ruth tries to arrange her hair and clothes to hide unsightly scars. The doctors think that she has healed well:

> as if the parted flesh were all too eager to leap together again in its new configuration. In most cosmetic patients wounds seemed determined to mend in the old pattern, not the new, building up scar tissue in an attempt to make things as they had been, not as they now were. (p. 237)

I have discussed the textual representation of the female body changing shape, in relation to technologies of transformation and discourses of beauty, femininity and death. What is ultimately at stake, perhaps, is not the question of agency, or the expansion or reduction of form, but whether the skin is cut. In *Life-Size*, Josie attempts to read a book: 'topology: the study of those properties of figures that remain unchanged even when under distortion, so long as no surfaces are torn' (p. 35).

References

Ash, Juliet and Wilson, Elizabeth, *Chic Thrills: A Fashion Reader* (Pandora, 1992)

Bakhtin, Mikhail, *Rabelais and His World*, trans. Helen Iswolsky (Indiana University Press, 1984)

Barthes, Roland, *The Fashion System* [1967], trans M. Ward and R. Howard (California University Press, 1990)

Benthien, Claudia, *Skin: On the Cultural Border between Self and the World* [1999] (Columbia University Press, 2002), chapters 3–6

Bronfen, Elisabeth, *Death, Femininity and the Aesthetic* (Manchester University Press, 1992)

Brookes, Rosetta, 'Fashion Photography: The Double-Page Spread: Helmut Newton, Guy Bourdin and Deborah Turbeville' in J. Ash and E. Wilson, eds, *Chic Thrills: A Fashion Reader* (Pandora, 1992), 17–24

Colebrook, Claire, *Gender* (Palgrave, 2003)

Craik, Jennifer, *The Face of Fashion* (Routledge, 1994)

Davis, Kathy, *Reshaping the Female Body: The Dilemma of Cosmetic Surgery* (Methuen, 1995)

De la Haye, Amy, *The Cutting Edge: Fifty Years of British Fashion 1947–1997* (V&A, 1997)

Douglas, Mary, *Purity and Danger: An Analysis of Concepts of Pollution and Taboo* (Routledge, 2002)

Ebersole, Lucinda and Peabody, Richard, eds, *Mondo Barbie: An Anthology of Fiction and Poetry* (St Martin's Press, 1993)

Fiedler, Leslie, *Freaks: Myths and Images of the Secret Self* (Simon & Schuster, 1978)

Hurley, Kelly, *The Gothic Body: Sexuality, Materialism and Degeneration at the Fin de Siecle* (Cambridge University Press, 1996)

Hollander, Anne, 'Accounting for Fashion', *Raritan* (Fall 1993) 13: 2, pp. 121–32

Isherwood, Lisa and Stuart, Elizabeth, eds, *Introducing Body Theology* (Sheffield Academic Press, 1998)

Lacan, Jacques, *Ecrits*, trans. A. Sheridan (Norton, 1977)

Merleau-Ponty, Maurice, *The Primacy of Perception*, ed. J. M. Edie (Northwestern University Press, 1964)

Orbach, Susie, *Hunger Strike* (Penguin, 1993)

Peterson, Shirley, 'Freaking Feminism: *The Life and Loves of a She-Devil* and *Nights at the Circus* as Narrative Freak Shows' in R. G. Thomson, ed., *Freakery: Cultural Spectacles of the Extraordinary Body* (New York University Press, 1996)

Poovey, Mary, *Making a Social Body* (University of Chicago Press, 1995)

Russo, Mary, *The Female Grotesque: Risk, Excess, and Modernity* (Routledge, 1994)

Scarry, Elizabeth, *The Body in Pain* (Oxford University Press, 1985)

Showalter, Elaine, *Sexual Anarchy: Gender and Culture at the Fin de Siecle* (Viking, 1990)

Shute, Jenefer, *Life-Size* (Minerva, 1992)

Silver, Anna Krugovoy, *Victorian Literature and the Anorexic Body* (Cambridge University Press, 2002)

Stewart, Susan, *On Longing: Narratives of the Miniature, the Gigantic, the Souvenir, the Collection* (Duke University Press, 1993)

Tanner, Laura, *Intimate Violence: Reading Rape and Torture in Twentieth-Century Fiction* (Indiana University Press, 1994)

Thomson, Rosemarie Garland, ed., *Freakery: Cultural Spectacles of the Extraordinary Body* (New York University Press, 1996)

Warner, Marina, *From the Beast to the Blonde: On Fairy Tales and their Tellers* (Chatto & Windus, 1994)

Weldon, Fay, *The Life and Loves of a She Devil* (Sceptre, 1983)

Welsh, Louise, *The Cutting Room* (Canongate, 2002)

Wigley, Mark, 'Untitled: The Housing of Gender' in B. Colomina, ed., *Sexuality and Space* (Princeton Architectural Press, 1992), 327–89

Wolf, Naomi, *The Beauty Myth* (Vintage, 1991)

Wood, Christopher, *The Pre-Raphaelites* (Weidenfeld & Nicolson, 1981)

3

Cutting Edge: Witnessing Rites of Passage in a Therapeutic Community

ELIZABETH BAXTER

In this essay I am attempting to understand something I have not experienced myself. Although I have been alongside people for whom self-harm through cutting is their reality, I cannot even begin to come near to understanding the depth of pain and rage that leads someone to so deliberately self-harm. Yet through this accompaniment I recognize glimpses of connection with the Jesus story, which has to be the story of the body of Christ/Christa today, and *I am* part of that body and a witness to its being and becoming. This is the *I am* body, living, moving, and having its being and becoming desecrated, for 'our bodyselves become the ground upon which God moves through, with and among us' and they 'are the nature and destiny of God' (Heyward, 1989, p. 71 and p. 33).

Living in a therapeutic community with a Christian foundation, I find myself asking what it means to be a witness in the Church today, to the healing of the brokenhearted. Who are the witnesses, and what has the one whose pain and process I witness been witness to, for research has identified witnessing as one of the predominant factors where an ethic of 'might is right' is learned and well mastered (Lines, 2006, p. 15)? And primarily, how may someone so wounded be a witness to me of the real presence of the *I am*? I do not suggest I have any answers, but I will attempt to find a chink of light in this vast body of human experience, offering perhaps a small glimpse of hope in a sea of despair.

Learning from the 'signifying practice' (see Butler, 1990) of cutting rituals, my question becomes more focused as I ask how the witness of the community to such rites of passage may bring some form of healing into a wounded situation. My experience leads me to believe that coming to a therapeutic centre is a symbolic action in and of itself, and the healing process is already in action as the rite of passage has already begun. I would like to be able to dream of the possibility of Christian communities as expressions of church, becoming safe enough to be therapeutic centres, where a person for whom space and place has been so unsafe may yet find her own safe space in which to act out her healing rituals. I found a new key to unlock some of my own understanding when someone whose pain I had been witnessing reached out and held me, whispering tearfully, 'this is the first time I have ever felt safe enough to feel unsafe'.

Mortification of the flesh has been part of human ritualistic behaviour expressed in different ways in different generations and cultures. Blood has held symbolic powers of healing. The spilling of blood gives life during birth and takes away life at death. Rituals include blood sacrifices, blood-letting, ecstatic stigmata, drinking of wine at the Christian eucharistic ritual, initiation rites of cutting and psychological release of ill-will known metaphorically as 'getting rid of bad blood'. Mortification of the flesh is found at the heart of Christian faith and its doctrines of salvation, and the Catholic Church canonizes those who mortified their flesh. These Saints have become intercessory agents for the sick as well as receiving salvation for their suffering. The psychiatrist Edward Podvoll suggests that the history of images of self-harming reaches at least as far back as the Passion of the Cross (see Podvoll, 1969, cited in Gardner, 2001, p. 136). The Old Testament refers to the prophets of Baal ritualistically cutting themselves,[1] a practice forbidden to the Israelites,[2] and the Gospel narrative includes the story of the 'Gerasene demoniac' who bruised himself with stones.[3] A tradition of mystical Islamic healers in Morocco has been to work themselves into a frenzy and slash open their heads in ritual while sick people would dip bread or sugar cubes in the healer's blood and eat them. The blood of the healer becomes the

1 1 Kings 18.28.
2 Leviticus 19.28, Deuteronomy 14.1.
3 Mark 5.5.

healing medicine. In shamanic cultures shamans endure terrifying sickness, dreams and visions and dismemberment of their bodies – their bones and flesh are then reassembled (re-membered) and the shaman becomes the wise healing person (Strong, 2000, p. ix). Sufi mystics – whirling dervishes – slash heads, hammer spikes into their skin, swallow glass and razor blades and feed their blood to others in order to drive out evil spirits and for healing. The West's fascination with the bodies of other cultures has led to the postmodern primitive 'New Flesh' scene, de-naturalizing and de-stabilizing the cultural constructions of the western ideal of the body, transgressing mainstream acceptabilities:

> The progenitors of the New Flesh . . . are already among us. Their influence can be detected in the enthusiastic uptake of non-functional, decorative body modifications like piercing, tattooing and scarification. These are the signs of a palpable refusal to be bound by the previously prescribed limits of the body and an attempt to transcend it by transforming it, by undergoing a process of transmutation. (Sherman, n.d., p. 59, cited in Fernbach, 2002, p. 15)

I would argue that the modern-day 'cutter' is buying into this milieu and has found a deconstructive way forward to express her pain and terror, to be heard and to find some release, for 'the body is still the map on which we mark our meanings' (Warner, 1985, p. 331).

An estimated 170,000 cases of self-harm come to the attention of UK hospital staff each year and 24,000 are aged under 25. The charity Childline reports that it counselled 4,000 children about self-harm in 2004, a 30 per cent rise on the previous year. A 2000/01 survey of 6,000 teenagers for the Samaritans, conducted by the Centre for Suicide Research at Oxford University, found that 10 per cent had self-harmed. The Samaritans' research in 41 schools was summed up in a report, *Youth and Self-Harm: Perspectives*. It found that girls were four times more likely to self-harm than boys, with cutting more common than poisoning. (This is why I refer to the female gender in this essay.) Self-harm was also more prevalent among white pupils.[4] Catherine

---

4 *Public Health News*, 15 August 2005, 'Self destruct', p. 9.

McLoughlin, chair of the national inquiry into self-harm, says, 'Young people want to talk about this and want to have a plan to manage it. Many of them don't want to give it up.'[5] For many the ritual is carefully set out, ordered, disciplined and obsessively prepared, sometimes leading to careful patterning or deliberate dangerous action. This rite of passage is spoken of as 'The syndrome of delicate self-cutting'.[6] Even following a healing of the wounds there may be ritualistic interference with them, picking at scabs and reopening scars.

What then may the adolescent be witnessing to through this dramatic and ritualistic action, and how should the witnesses respond?

Whatever our community or family, we often become witnesses to rites of passage becoming especially acute with adolescents who create their own initiation rites which get jumbled up in and among western society's initiation structures, such as legal ages for behaviour, confirmation and senior school. Dress, music, addictive behaviour and experimentation are all part of these rites for young people from a relatively stable background, but for those whose childhoods have been shattered through abuse, neglect or violence, rites of passage are often expressed differently and dangerously through self-harm and manifested in different ways. Generally, but not entirely, women and girls act out self-harm interiorly through eating or cutting behaviours, while men and boys tend to act out exteriorly through dangerous activities with peers or dramatic action in often pre-planned solitude. Dangerous peer behaviour with adolescent boys and cutting behaviours with adolescent girls correspond with many tribal rites of passage, such as the stick-fighting of boys and the cutting of lips and breasts by girls in the Suri people of Ethiopia.[7]

Rites of passage for adolescents expressed through the shedding of blood may distress adults, but are often just part of growing up. For example, before the threat of AIDS boys would play at becoming blood-brothers, and teenagers would pierce body parts at the back of the class-

5 *Public Health News*, 15 August 2005, 'Self destruct', p. 10.

6 *British Journal of Medical Psychology* 42 (1969), pp. 195–205.

7 BBC 2, Monday 10 January 2005, *Tribe*, Bruce Parry lives among the Suri people.

room! More sophisticated body-piercing is now practised in the West as a norm, with tattoos for adolescent girls and body-piercings for both genders. The whole of society in the West witnesses these rites of passage, but they cannot be put in the same frame as adolescent self-harm, through cutting, which may also be the outcome of the biochemical changes during puberty activating structural damage done in childhood trauma affecting the interaction of brain, hormones and environment.

To further my understanding I have to ask why so many people deliberately harm themselves through cutting rituals. Favazza attempts two answers:

> The short answer . . . is that it provides temporary relief from a host of painful symptoms such as anxiety, depersonalization, and despera- tion. The long answer is that it also touches upon the very profound human experiences of salvation, healing and orderliness. (Favazza, 1996, cited in Strong, 2000, p. 34)

I suggest that this ritual finds its profundity in the scarring of the skin, for scars are richly symbolic. They are a permanent record of both the pain and the healing. Favazza is once again insightful:

> The scars of the process . . . signify an ongoing battle and that all is not lost. As befits one of nature's great triumphs, scar tissue is a magical substance, a physiological and psychological mortar that holds flesh and spirit together when a difficult world threatens to tear both apart. (Favazza, 1996, cited in Strong, 2000, p. 35)

Rituals make connections particularly between a passage of time, and 'otherness' or transcendence, and Fiona Bowie argues that rites of passage can be seen as archetypal ritual processes, encompassing in their simple threefold structure a pattern underlying all rituals (Bowie, 2000, p. 158). Van Gennep defines this structure in the three stages of separa- tion to transition to incorporation or reaggregation, or preliminal to liminal to postliminal (cited in Bowie, 2000, p. 162); the cutter travels through these three stages, and in the second stage the direct damage to the skin is particularly symbolically meaningful, becoming a route for transformation involving a transcendent aspect of religious belief. The skin acts as a 'medium for communication, (and a) container for the sense of self' (Gardner, 2001, p. 33). Body and skin becomes the locus for anxiety, fear and difference, as well as eroticism and comfort. Primarily there is a fleshing out of injustice perpetrated on the abused. This may include actual bodily abuse, as well as societal and religious abusive injustices, as Camryn, a 19-year-old Australian cutter writes in her poem 'Escape':

> She pays such a terrible
> price for her sin and
> at last the outside
> matches the in
> justice.
> (cited in Strong, 2000, p. 1)

The wounds and scars on the skin hold the symbolic meanings, representing earlier history/herstory, for 'scars are stories, history written on the body' (Harrison, cited in Strong, 2000, p. 17). There is a desperate attempt to communicate and tell the story, when the verbal telling has been silenced through physiological and psychological damage often through those societal and religious projections, for 'what is carved in human flesh is an image of society' (Douglas, 1966, p. 117). Scars may be used to 're-member' events when the mind is in so much turmoil that memory is affected. A scar will record a time of trauma, precipitated by a particular event at a particular time, a language written on the body through blood, scars and open wounds. The skin tells the story as the cutting has become a 'substitute' for the pain inside – a tangible, physical pain that can be controlled and released. This substitutionary aspect echoes the substitutional atonement theories in Christian tradition, in particular, words attributed to Saint Peter, 'He himself bore our sins in his body on the cross, so that, free from sins, we might live for righteousness; by his wounds you have been healed.'[8] Such theories remove responsibility

---

8 1 Peter 2.24.

from those who cause the harm and destruction. The innocent one is punished for the sins of the perpetrator of crime, and this is glorified. Such sentiments are borne out in hymnody such as 'daring shame and scoffing rude, / in my place condemned he stood, / sealed my pardon with his blood',[9] and 'See from his head, his hands, his feet, / sorrow and love flow mingled down, / did ere such love and sorrow meet, / did thorns compose so rich a crown?'[10] I would argue that this unconscious echo in the mind and body of the abused person has often been perpetuated through the collusion by churches with such doctrines, and this urgently needs to be addressed.

For most people tears are part of the language of pain, but for others there are no tears, there is only numbness, or the tears that there have been are too little to release the pain. It may be that the child's tears were responded to by adults with violence or dismissal. For many people other forms of release come through verbal communication, but an abused person may well have learnt experience of being unable to breathe or shout out as well as learning methods of secretive behaviour. Their words may have been denied or minimized by adults, or they may have internalized the aggressive verbalization of adults around them, and unable to release it through sound, release it now through cuts to the body. The process of puberty may cause severe anxiety around unintegrative body changes, reaffirming lack of worth, disgust and detestation of the body, especially those parts which have been particularly molested. Some girls may control their menstrual cycle by anorexic behaviours while simulating through controlled cutting behaviours, for cutting becomes controlled bleeding rather than the uncontrollable bleeding of menstruation. Many people believe they cannot speak of their trauma because harm may come to the listener, who will think they are evil. Many of us who accompany traumatized people have heard the stories of a therapist becoming ill or having an accident shortly after a session. Other adults are then 'protected' by more silence. This may be a repeat of what happened in childhood, and the agitation to cut becomes

---

9 Isaac Watts.
10 Isaac Watts.

stronger and the scars will demonstrate the internal chaos and fear, for cutting is usually precipitated by the feeling of utter loss and abandonment, symbolic of the words attributed to Jesus on the cross, 'My God, my God, why have you forsaken me?'[11] This he spoke before the words 'it is finished'.[12] The cutter will bring a temporary ending from the pain of abandonment, for she does not allow herself to abandon herself; rather than a cry of suicide, it becomes a cry leading to the possibilities of a brief glimpse of resurrection, while initiating the witness into her world.

> The skin becomes a battlefield as a demonstration of internal chaos. The place where the self meets the world is a canvas or *tabula rasa* on which is displaced exactly how bad one feels inside. (psychologist, Scott Lines, cited in Strong, 2000, p. 29)

The journalist Marilee Strong calls the cutters she spent time with heroes and heroines, and found hope through their search for a brighter future (see Strong, 2000, Acknowledgements and Introduction). Although such a future may not be possible as damage may be irreversible, nevertheless the action taken in cutting is a reminder to the cutter that she is still alive, the 'deadness' of her 'being' is interrupted and as the fresh blood flows there is fresh cause for hope.

> 'Thus, with a few strokes of the razor the self-cutter may unleash a symbolic process in which the sickness within is removed and the stage is set for healing as evidenced by a scar.' (Favazza, 1996, cited in Strong, 2000, p. 35)

In many situations, hope may well not be realized. I recall time spent with Rosie, whose whole body was scarred with ligature, cutting and burning scarring. Her scars were a mixture of self-infliction and inflicted in abusive rituals perpetrated on this lovely woman who witnessed love and trust to me. Sadly the stage she had set for her healing was not freed

---

11 Matthew 27.46.

12 John 19.30.

enough from the abusive players in her life, and I still have a poem she wrote about the love she found during the time in the community. I hold that as dear, as some weeks later her aunt wrote to say she had finally killed herself through methane gas at the back of her caravan. My hope for Rosie now becomes the hope she may have sought for in her final action.

People working through their own rites of passage will take charge of their ritual, and some cutters find comfort, strength and security in their stash of blades, or blood stains they have pressed in a journal, or a vial of blood they keep on display. The need to take control of what feels out of control leads to controlled cutting practices taking control of one's own body. If a person's abuse has led to bleeding, this can be either counter-acted or re-enacted, through self-cutting, and blood may be drunk, tasted or smeared; such behaviour is not far from that of other rituals mentioned at the beginning of this essay. The Christian rituals of the sacrament of the mass, with benediction and revering of relics, especially those which are supposedly blood-stained, may have been part of the person's background, and she may buy into it as the priest of her own sacramental action. She will choose carefully where this is to take place and may claim it by ritually cleansing the place before the cutting begins, laying out cutting implements and healing cloths in ritualistic fashion.

Some people choose witnesses to their process, and these will be chosen carefully. Susan asked me if I would witness her therapeutic process. She led me to a large room where she had set out on the floor around one hundred A4 drawings and paintings of her own. Here was a reflection of her therapeutic journey over the years, and she stood back as I silently moved from one to the other, until I felt I had witnessed what she had asked me, and I then stood with her, with no words, just a touch of hands. Here was a journey of abuse and terror, leading to raw emotion, rage and fury, to self-acceptance and a peaceful spirit. The witnessing ritual became an integral next step for Susan as she found the courage and wisdom to move on from the place of victim to survivor, and from survivor to a fuller awareness of who she may yet become – her *I am.*

The *I am* witnesses primarily to herself, breaking out of the self-policing (see O'Grady, 2005) which has dominated and immobilized her; and, refusing to engage with the dominant cultural norms of internalizing the abuse, she 'opens space for the exploration of alternative, preferred self-relations and increases possibilities for active participation in identity making [. . . revealing] the potential for renegotiating given relations of power' (O'Grady, 2005, p. 35). Through this subversive action the *I am*, whose underwear has been stripped away through abusive practice, now parades her innerwear as outerwear (for other usage see Fernbach, 2002, p. 15), challenging her inner fears about the crossing of the boundaries of her own body and inner anxieties arising from the transgression of boundaries within the social body (Douglas, 1966, p. 3). For without the 'marks', the cutter 'sees herself' as 'unremarkable' (see Mascia-Lees and Sharpe, 1992), indeed she does not 'see herself' at all. With the 'marks' she is made whole again and becomes a witness to her healing action. Fakir Musafar, an exponent of ritualistic body play, made a similar point regarding lack and completion, in his discussion on tattooing. Fakir associated the out-of-body experience with a state of completion (cited in Fernbach, 2002, pp. 111–14), and I surmise that the cutter who disassociated into an out-of-body experience during the abuse is 'redeeming' that experience.

An important question to be asked is: How may a person be able to 'see herself' in abusive situations? How is she able to become a witness both to her abuse and to her redemption? A key to this, I would suggest, is the dissociative state, a strategy for survival. According to the international version of the *Diagnostic and Statistical Manual of Mental Disorders*,[13]

The essential feature of the Dissociative Disorders is a disruption in the usually integrated functions of conciousness, memory, identity, or perception of the environment. (cited in *Counselling and Psychotherapy Journal*, April 2004, p. 24)

---

13 American Psychiatric Association (1995), *Diagnostic and Statistical Manual of Mental Disorders*, 4th edn, International Version, Washington, DC, American Psychiatric Association.

This mind/body split is a psychological strategy, and may give cause to the abused to witness the abuse from an altered state, or to 'absent' herself from any witness to the abuse, repressing any memory. In this way she overturns any whiff of panoptical power structures (see Foucault, 1979), transgressing normative boundaries and 'charting . . . a personal history [*herstory*] of *resistance* to the abuse and its ongoing effects, including those that continue to be reinforced by the broader culture' (O'Grady, 2005, p. 39, my italics and addition). In order to survive she may even teach herself to believe any physical effects or injuries are due to something other than abuse. She may use terms about herself such as 'she is not me'. The key to an understanding of this is the 'sense' (when the 'senses' are dulled), of the absence of the *I am*.

[Dissociation] . . . begins with the child's self-hypnotic assertion '*I am* not here; this is not happening to me; *I am* not in this body.' (Mellon, 1996, p. 15, my italics)

Dissociation learnt as a child may become a conditioned response causing disintegration and fragmentation, and an urgent requirement for reintegration. There may be a depersonalization accompanied by derealization, a disconnectedness from reality. There are times when the numbness goes and the pain is so acute that the person will cut to release the pressure building up – like a boil to be burst. The sight and even taste of the blood will become a release and the person will feel real and alive again. She will be reassured that she exists, and may lovingly care for the wounds, helping in the healing process.

Stelarc, a simulation body performer, whose work is about the disavowal of his body, refers to his performances as 'body-by-pass' events, and writes, 'what I am doing is bypassing the normal thresholds of the body . . . it's the primal urge to transcend your physical limitations' (cited in Fernbach, 2002, p. 111). The cutter who has so often by-passed her body during abuse, through dissociation, acts out this experience once again, but this time, as a redemptive act, wilful and controlled, often with ritualistic preparation and tender care. There is a tension between the disavowal of the body and the re-acceptance of it as the cutter seeks to transcend her physical limitations which have been further curtailed through intrusive and invasive abusive practice by others. She acts out 'ascension' leading to glory and fulfilment. This moment of glory is short-lived, and her action becomes repetitive and addictive, a continual action of 're-membering'.

Both Stelarc and Fakir work on a mind/body dualism, not feeling the pain when the skin is pierced but becoming the observer and recorder of bodily sensation as the body feels the pain (see Fernbach, 2002, p. 113). The person who has had to learn the survival technique of dissociation will need to reintegrate mind and body before she is able to let go of the practice of cutting. This process is a long and painful journey in itself, and even with the best psychotherapist and the safest space within which to work, this may not be enough to undo the profound damage done to a person's very being, the very murder of her soul.[14] She may have to continue to be a survivor through her redemptive rituals, and a loving, accepting community will need to be alongside her in those actions. These in turn may minimize susceptibility to the shame she feels from having been shamed so violently (Millar, cited in Pattison, 2000, p. 118). She must not feel from the community that her actions are shameful, for they become for her empowering actions to kill shame, by the mortification of the body (Kinston, cited in Pattison, 2000, p. 118). Christ was shamed by the community, through death as a common criminal, stripped naked and ridiculed. The bodily resurrection tradition of Christian faith transcends this shaming, and the cutter enters into the same transcendence through her 'ascension' experience.

An integral aspect of the cutting ritual is the period of time leading up to it. This is a painful time of transition, a crossroad. It is in this space that the person may be getting in touch with her own wisdom, for it is 'at the crossroads' that wisdom 'takes her stand'.[15] Her wisdom, however, will be damaged by the abuse she has experienced, and her understanding will be askew. Nevertheless, the community must respect her honour, her own enlightenment and her own decision to self-harm. This is her

---

14 Leonard Shengold's term 'Soul Murder' referring to effects on abused children.

15 Proverbs 8.2.

power, her wisdom, her way forward out of the pain. Perhaps for the first time she is taking control of her own life. To have come this far is a courageous step. She is making it clear in her own way that she is a survivor, yet the intense and immense agitation building up from the depth of her being, her *I am*, leads her to this dramatic ritual. Some people describe the feelings leading up to a cutting ritual, as 'about to explode', and we may only surmise the devastating and fragmented effect of that possibility. The *I am not* creates a loss of sacrality, a loss of real presence, a dis-membering. For effective re-membering, the community is required to be real and safe enough to hold and witness the pain and to heal the brokenhearted, by re-establishing real presence, the *I am*. The person herself may find her own *I am* through the grounding experience of cutting and seeing for herself her own blood flowing. Favazza calls self-injury 'a morbid act of self-help' 'converting chaos to calm, powerlessness to control' (cited in Strong, 2000, p. 43). It is essential for the community to acknowledge this ritual, for as Alice Millar recalls from her own experience, 'an unacknowledged trauma is like a wound that never heals over and may start to bleed again at any time' (cited in Strong, 2000, p. 85). However, a compassionate accompaniment may lead towards finding other, safer, grounding strategies, not primarily for the sake of the community, but for the sake of the person who is to gain a sense of her immense worth, indeed, of her reflection of the *I am* to the community, for here is Christa bleeding yet again, redeeming shameful acts of betrayal and denial, perhaps from the community to which I belong, and indeed, through my accompaniment I may feel personally attacked, as she attacks her body, which becomes both mine and hers, entwined together as part of the body of Christ/Christa.

> Survivors who self-mutilate consistently describe a profound disso-ciative state preceding the act. Depersonalisation, derealisation, and anesthesia are accompanied by a feeling of unbearable agitation and a compulsion to attack the body. (Herman, 1994, p. 109)

This attack on the body is an attack on the community, the community the survivor was supposed to be able to trust, the family, the youth club, the church. The body of Christ/Christa will be a body able to bear this attack, to bleed and rage with the attacker, and to gather her afterwards gently bathing the wounds together. Yet it is not enough to bathe wounds. The very rage itself can be turned around from self-destruction to new wise action for change, discovering wisdom again as she stands at the crossroads of a changed vista, for nothing can be the same again. The many voices of the community harmonize in solidarity as they cry out for justice, freeing up the lost and silenced voice of the wounded one. New and deeper cuts have to be made in the systems of oppression that cause such abuse. The very community that bathes the wounds needs to look to itself to discover the betraying and denying within its own embodied way of being, for while the community is abusive in its language, symbolic and action, the *I am* becomes both the abuser and the abused, as a research participant diagnosed with Dissociative Identity Disorder describes:

> I have DID and there is an alter . . . Sometimes when I consciously self-injure she will come out and finish the job. I will not know what damage has been done until I wake up the next day. I become so detached that it is like I become in a trance-like state and it is like **I am** (my bold type) watching someone else doing the cutting. (see Sutton, 2004, p. 27)

Rose (1997, p. 151) argues that the 'alter' is the persecutor who acts as a misguided protector, and I believe we have licence to make connections with the way in which the Church has used trinitarian doctrine to play one 'person of the trinity' off against another, for example the friendly Jesus, the judgemental Father and the powerful, guiding Spirit, leading to confusing altered states making different and often abusing demands on the religious person who hears different voices, and acts accordingly. How much more should the religious community take responsibility for such projection, for now the wounded person, the fragmented *I am* will need the reassurance of safe, grounded space, the still, harmonious voice of acceptance, peace, and the 'edgeless love' Gillian Rose wrote about, commanding 'the complete unveiling of the eyes, the transparency of the body' (Rose, 1997, p. 98).

In my attempt to find an understanding of witness to christic action, I turn to the experience of Chris Nicholson, who worked at Jacques Hall Therapeutic Community between 1998 and 2004. He suggests that adolescents are seeking to create or recreate the self through self-harm. Such behaviour, he argues, 'can engender in the witness the recognition of wounds and the desire to comfort' (Nicholson, 2004, p. 34). However, he suggests that cleaning and dressing the wounds may be inappropriate, rather it may be important for the witness, however disturbing the experience, to stay with the young person, with the wounds (if they are superficial), and with the blood, to be a witness to the pain the young person is acting out that was caused to her by an adult. He writes, 'the cut to the child's self also cuts the adult witness who is forced to stay with the painful wound' (Nicholson, 2004, p. 35). If the wound is bandaged the pain is hidden once again. It becomes a secret and the young person will withdraw back into herself and into a place of denial. Part of the witness in such situations is to act differently to the abusive adult in the person's memory, or to those who did not listen previously. Listening is essential, for in mid-journey a self-harmer cannot hear our words of comfort, she needs to be heard through our witness of her action. This form of rite of passage for the troubled adolescent is reminiscent of the story of Jesus in the garden of Gethsemane calling his disciples to witness his agony. 'Stay awake with me,' he says. 'Could you not stay awake with me one hour?'[16] '. . . in his anguish he prayed more earnestly, and his sweat became like great drops of blood falling down on the ground.'[17]

Reconciliation is at the heart of the Christian faith, and attempts by adolescents to achieve acceptance by family or society, through self-harm, are 'pacts, unconscious and sealed with blood, indicating the adolescents' desire to be reconciled with society' (Favazza, 1996, cited in Nicholson, 2004, p. 41). An early church hymn used similar language to the above, 'through [his beloved Son] God was pleased to reconcile to himself all things . . . by making peace through the blood of his cross'.[18]

---

16 Matthew 26.38–40.
17 Luke 22.44.
18 Colossians 1.20.

Reconciliation is understood in different ways; for example, a distressed girl may be anorexic or traumatized through abuse, causing her periods to cease. She may start to cut in order to release her flow of blood, so she may feel reconciled with society's expectations of her.

Our witness of the person, the pain and the blood, becomes part of the reconciliation process. As such a witness we become the priest enabling the rite of passage towards reconciliation and peace. Brian Thorne explores these ideas in his discussion around ideas of psychotherapist as priest as he suggests that counsellors and psychotherapists offer hope as 'potential substitute family members' (Thorne, 1998, pp. 40–2 and 2003, see prologue and first chapter).

One of Edward Shillito's poems expresses this relationship, the cry of the wounded distressed longing for the balm of Christ, who experiences the wounds in his own body and whose scars bring grace. Those who claim to be the christic body are called in this poem to 'draw . . . near . . . when the doors are shut'.

> If we have never sought, we seek Thee now;
> Thine eyes burn through the dark, our only stars;
> We must have sight of thorn-pricks on Thy brow,
> We must have Thee, O Jesus of the Scars.
>
> The heavens frighten us; they are too calm;
> In all the universe we have no place.
> Our wounds are hurting us; where is the balm?
> Lord Jesus, by Thy Scars, we claim Thy grace.
>
> If, when the doors are shut, Thou drawest near,
> Only reveal those hands, that side of Thine;
> We know to-day what wounds are, have no fear,
> Show us Thy Scars, we know the countersign.
>
> The other gods were strong; but Thou wast weak
> They rode, but Thou didst stumble to a throne;
> But to our wounds only God's wounds can speak,
> And not a god has wounds, but Thou alone.
> (Edward Shillito, 'Jesus of the scars', n.d.)

The *countersign* is the key to this relationship. The identification is at the heart of this rite of passage. For Christians accompanying a person self-harming through cutting, there can be no greater identification. The Eucharist, the Communion, the Mass, bears this out in the words of Jesus, spoken by the minister or priest, 'This is my body, this is my blood . . . take eat . . . drink . . . to re-member me.' In this therapeutic accompaniment, the rite of passage Christians experience in the Eucharist corresponds with the rite of passage the distressed person is travelling, and we become witnesses as Shillito's poem grounds us in the vulnerability and wounds of the *I am*.

Rites of passage in many cultures use cutting as part of initiation into adulthood. This has often been associated with letting out the blood of the mother who has nourished and nurtured the child until puberty. This wrench from the mother, through violation of the body and permanent separation, may be seen as an archetype in the Christian ritual of baptism, when a mother's birth is not enough, and is seen as unclean and even demonized. The child is often taken from the mother's arms by the minister, baptized and shown to the 'new' family within which the child has been initiated, and then placed in the care of 'God-parents'. In this initiation rite evil is renounced, and the birthing and nurturing one – the mother – is abandoned. Even Julian of Norwich, a fourteenth-century mystic, whose writings inspire many people today, spoke of the crucified Jesus as her true mother, reflecting again on the shedding and ridding of the mother's blood, the feminine, that the Father may be glorified. It needs to be considered that the self-harming adolescent girl may be acting out an archetypal rite found at the heart of Christian faith and she may be attacking 'the undifferentiated and internalised mother figure' (Gardner, 2001, p. 73).

> Attacking the external body as a way of managing the fantasised mother inside emphasises the blurring of the boundary between 'inside me' and 'outside me' . . . Cutting the skin gives expression to the need to cut the ties and sever the connection with mother. It establishes a sense of body edge, and gives the cutter a powerful sense of ownership of her own body and her own blood. Repeated cutting

increasingly tethers the young woman to her body as the locus for the solution to problem feelings. Thus self-harm not only acts as a self-soothing comfort, but . . . can develop into a form of perverted self-mothering. (Gardner, 2001, p. 73)

In addition to religious projections supporting the loss of mother care, there are all the abused and neglected children who have no parental example of care at all. These children will have learnt the hard way to 'care' for themselves, and if they become self-harmers, will have an automatic response to the soothing of their pain through seeking to heal the wounds they have inflicted on themselves. Creating a tactile experience through cutting may provide a temporary pleasurable and soothing feeling rather than the deadness experienced previously. Traumatized children often draw themselves without arms as well as cutting their arms in later life. Perhaps they have internalized the longing of being held within loving arms, the arms of the mother. The symbol of the crucifix expresses the torture which an abused person may identity with, while it may also offer a contradiction, with the arms of Jesus stretched out, for them, towards them, around them.

Self-harm may also act as a pattern of reversal for both the witness and the self-harmer. The story of Mary Magdalene is an example of this reversal. Jesus witnessed her pain and she found healing. At the cross, she witnessed the pain of Jesus, and he came into resurrection. In their meeting at the tomb they encountered relational mutuality. This role reversal takes place within the self-harm process as uncontrolled abuse is acted out in a controlled way. In most therapeutic work the feeling of being out of control is gradually replaced by the 'client' taking control of her process and her life. What seems to be the place of authority shifts. In witnessing self-harm in an adolescent, the adult–child relationship is reversed as the witness becomes the 'child', feeling the pain, being with the wound, in order to understand the child's former experience which s/he is acting out. This therapeutic relationship becomes profoundly intimate and may echo the words attributed to Saint Paul: 'I am crucified with Christ, nevertheless I live, yet not I but Christ, lives in me.'[19]

19 Galatians 2.20.

So who were the real witnesses at the cross? Not the soldiers that jeered, or the disciples who ran and watched from a distance, but the women and the beloved disciple who stood by the foot of the cross, staying with the bleeding man, becoming part of his pain, feeling it, and witnessing his rite of passage. It is only when he is assured of their dedicated witness to this that he is able to complete his rite of passage and leave them, and they become his body on earth.

Roger Grainger argues for ritual as a three-phase shape, the pre-liminal phase, the liminal phase and the post-liminal phase (see Grainger, 1988). The witness to the person's process of cutting is likely to be involved in all three phases, and experiences that place of liminality and transition, with all the fear and struggle that being a witness of such a painful process brings. The professional therapist will need supervision of this journey, and other witnesses will need support and affirmation from the community.

Self-harm is often understood as a form of inverted aggression, a defensive mechanism, the dreadful feel and the feel of dread of being possessed in today's world where everything is ordered and has its place and time. In her work on self-harm, Gardner coins the phrase 'the encaptive conflict' as a state where the fear of being possessed conflicted with the fear of rejection and the psychic conflict led to a defensive compromise (Gardner, 2001, p. 58). In self-harm, the compromise is the violence to self rather than to the other. There is a deliverance from the pain of the encaptive conflict and the experienced enslavement to an inner tyrannical and conflictual object relationship. Such a conflict of terror needs to be held and embraced rather than turned away or cast out. To shout religious words in an authoritarian manner to such a person is a complete misunderstanding of what it means to be a witness. Witnessing to the compassionate love of Christ/Christa, and acting it out in and through community, helps towards the healing of those who fear their 'demons', those abusive powers projected onto them by others, making them feel as if those powers completely possess their body and soul. Such a person may need medical support and a psychiatrist may be the witness to feel the pain, and the distressed person will need to be held and healed by the body of Christ, whose own wounds were felt even more acutely when 'darkness covered the land . . . while the sun's light failed . . . and the earth shook . . .'[20] and the very cosmos became the witness to the pain and anguish of the world.

Luke's Gospel recalls how the people who had gathered for the spectacle of crucifixion 'returned home, beating their breasts'.[21] Those who beat their breasts were projecting the violence back on to themselves in a futile gesture because they had watched a violent spectacle, rather than become witnesses of the depth of pain of one with whom they had a relationship of love. Meanwhile the true witnesses continued to watch.

Those who process through these rites of passage witness to a community, which Roger Grainger refers to as the 'charmed circle', as they may know much more about life than those who witnessed their journey, 'for . . . their rejected condition becomes their skill, their special contribution; the sympathy and understanding which it has brought them, they give to others within the charmed circle' (Grainger, 1988, p. 60). This circle will widen to embrace them, and they in turn will accompany others on their rite of passage.

I have touched on issues arising from my original questions only to be more aware that often our body or mind becomes ill and literally stops us in our tracks, becoming symbolic of what we need to do – to give ourselves permission to both know and feel our own vulnerability. We may intuitively find our way to places far from home and work, thinking we are coming for one reason, only to find we have an important interior journey to travel. This may be an unexpected experience both for ourselves and for those who welcome us to their homes, communities and churches. In different ways we need to be ready for the unexpected in order to become witnesses to glimpses of hope in our own lives and the lives of others. The churches often talk about mission and witnessing with healing as an optional extra. It is an urgent matter for mission and healing to be brought together in order for witnessing to take on a new dimension, and for churches to dare to become therapeutic communities. Every person has the capacity to be a healer and has the ability to witness to the pain of another. The Jesus story corresponds to the rites of

20 Mark 15.33; Luke 23.44; Matthew 27.51.
21 Luke 23.48.

passage of human living, and Christian calling is to witness diverse human living, the *I am* incarnated in the unexpected.

Acknowledgement

The Scripture quotations contained herein are from the New Revised Standard Version Bible, copyright 1989, by the Division of Christian Education of the National Council of the Churches of Christ in the USA, and are used by permission. All rights reserved.

References

Bowie, Fiona (2000), *The Anthropology of Religion*, Oxford: Blackwell.

Butler, Judith (1990), *Gender Trouble: Feminism and the Subversion of Identity*, New York and London: Routledge.

Douglas, Mary (1966), *Purity and Danger: An Analysis of Concepts of Pollution and Taboo*, London: Routledge & Kegan Paul.

Favazza, Armando R. (1996), *Bodies Under Siege: Self-Mutilation and Body Modification in Culture and Psychiatry*, 2nd edn, Baltimore: The Johns Hopkins University Press.

Fernbach, Amanda (2002), *Fantasies of Fetishism: From Decadence to the Post-Human*, New Brunswick, NJ: Rutgers University Press.

Foucault, Michel (1979), *Discipline and Punish: The Birth of the Prison*, Harmondsworth: Penguin.

Gardner, F. (2001), *Self-Harm: A Psychotherapeutic Approach*, London: Brunner-Routledge.

Grainger, Roger (1984), *A Place like This: A Guide to Life in a Psychiatric Hospital*, Worthing: Churchman.

Grainger, Roger (1988), *The Message of the Rite: The Significance of Christian Rites of Passage*, Cambridge: Lutterworth Press.

Herman, Judith L. (1994), *Trauma and Recovery: From Domestic Abuse to Political Terror*, London: Pandora.

Heyward, Carter (1989), *Touching our Strength: The Erotic as Power and the Love of God*, San Francisco: HarperSanFrancisco.

Lines, Dennis (2006), *Therapy Today: The Magazine for Counselling & Psychotherapy Professionals* 17.7 (September).

Mascia-Lees, Frances E. and Patricia Sharpe (1992), 'The Marked and the Un (re) Marked: Tattoo and Gender in Theory and Narrative', in Frances E. Mascia-Lees and Patricia Sharpe (eds), *Tattoo, Torture, Mutilation, and Adornment: The Denaturalization of the Body in Culture and Text*, New York: State University of New York Press, pp. 145–67.

Mellon P. (1996), *Multiple Selves, Multiple Voices: Working with Trauma, Violation and Dissociation*, Chichester: John Wiley and Sons.

Nicholson, Chris (2004), 'The "Rites of Passage": Gender-Specific Initiation Rites in the Understanding of Self-Harm, and Creating the Self through Self-Harm', *Therapeutic Communities* 25.1.

O'Grady, Helen (2005), *Woman's Relationship with Herself: Gender, Foucault and Therapy*, Women and Psychology, London and New York, Routledge.

Pattison, Stephen (2000), *Shame: Theory, Therapy, Theology*, Cambridge: Cambridge University Press.

Podvoll, Edward (1969), 'Self-Mutilation within a Hospital Setting: A Study of Identity and Social Compliance', *British Journal of Medical Psychology* 42, pp. 213–21.

Rose, Gillian (1997), *Love's Work*, London: Vintage.

Shengold, Leonard (1989), *Soul Murder*, New Haven: Yale University Press.

Sherman, Lisa (no date), 'Eros Ex Machina', *Skin Two* 26.

Shillito, Edward (no date), *Jesus of the Scars, and Other Poems* (published shortly after the First World War).

Strong, Marilee (2000), *A Bright Red Scream: Self-Mutilation and the Language of Pain*, London: Virago.

Sutton, Jan (2004), 'Understanding Dissociation and its Relationship to Self-Injury and Childhood Trauma', *Counselling and Psychotherapy Journal* 15.3.

Thorne, Brian (1998), *Person-Centred Counselling and Christian Spirituality: The Secular and the Holy*, London: Whurr.

Thorne, Brian (2003), *Infinitely Beloved: The Challenge of Divine Intimacy*, Sarum Theological Lectures, London: Darton, Longman & Todd.

Warner (1985), *Monuments and Maidens: The Allegory of the Female Form*, London: Weidenfeld & Nicolson.

4

Mutilations and Restorations: Cosmetic Surgery in Christianity

MARCELLA ALTHAUS-REID

Nonnus, by giving (Pelagia) the clothes of a man, not only accepts but even approves of Pelage's decision to leave behind her former identity as a woman and start completely anew. (Lowerre, 2005, p. cvi)

But the feminine can also countersign the author's irony. She would speak of the author, she would state or show the author in her mirror. (Derrida in Attridge, 1992, p. 331)

I am starting these reflections by quoting from a commentary on the life of St Pelagia, a transgendered saint from the fifth century. Pelagia was a dancer and entertainer who had the radical makeover that conversion required of a woman in her time, and which was the site of conflictive messages of idealized womanhood but also of the complete denial of any trace of femininity. The conflict of female interpretation in Christianity, however, is not new. Pelagia's transgenderism (if we could use this concept in the context of the Fathers of the Church) was not unique, and needs to be located at the crossroads of theology and gender impossibility. Several examples survive of cross-dressing female spiritual women such as Tecla, Eugene, Mary of Egypt or Maryne, and although some may have been, following our contemporary understandings of sexuality and gender identity, genuine cross-dressers, others may have used transgenderism in a more superficial way. For some it might have been a cosmetic procedure, in order to remove the female appearance which was an obstacle to entry into a monastery. In that sense, Pelagia was a mirror in which Bishop Nonnus could reflect his own image. Genuine spiritual vocations in a world where the female gender was under curfew required a commitment to certain physical changes, in terms of clothes, hairstyle, voice tone, posture as well as the observation of certain gender codes such as measuring the expression of emotions in the way to which men were accustomed. However, we shall never know about the real sexual identities of the cross-gender saints: the testimonies which survive, such as in the *Vitae Patrum*, were written for male readers and carry their own theological and colonial limitations. And yet they function as powerful metaphors at a time when issues of gender identity, spirituality and physical appearance still suffer from the influence of Christianity as a project founded on norms of homogeneity in issues of gender and sexuality.

The transgender saints present a particular paradox. On the one hand they remind us that a Christian woman always needs to become what she is not, which is the meaning of conversion in the narrative of gender in Christianity. On the other, they bring the possibility of taking charge of bodily transformation. After all, the body is a cultural product and not a given. What we take for granted as 'natural' for a woman's body is in reality a highly ideologized product, involving her depth of voice tone, her hair line, her stature, which may betray a cultural understanding of nutrition among genders. Let us start with the first point: a woman must start anew, as if her exteriority has commoditized what Ken Stone has called the heterosexual contract of Genesis (Stone, 2006, p. 5). In the meta-narrative of primordial sin, that 'Eve of destruction' of the scriptural narrative, a woman's body is a signifier of that contract. The cosmetic unravelling needed is related to a process of restoration, which in the case of Eve began with a retro-projected utopia of a primordial disobedience to all the laws, signified by the divine law. Physical punishment is the supplement of this divine primordial female transgression, and the biblical primordial mother cannot be understood without a history of body transformation. Effectively, from there her body will suffer alterations: she will be cosmetically changed by being named. Her body will also be historically a site to host physical violence; women subjected to domestic rape (according to their lords' desire) and women subjected to the pain of child-birth in their vocation as mothers. The subjection of women, in the Bible and in the Church, is but a liturgical continuation of these stereotypes of the female body.

By this route within Christianity the woman does not exist as herself: she needs to be referred to and reminded of the illusion of an original or pure womanhood. However, the references for that lie not in Genesis; they precede Genesis. If anything this text reminds us of the situation of Israel in certain historical periods. It provides us with a narrative of restoration, a nostalgia to be what one is supposed to have been, not experimentally but by virtue of the authority of the text. The Virgin Mary was created out of this need. She is represented not simply as a spiritual ideal, but as an ideal of youthfulness according to the aesthetic norms of European culture which extend to a pale skin and an aquiline rather than a Semitic nose. Cosmetic surgery might well claim to stand as a successor to the Christian tradition in its offer to restore a woman's body to its original form, from which ideal, spiritual and aesthetic, it has fallen. Cosmetic surgery may not be a procedure indicated in the Bible (except perhaps in circumcision) yet the hermeneutical principle is there. Even the most natural functions of the female body are condemned as pollution, requiring ritual acts of purification and restoration.

Epistemological (fetishist) challenges

One of the most important contributions that feminist theologies have produced in the past 30 years has been in their reflections on the female body in the discourse of Christianity. The supposed invisibility of women's bodies in Christianity has obscured the fact that ultimately the body, and the female body in particular, is the perverse reference which haunts Christianity. If we might use the metaphor, there is a hermeneutics of mutilations, quasi-surgical, which historically seems to have been in conflict with the appearance of Otherness, which in this case women represent in Christianity. To this haunting from rewritten bodies in Christianity we arrive at what Lisa Isherwood has conceptualized as the 'spiralling of incarnation' (Isherwood, 2004, p. 141). By this Isherwood calls our attention to the process of continuously situating the female body as a theological source and also as a privileged context for reflection. The epistemological challenge is immense, especially if we leave behind heterosexual ways of knowing which partake of binary systems of interpretation, the very ones that precisely we are trying to overcome.

From a Queer theological perspective, incarnation acts as a classical fetishist act which does not accept the construed frontiers between the material and the spiritual but transgresses them both. Could it be that the hermeneutical spiralling of incarnation from Isherwood works also in a fetishist theological way? Somehow, yes. The theological frontiers between women's bodies and spirituality become even interchangeable, but the same fetishist knowledge is present in Jesus' incarnation when the divine eats, feels sick and bleeds to death. However, fetishist knowledge has been suppressed because it contradicts the need of restoration to an original body that Christianity claims. There are several consequences, reflected in the suppressed bodies of knowledge that, like fetishism, destabilize the logic of traditions and the quest for the pure, conceptually, dogmatically, physically and aesthetically.

In the history of Christianity female bodies have been inscribed in different signifiers of power struggles. The female Christian body has been marked, cut and tattooed with heteropatriarchal 'divine signifiers' which have not only constructed different and contradictory concepts of womanhood but also act as a mechanism for disciplining womanhood. A key aspect of that has been, as already noted, the delegitimization of God's original fetishist act in Jesus. I am already hinting here that there is a certain mutilative characteristic in Christian hermeneutics, which might function ideologically in a way that connects with cosmetic surgery as well as with other issues concerned with reducing the body, as for instance in self-mutilation and anorexia. We are referring here to the disciplining of women's bodies, including amputations and medications as organized under secular and religious law. In any case, the woman's body needs to be limited and pruned. I deliberately homologize the discipline techniques historically used for women's bodies (even as they differ culturally) as cosmetic, to emphasize that they are actions belonging to the superficial and transient, the realm of *anathema* (adornment).

Yet, they are part of a capitalist divine exchange system in which women's bodies are supposed to give meaning in a Christian globalized ethics. At a certain point in this mechanism of the divine exchange rate the contextual becomes *kerygma*. As in a fundamentalist parable the ephemerons become teleology and the disciplining of women's bodies becomes the objective of Christianity and in a way its ultimate meaning. Curiously, the so-called secular societies, by rebuking fetishist knowledge and insisting on a logic of women as frontiers between flesh and spirit, have incarnated the true hermeneutics that I have called mutilative, as developed during the early days of Christianity.

Let us now consider these elements in more detail. First of all, let us proceed to reflect on how the Law of the Father requires a cosmetic implementation. Or, to put it in a different way, how the ideology of cosmetic exchanges is a supplement to the Father's disciplining capacity in relation to the 'lack' which characterizes women. Second, we can proceed to unravel how, in the present time of capitalist expansion, the restorative body project of Christianity has been extended into new fields, such as organizing the disciplining of female identity around issues of merchandise values. Finally, we need to reflect on Queer theology and its transsexual acts through which it problematizes the call to restore an original woman's body and also insists on the right to disrupt women's bodies. In this it aims to liberate them from what could lead to an hegemoneous, harmonic agreement which will only reproduce the heterosexual contract of Genesis, if not in form, then in spirit.

The Law of the Father

The Law of the Father (or Phallus) is a concept from Lacan which refers to the submission to language rules governing the symbolic order (Lacan in Marini, 1992, p. 173). It is the primordial origin of hegemonic divine orders. The cosmetic or alterative body procedures to which we are referring are inscripted in theological language, and require a hermeneutics of suspicion. The Law of the Father (YHWH) in the Scriptures requires bodily changes: the angel at Peniel changed Jacob's name to

Israel, only after the angel had put Jacob's hip out of joint, leaving him with a limp (Genesis 32.25-8). Not only biblical heroes suffer physical disabilities inflicted upon them for having fought with God: Greimas draws attention to the physical marking of the hero in Russian folktales. Mutilative hermeneutics confer deep meaning on acts of the cutting of genitalia, the specific covering of the body to disguise/modify the natural female appearance, the seclusions and rituals of extreme cleansing during women's bleeding experiences such as menstruation and after birth. All have left their marks in the body of the believer. These are not just scars, but hermeneutically speaking, they are pedagogical procedures. The way that a woman covers her head in worship, the fashion in which eyebrows should curve (or not) and the narrowness of shoes which require a surgical procedure of eliminating a toe, are all linked. The Law requires meaning by mutilation because there are power struggles behind an ideology of incompleteness or lack. In fact, the crucifixion itself seems to act as the teleological divine act where the body needs to be ultimately cut and crushed in order for God to be Godself again. God seems here to depend on the survival of dualist thinking, either one or the other: the Christ body should be crushed or the spirit will not be free.

Curiously, God the Redeemer in Jesus has not had the theological narrative strength to deconstruct the exteriority to which women in particular have been subjected, in order to restore an original divine and bodily imprint of female identity. That exteriority, to use a concept from Derrida, has provided the Christian requirement of surgical modifications or reconstructions which are crucial for processes of Christian identity formation. Here we are confronted with two problems. First, Christianity is an identity marker in a hegemonic struggle with sexual identities. Second and paradoxically, following Derrida, the true identity of Christianity resides in the fact that Christian self-identity is not equal to itself: it contains multitudes. Yet, we are all supposed to receive the same shape of nose in the operating theatre of conversion in the cosmetic clinics of Christianity.

Capitalist restorations

The God of the Bible, and specifically the Hebrew Scriptures, seems to require extreme body restoration. Why and how? It is basically by positing a divine ordered body which does not fit in with the narrative of creation. But this in itself is a quite subversive concept. It really means that there is no original to which we should return. Yet, the rituals of circumcision and pollution and/or the covering and re-positioning of women's bodies, serve the purpose of resituating bodies in respect of what God theologically wants them to be. Although we do not have an explicit text of how bodies should fit divinely, we do have the construction of exteriorities or supplements which act as the ideal of 'pure' bodies' sacramental desirability. That is, the ideal female body as expressing an understanding of a relationship with God. For that, women's bodies require medication. However, the process of surgical manipulation of female bodies does not end here. In turn, the ideal body also becomes a double exteriority in relation to men's bodies, for instance, as sources of sensual temptation or impurity. It seems that female bodies are then condemned to be permanent exteriorities, denouncing somehow the impossibility of heterosexuality. This happened because a system such as heterosexuality depends on the permanent supplanting of femininity in the discourse. Femininity needs to be adorned, accessorized continuously, to produce the maximum effectiveness in its sexual representation system. Cosmetic surgery is a display of the impossibility of the feminine heterosexual: it does exist and it needs constant acts of violence against the woman's body.

The global expansion of capitalism and technology has only profited in the marketing of a product already tried and tested. Such a product is the heteropatriarchal body of women. The gap in the market, or window of opportunity, for selling cosmetic surgery may have been provided by the crisis of sexual identity in postmodernism and the need to reinforce what we have called the supplement of heterosexuality: we should be all the ideal girls of the ideal postcards. Or virgin Marys, young, white, slim, with the perfect nose. We should not forget that the Virgin Mary has been not only a divine but also a ruling aesthetic criterion for many centuries.

Obviously, women also know that there are marketable opportunities in investing in youth and/or bigger breasts. However, the paradox is that the surgically modified body produced in the high capitalist societies is an image closer to that of the Christian heteropatriarchal, pure, original body. Capitalism, as the ultimate blasphemous church, has produced its own Frankensteins, and in more than one way, if we consider the physical sufferings and even death produced by cosmetic surgical procedures. The triumph of capitalism lies here, in this embodiment or incarnation of bodily ideals by making women's bodies into ideological laboratories.

Transsexualities

Let us now go back for our final reflection to Pelagia's story. Up till now we have been considering how the hermeneutics of bodily restoration has been inscribed in Christianity, by the Church. It has involved claims of an original purity to which believers, and especially women who signify exteriority, need to refer. This is what Pelagia did. Liturgically, the fact that women cover different parts of their bodies during mass has constituted a sign of the cosmetic cutting and reassembling of female bodies required in the separation of the sacred from the profane. Cosmetic surgery is not just a 'secular' enterprise, but part of a deeper Christian hermeneutics responsible for the understanding of perfection, part of a theological understanding privileging purity as youthful beauty in women. However, beauty and youth are also subject to race and class negotiations. Christian cultural imperialism has its own colonial aesthetics requiring subversion. What we are saying now is that cosmetic surgery cannot be understood as a cure to restore the original body of heterosexual systems: such an original body does not exist. By the same logic, it is wrong to consider that our female bodies enjoy some virtue by refusing cosmetic alterations. To prohibit cosmetic surgery will not give back the virtue of a lost, pure, original body to women: there is virtue neither in wrinkles nor in Botox procedures. However, what is interesting is that in some feminist discourses, such virtue is claimed to exist in the declaration that the female body has some naturality which cannot be lost. Thus in the 1960s some American feminists refused to shave their legs. By contrast, in some Latin American patriarchal cultures, legs have never been shaved, to differentiate white women from indigenous women, who seldom have much body hair.

The tension here is one of legitimization and transgression. While the market structures of exploitation regarding what we have called the hermeneutics of mutilation are to be condemned, so also should we condemn the claim of a natural woman's body, kept clean of cosmetic interventions. In fact, following Queer theory, genders are performative acts which depend on cosmetic excesses, including tattoos, bird masks, leather, S/M vinyl clothes, imposing high heels. They can also be supplemented with fake breasts or alterations in voice tone. Paraphrasing Derrida, we are always drugged (Derrida, 1995, p. 244). Maryne, another cross-dresser saint, as Pelagia, drugged her own body in a way, by disciplining it as a male body in such a way that other monks found her (him) attractive sexually as a young monk, a sexual temptation to which they were accustomed (Lowerre, 2005, p. xcvi). Did Pelagia lie? Or was she guilty of cosmetic surgery? The fact is that there is no life without contamination or adulteration. In Christianity contaminations proceed not only from the constraint of heteropatriarchalism and the woman's body as a product, but also from ideological constraints.

Yet transsexualism and transgenderism remind us that sexual identities can only be found grounded in earthquakes: their only commonality is their continuous and slippery _différence_. A woman's identity in the struggle against gender and sexual legitimacy systems requires subversive procedures, which could sometimes be cosmetic procedures. As queer theologies reflect on the debasing and permanent inscriptions of Queer bodies as transgressive acts, it is useful to remember that sometimes our bodies are inhabited by multitudes. To give hospitality to our own fragmentations may require sometime acts of transformations. At the end, as we receive the body of Christ in the host, and Christ and ourselves merge, we are supposed to lose the illusion of identity in the midst of the Eucharist: the Divine requires a new nose and I require a sense of the divine. A sense of aesthetic experience is exchanged. Fetishist knowledge may provide the clue to the understanding that the

Christian hermeneutics of mutilations and restoration carries in itself its own transgressive project, so the author (or the Law of the Father), will not see himself in her mirror again.

References

Attridge, Derek, ed. (1992), *Jacques Derrida: Acts of Literature*, London: Routledge.

Derrida, Jacques (1995), 'The Rhetorics of Drugs', in *Points . . .: Interviews 1974–1994*, ed. Elizabeth Weber, Stanford: Stanford University Press.

Isherwood, Lisa (2004), 'The Embodiment of Feminist Liberation Theology: The Spiralling of Incarnation', in Beverley Clack, ed., *Embodying Feminist Liberation Theologies*, London: Continuum.

Lowerre, Sandra (2005), *The Cross-Dressing Female Saints in Wynkyn de Worde's 1495 Edition of the Vitas Patrum*, Frankfurt: Peter Lang.

Marini, Marcelle (1992), *Jacques Lacan: The French Context*, New Brunswick: Rutgers University Press.

Stone, Ken (2006), 'The Garden of Eden and the Heterosexual Contract', in Ellen Armour and Susan St Ville, eds, *Bodily Citations: Religion and Judith Butler*, New York: Columbia University Press.

5

This Body Trans/Forming Me: Indecencies in Transgender/Intersex Bodies, Body Fascism and the Doctrine of the Incarnation

MARTÍN HUGO CÓRDOVA QUERO

And the Word Became Flesh.[1]

When we renounce being the typical male of the system, the strong, dominating male, then they immediately install us within the feminine realm. But it is not a matter of any feminine one; to the sweet and glamour we are asked to add an image and a body that should be the most clear and exuberant possibly. There is a demand associated to a noticed, reinforced performance . . . [2]

I feel / like Clark Kent / ducking into a phone booth
/ to emerge / as Wonder Woman.[3]

---

1 John 1.14a. Quotations from the Bible in this article are taken from the *New Revised Standard Version* (Oxford: Oxford University Press, 1977).

2 Lohana Berkins, 'Eternamente Atrapadas por el Sexo', in Josefina Fernández, Mónica D'Uva and Paula Viturro, eds, *Cuerpos Ineludibles: Un Dialogo a Partir de las Sexualidades en América Latina* (Buenos Aires: Ediciones Ají de Pollo, 2004), p. 22. Translation mine.

3 Veronica West [Beth Westbrook], 'Secret Identity', in Mary Boenke, ed., *Trans Forming Families: Real Stories About Transgendered Loved Ones*, 2nd edn (Hardy, Va.: Oak Knoll Press, 2003), p. 20.

Introduction

Flesh, corporality, passions, feelings, eroticism, identity . . . There is a whole universe of multiple worlds contained within the notion/s of *body/ies*. What do we really mean when we talk about body/ies? Is there a single definition? Can we change/alter our body/ies? Does theology have something to say about body/ies and their constructions? Can we relate this to Jesus, to God, to the Virgin Mary, to the Saints, or to the Church? Is a spiritual(ized) realm the only way to inscribe body/ies in the religious discourse? If God incarnated in the creation through Jesus Christ, can Christology embrace *all* the dimensions of corporality? Can we have agency over the construction of our body/ies and our identity? Do those two realms match all the time? These are questions that burn deeply within us when addressing issues related to the intersection of body/ies and theology.

Even so, we want to enquire further by connecting these questions to a particular case: the experiences of transgender[4] and intersex[5] people.

---

4 Through this article I will use the term *transgender* instead of the term *transsexual*. In understanding both terms, I follow Mollenkott, who defines this issue as follows: 'At first, the term transgender referred only to people who had changed their gender but not their genitals – for instance, a man who uses estrogen, lives as a woman, but has no plans to undergo sex-reassigment surgery. (Now, such a person would be called a non-operative transsexual.) But gradually, the term has been extended to include intersexuals, transsexuals, cross-dressers, drag queens and kings, androgynes, and anyone else who feels "otherwise" from society's gender assumptions' (Virginia Ramey Mollenkott, *Omnigender: A Trans-Religious Approach* (Cleveland, Ohio: Pilgrim Press, 2001), p. 40). Shapiro also contributes on this (in relation to transsexualism): '[The designation of] those who feel that their true gender is at variance with their biological sex; more specifically, to designate those who are attempting to "pass" as members of the opposite sex; and, most specifically, to designate those who have either had sex change surgery or are undergoing medical treatment with a view toward changing their sex anatomically' (Judith Shapiro, 'Transsexualism: Reflections on the Persistence of Gender and the Mutability of Sex', in Julia Epstein and Kristina Straub, eds, *Body Guards: The Cultural Politics of Gender Ambiguity* (London: Routledge, 1991), p. 249).

5 '"Intersex" is a general term used for a variety of conditions in which a person is born with a reproductive or sexual anatomy that doesn't seem to fit the typical

Hence, doing this takes us to unknown terrain, especially since this article attempts to introduce a third element: the doctrine of incarnation. Whether rocky or soft, the soil under our feet does not give us any sense of comfort while doing this. In other words, when we look at the intersection of issues of transgender and intersex people and the doctrine of the incarnation, many other questions strongly arise. Moreover, when we look at the performativities of transsexuality, especially in terms of sex reassignment surgeries, transgender transitioning, the display of chosen gender *vis-à-vis* body genitalia, and, even, issues of body modifications,[6]

---

definitions of female or male. For example, a person might be born appearing to be female on the outside, but having mostly male-typical anatomy on the inside. Or a person may be born with genitals that seem to be in-between the usual male and female types – for example, a girl may be born with a noticeably large clitoris, or lacking a vaginal opening, or a boy may be born with a notably small penis, or with a scrotum that is divided so that it has formed more like labia. Or a person may be born with mosaic genetics, so that some of her cells have XX chromosomes and some of them have XY. Though we speak of intersex as an inborn condition, intersex anatomy doesn't always show up at birth. Sometimes a person isn't found to have intersex anatomy until she or he reaches the age of puberty, or finds himself an infertile adult, or dies of old age and is autopsied. Some people live and die with intersex anatomy without anyone (including themselves) ever knowing. Which variations of sexual anatomy count as intersex? In practice, different people have different answers to that question. That's not surprising, because intersex isn't a discreet or natural category. What does this mean? Intersex is a socially constructed category that reflects real biological variation' ('Frequently Asked Questions: What is Intersex?' in *Intersex Society of North America*, http://www.isna.org/faq/what_is_intersex (accessed 4 May 2006)). Mollenkott contributes to describe the major categories of intersexuality as: Androgen Insensitivity Syndrome (AIS), Partial Androgen Insensitivity Syndrome, Progestin Induced Virilization, Adrenal Hyplasia, and Klinefelter Syndrome (cf. Mollenkott, *Omnigender*, pp. 45–7).

6 Strictly speaking, 'Body modification (or body alteration) is the permanent or semi-permanent deliberate altering of the human body for non-medical reasons, such as spiritual, various social (markings), BDSM "edgeplay" or aesthetic. It can range from the socially acceptable decoration (e.g., pierced ears in many societies), to the overtly religiously mandated (e.g., circumcision in a number of cultures) to corporal punishment, to provocative statement by the rebellious (e.g., tongue splitting), some even get physically addicted to the andrenaline/endorphine release associated with a painful procedure in a way analogous to that experienced

the whole panorama gets totally blurred. We suddenly discover that body/ies are not confined to a binary male/female dichotomy, but much more varied than we thought. In addition, all these issues cannot be understood in full without paying attention to their intricate interrelation with a twofold social/cultural/legal mechanism of regulation of these issues: body fascism and hetero-normativity. I understand *body fascism* as the policing, controlling and punishing of bodies which do not conform to hegemonic constructions of bodies in society. They are idealized and used to rule other body/ies that are considered deviant because of

by those who self harm. Some people experience an abstract but distinct compulsion to modify their body that appears to have no underlying or external reason. Nearly every human society practises or has practised some type of body modification in its broadest definition, from Maori tattoos to Victorian corsets to modern breast implants. Some futurists believe that eventually humans will pursue body modification with more advanced technological means, such as permanently implanted devices to enhance mental and physical capabilities, thereby becoming cyborgs. For the substantial number of people with heart pacemakers and brain implants such as cochlear implants and electrical brain stimulators for Parkinson's disease, this is already a reality' ('Body Modification', in *Wikipedia: The Free Encyclopedia*, http://en.wikipedia.org/wiki/Body_modification (accessed 4 May 2006)). However, when I refer to the expression *body modification* I am also considering other areas, as there are many everyday situations where body/ies are modified. Nonetheless, we do not often think of them as body modification. Some of those situations are the result of the following: (1) compulsive (hetero)normative social expectations, such as diets, skin whiteners, plastic surgeries and surgical modifications (for example, women removing their last rib in order to reduce the size of their waist or injecting silicones in order to enhance their breast); (2) attempts to recover bodily balance, such as diets or exercise in order to reduce cholesterol, prevent diabetes, heart diseases, etc.; (3) privation of food or shelter, such as undernourishment, poverty, wars, homelessness and uprootedness; (4) collateral effects of other situations, such as anorexia, bulimia, depression, etc. that compulsorily push individuals in society to be in a certain physical way; and (5) tattooing and piercing, which sometimes, as in the case of some Pacific Islander regions, are a cultural expectation and a highly prized act. Although this list does not seek to be 'the ultimate list of body modification', it opens up our view of the issue to more complex realms. Issues of weight are also connected to the realm of body fascism, especially to the aesthetic rejection of over-weight people. For a study about this issue, see Kathleen LeBesco, *Revolting Bodies? The Struggle to Redefine Fat Identity* (Boston, Mass.: University of Massachusetts Press, 2004).

their inadequacy to those hegemonic constructions of body/ies. This is connected to issues of discrimination and punishing of those who remain bodily deviant.[7]

When our journey takes us deeper into this terrain, we need extra cartographies for the route as, I assume, it is a passage-way that the reader/s probably never transited before. Nevertheless, this entire journey implies a challenge that academic reflection may consider worth the trek, maybe *to boldly go where no academic reflection has gone before*. As a result, this article attempts to seek adventure in this terrain. If this daunting landscape seems to be occluded for the majority of heterosexual people, and more often only visible to transgender and intersex people in their everydayness, this does not mean that it is not an issue that cuts across the study of human sexuality. Consequently, an interdisciplinary dialogue among many cartographies is necessary for the unfolding of the topics at hand.

In sum, by tying in some aspects of the development of the doctrine of the incarnation as a core Christian doctrine, this article seeks to unpack and explore how the issues of body/ies in relation to the transgender and intersex experience relate to this doctrine; and how theology has intertwined this doctrine with body fascist ideologies coming from a hetero-patriarchal system of domination in relation to their acceptance and salvation. What bodies are incarnated? What bodies are saved? What bodies are resurrected? I have questioned elsewhere what would happen if Mary were a lesbian, or Jesus bisexual, or transgender or inter-

---

7 On this the online magazine *Sportsteacher* refers to this problematic in the following terms: 'What is body fascism? Body fascism is a problem that has evolved out of western society's obsession with thinness. Body fascism is defined as: The severe intolerance in self and others of any weight or shape that doesn't resemble idealised bodies portrayed in media images. These images are usually of extremely thin young women with noticeable lack of curves, often looking pre-pubescent or androgynous. In men, the idealised form is muscular and well toned, with broad shoulders and narrow hips. Body fascism involves severe criticism of other people's size and shape, often resulting in the rejection or bullying of those who don't conform to a specific body type' ('Body fascism: Another form of discrimination?' in *Sportsteacher*, 25 February 2005, http://www.sportsteacher. co.uk/news/editorial/01autF_bodyfascism.html (accessed 4 May 2006)).

sex. Can Jesus, the Trinity, or Mary the Virgin, embrace those gender constructions and those performances of sexuality? What if we change our bodies? Furthermore, what if Paul the Apostle was formerly a woman named Paula who underwent a process of transition to *become* Paul? These in/decencies certainly do trouble us. Nonetheless, it must be highlighted that to enter this terrain and explore its geography is an extremely important journey towards the construction of both a contemporary Christology and, following Marcella Althaus-Reid, an *indecent theology* of transgender and intersex body/ies in a liberationist and qu(e)er(y)ing way.[8]

'My body and me': struggles towards self-understanding

A bedroom . . . The camera shows a couple, a man and a woman, getting dressed for a party. Their conversation, mixed with kisses and hugs, revolves around the new neighbours who just moved in, and how this couple perceives them. Focus changes abruptly. In another bedroom . . . the film takes us to witness another busy couple also getting dressed for a party. The festive tone of the first couple has now changed to a more serious tone of this second couple. As the dialogue unfolds, it lets us know that this man is a co-worker of the new neighbours. Suddenly, their dialogue is interrupted by the appearance in the bedroom door of their little son, whom they address as Jerome. Both couples are going to the same party. Change of focus again.

Another bedroom . . . and the film introduces us to a third couple. As we inspect the images of the environment, we realize they are the new neighbours the previous two couples were talking about. While trying

---

8 Marcella Althaus-Reid defines *Indecent Theology* in the following way: 'I am using the term "Indecent Theology" to refer to a Queer Theology whose hermeneutical circle is informed by Latin American Liberation Theology and therefore is based on a political praxis of liberation. I use the concept of "indecency" because the axis of decency/indecency is constitutive of the regulation of the order of society in my own country, Argentina, and especially for women' (Marcella Althaus-Reid, *The Queer God* (London: Routledge, 2003), p. 172, n. 1).

to get dressed, there are intermingled images of the busyness of getting everything ready for the party. Children are also running and getting ready. While preparing one table, the new neighbours are still getting dressed and we hear the woman asking the husband for her red shoes. While they continue moving, the camera moves to a new place. We move with the camera facing the wall, the roof, and finally we enter through the window of the second floor to another bedroom. There we find a little girl applying make-up to her face. She is wearing her mother's red shoes. She expertly applies her lipstick as she constantly admires her reflection in the mirror. Wearing a beautiful pink princess dress, the little girl chooses an earring. While she is doing that, we are taken downstairs where the grandmother is arriving for the party. This is the opening scene, 'Going to a Party', of the film *Ma Vie en Rose* (My Life in Pink),[9] which paints a picture of what seems to be a quiet middle-class suburban neighbourhood. However, the film would bring more information about these people in the following scene.

Scene 2, entitled 'Welcome to Our Home', shows all the families arriving at the house of the new neighbours. While everyone is making themselves comfortable at the party – adults having a drink and children *attacking* the snacks table – the new neighbours are asked to introduce themselves. Consequently, the father introduces his wife, the grandmother and the two sons. Then he goes to introduce Zoe, the daughter, but she does not appear immediately. Everyone is expectant to meet and pay homage to the new girl in the neighbourhood. Suddenly, we see the little girl coming down the stairs. Slowly she moves towards the curtain that covers the window connecting the living room with the backyard. When she finally emerges, everyone claps, except the girl's family, who look disappointed. We arrive at a cleavage point in the narration of this house-warming party. We move to the next scene.

Scene 3, 'Ludovic', introduces us to a dramatic moment in the film. After emerging from behind the curtain, another girl runs towards the little girl and exclaims: 'my princess dress'. Everyone is astonished while not understanding the situation. Consequently, the father, in disappoint-

---

9 *Ma Vie en Rose*, dir. Alain Berliner, Sony Pictures, 1997.

ment, introduces the little girl to a surprised audience as 'that's our son
. . . the *joker* one. It's his favourite joke.' Everyone, relieved, laughs and
claps celebrating the sense of humour of the now *boy*, Ludovic, who is still
in his/her pink princess dress while looking at everyone disappointed and
shocked. At this point, our perception of the film is paralleled with our
own surprise and uneasiness. In the film the mother takes Ludovic to the
kitchen to wash her/his face and to change her/his clothes, while the father
announces, 'Let the party begin!'

In this very visual way we are immersed in a world that suddenly
changes. From the happiness of *a little girl* we are moved unexpectedly
to the unhappiness of *a little boy*, who looks just the same, before and
after. What changed are the definitions the adults in the film have in
dealing with Ludovic. The gender-bending of the film does not allow us
to find a quiet reaction to this unforeseen change. Nonetheless, we are
not out of place in this reaction. *Ma Vie en Rose*, by the Belgian director
Alain Berliner, also surprised the entertainment industry in 1997 for the
clarity and daily-life tone of its plot as well as its courage in taking the lead
in telling a story that is not common in mass media: transgender issues
and childhood.[10] The film is the story of seven-year-old Ludovic (played
by the 11-year-old actor Georges Du Fresne), born to a family of five.
Ludovic believes he is a girl trapped in a boy's body, a mistake that will
be (re)solved some day. Throughout the whole film we are witnesses of
Ludovic's constant internal battle to understand what is happening
around her/him and what is happening *inside* her/him. The situations in
the film get worse and worse as the non-acceptance of the neighbours
escalates to dramatic consequences.

In the midst of all this, we are witnesses of Ludovic's struggles. In scene
13 entitled 'XX or XY?' we are witnesses to a dialogue between Ludovic
and her/his sister Zoe. Ludovic, lying in bed, is worried as s/he realizes
how the world of the adults has become unbearable for her/him. Ludovic

---

10 The director Berliner is also conscious about this. In the website of the
movie, he is quoted affirming this: 'To my knowledge, no one has covered this
topic at this age before, the age when the question of sexual identity appears' (*Ma
Vie en Rose* (official web page), http://www.sonyclassics.com/mavieenrose
(accessed 5 May 2006)).

asks if s/he is a boy or a girl. But Zoe replies with a statement: 'Look, it's easy at your age. The hassles come later.' However, Ludovic is not convinced with the answer and re-asks the question, upsetting Zoe. Nonetheless, she tries to help Ludovic by showing her/him a notebook with a classroom explanation of biology. According to the notes, what makes a 'boy' or a 'girl' is the genetic distribution, that is, XY for boys, and XX for girls. Ludovic is still unsettled with the explanation and goes further by asking if God is not involved in the decision. Zoe very naturally replies affirmatively. This is the last piece for Ludovic to find an answer. By constructing a mix of classroom science and religious assumptions, Ludovic is able to find a satisfactory answer for her/him. While Ludovic lies in bed, the camera takes us to her/his inner imagination.

In beautiful images the film introduces us to the mind of little Ludovic, picturing how that process went for him. We see the hands of a God in heaven, so from this God's place we can see the whole neighbourhood below. This God has a book from which God reads the names of all the boys and girls who are awaited by expectant mothers on earth. God reads from it 'Ludovic Fabre: girl' so this child takes some 'chromosomes' represented by silver 'X' and 'Y' letters. God sends them from a cloud to the house of Ludovic, where her/his family is awaiting. However, the silver 'XXY' chromosomes did not go down correctly into Ludovic's house – one of the 'X' chromosomes falls into a rubbish bin, and the other 'X' and the 'Y' manage to go down the chimney. Consequently, Ludovic now has an explanation for what is happening to her/him. Coming out of her/his imagination, s/he exclaims: 'I know what happened to my X', and looking at a crucifix on the wall exclaims, 'Wise guy!'

Scene 14, entitled 'I'm a Girl-Boy', finally completes the explanation of what Ludovic understood about her/himself. In this scene, Ludovic and Jerome go to the girls' restroom at school. After using the toilet and telling Jerome that everyone looks almost the same from the physical exterior, Ludovic explains: 'You have to understand that I am a *girlboy*.' With this statement, Ludovic lays out two strong convictions, based on a twofold argument that to her/his age makes perfect sense: On the one hand, Ludovic believes that what is happening to her/him is a 'scientifically proven mistake that God will fix soon', making Ludovic finally a girl.

On the other hand, Ludovic asserts that God has the authority to turn things back to their *normal* state – in this case, changing Ludovic from a *boy* (something *wrong*) to a *girl* (something *right*). I deliberately use the terms *right/wrong* as the plot of the film constantly plays between both poles. An *(ab)/normal* binary is central to complete the point of view of both the adult characters and Ludovic. However, we soon find out in the film that clear-cut polarizations are not suitable to understand the complexities of the central argument in the overall plot. The film playfully intertwines these commonly assumed binaries with the multiple and complex worlds behind them. The binaries are unpacked in Lodovic's life, family, neighbourhood, school and work environments revealing the multiple issues, dynamics and experiences in all the characters related to Ludovic. As a result,

> The film makes clear that society quickly extends the transgender *stigma* to the entire family. To many, no child could honestly want or choose to be transgendered. Therefore, it must be the parents' fault. What did they do to make their child this way? From there it's a short step to seeing the entire family as pariahs.[11]

Therefore, the film shows the multiple challenges that everyone in the family, neighbourhood and classroom face in their interactions with transgender Ludovic. By doing this, it opens up for us a whole new world that we do not find along the pathways of our daily life. The film has *que(e)ried* and *queered* our vision and finally we can *see* what has been *occluded* to our daily-life experiences.

Body/ies and identity are two of the main dilemmas Ludovic has to face in her/his daily life. Her/his body and her/his identity do not match. No matter how s/he dreams about it, every moment s/he tries to match them does not come easily. Maybe it will never come. Not only Ludovic, the main character of the film, but also many people around the world deal with multiple issues while trying to understand and live as trans-

---

11 Melanie Yarborough, '*Ma Vie en Rose*: Transgender, the Child and the Family', http://village.fortunecity.com/carnival/383/ludovic.htm (accessed 5 May 2006), emphasis mine.

gender or intersex people. In everydayness, segregation/discrimination *devices* – that I call *discursive and material technologies of other/ing* – form part of the common experience of transgender and intersex people. Experiences of acceptance and encouragement of their particular lives are rare.

Let me expand on this issue. How are discourse and its effects transformed into instruments to separate human beings and to assign to them labels/categories that produce segregation? Drawing from Foucault and Butler's notions of power and inspired by Sue Golding's book *The Eight Technologies of Otherness*,[12] I would like to organize this multiple-layered process into two main categories. On the one hand, the existence of *discursive technologies of other/ing*: exoticism, stigmatization, labelling, dehumanizing, demonizing and silencing; whose function is the assignation of a category through which *the other/s* are *defined* as *different* and *inferior* to that of the subject who holds the power of labelling/cataloguing.[13] On the other hand, the *material technologies of other/ing*: racism, classism, xenophobia, sexism, misogyny, body fascism, ageism, and ableism; whose function is to perform the segregating act against *the other/s*. Evidently, these lists of *technologies* are not definitive and may be modified, as they are working tools to understand ever-changing processes of power. In other words, they are simply instruments that help to

---

12 See Sue Golding, ed., *The Eight Technologies of Otherness* (London: Routledge, 1997), especially pp. xi–xiv.

13 I am aware that the way discourse is performed and how it is interpreted works differently according to the context and according to the positionality of the subjects. Beyond denying this fact, I speak here about the dominance effects from discourses related to gender and sexuality in relation to the experience of transgender and intersex people. In her thoughtful research, Tannen explains: 'In analyzing discourse, many researchers operate on the unstated assumption that all speakers proceed along similar lines of interpretation, so a particular example of discourse can be taken to represent how discourse works for all speakers. For some aspects of discourse, this is undoubtedly true. Yet a large body of sociolinguistic literature makes clear that, for many aspects of discourse, this is so only to the extent that cultural background is shared. To the extent that cultural backgrounds differ, lines of interpretation and habitual use of many linguistics strategies are likely to diverge' (Deborah Tannen, *Gender and Discourse* (Oxford: Oxford University Press, 1994), p. 20).

understand how a certain act works to make the other/s a segregated being, and therefore, entitled to be excluded. Judith Butler works this in her discussion about the power dynamics around three crucial issues: racism, homophobia and misogyny.

Butler defines those issues as parallel vectors of power, which are deployed as well as mutually legitimized within their own articulation of power. Consequently, they are not separated universes or worlds that touch each other sporadically. Here resides the importance of relating the effects of heterosexism as a part of power dynamics imbued within historic legitimation of the heteropatriarchal system, which reconstructs and reshapes itself throughout time. Butler affirms:

> It seems crucial to resist the model of power that would set up racism and homophobia and misogyny as parallel or analogical relations. The assertion of their abstract or structural equivalence not only misses the specific histories of their construction and elaboration, but also delays the important work of thinking through the ways in which these vectors of power require and deploy each other for the purpose of their own articulation. Indeed, it may not be possible to think any of these notions or their interrelations without a substantially revised conception of power in both its geopolitical dimensions and in the contemporary tributaries of its intersecting circulation.[14]

Nevertheless, following Butler, I conclude that all these *technologies of other/ing*, whether *discursive* or *material*, are vectors of a similar operation of power that is unilaterally exerted on *the other/s* in order to segregate/discriminate them; they reiterate each other, they co-opt each other and they interact together in order to produce hierarchies of *other/ing* that divide people according to different categories, privileging some, diminishing other/s.

This operation of segregating power has permeated all dimensions of societies. Not only society stigmatizes transgender and intersex people

---

14 Judith Butler, *Bodies that Matter: On the Discursive Limits of 'Sex'* (London: Routledge, 1993), p. 18.

but also religions do, especially Christianity. As we will see further in this article, Argentina is not an exception from this reality. Ludovic's explanation that God decides upon every fact of life – making everything *good* and fixing everything that goes *wrong* – is simply a nice dream. Furthermore, it also makes us realize that the binary good/bad is an unstable and subjective world. However, the reality is that people of faith usually believe that God's work is to punish those who deviate from the normal – which is determined by certain interpretations of morality, Bible readings and theological views, as well as cultural constructions that not only construct this reality for human being but also for God's job description. Most Christian churches perceive body/ies, gender and sexuality as dangerous areas that need to be controlled/policed in order to achieve holiness or salvation. From spiritual practices that censor the body as negative, to systems of hierarchies based on gender, sexual orientation, colour of skin, class or nationality, among many other instruments, Christian churches have obtained their power to legislate which body/ies fit to God's grace and which do not. The clearest way to do this has been using narrow interpretations of the body of Jesus and the incarnation as a way to then universalize those visions as *the* way of being human. Therefore, the lives of persons with a transgender or intersex experience do not fit readily into these assumptions. Furthermore, the expectations of broader societies regarding these matters are allied with the expectations of mainstream Christian churches, which are displayed in dogmas, in Bible readings, moral teachings and institutional organization. In the end, we find that there is little, if any, room for transgender and intersex people in those churches. The arguments are well known, ranging from citing the Genesis accounts of the creation of humankind, where 'male and female [God] created them',[15] to interpretations of Jesus' message, moral teachings and traditions, and to the Sermon on the Mount's theological statements. The result is hopelessness. The options are either to convert to mainstream assumptions of Christianity that exhibit a narrow understanding of body/ies, gender and sexuality or to remain outside traditional religious territory.

---

15 Genesis 1.27c.

I remember the debate that took place some years ago in Argentina on a new city legal code (called *Código de Convivencia Urbana*, or *Código*), which covered issues related to body/ies, gender and sexual identities. One of the issues discussed in the new *Código* was prostitution or soliciting money for sex services in the streets of Buenos Aires. The issue certainly sparked a never-ending debate in Argentina around the *travas*[16] in the streets of Buenos Aires. It was very interesting to see how broader society's right-wing movements allied with right-wing Roman Catholics and Evangelicals in support of certain points raised in that debate. It was unusual for these three groups to join forces to advocate a common agenda, and Argentina has many social issues where they could be allies, such as relieving hunger, countering unemployment, or speaking against the lack of political and economic rights affecting millions of Argentinians as a result of the globalization of neoliberalism. Sadly, these issues are not attended to by these groups. They are not easily agitated by these social ills to the point of mobilizing thousands of people into the streets of Buenos Aires to combat the injustices. The few Protestant churches and grass-roots Roman Catholic organizations that speak up about these issues are delegitimized and, consequently, their 'Christian roots' are questioned. Nevertheless, at the end of that tumultuous public debate, the Government of the Autonomous City of Buenos Aires proclaimed a new *Código* that regulated – among many other issues of legal interaction among citizens within the city – the places where sex services could legally be allowed.[17] This directly affected the lives of female and transgender

---

16 *Trava* is the slang term to designate transgender people in Argentina.

17 The importance of the *Código de Convivencia Urbana* resides in the fact that it eliminated the police edicts dictated for over half a century by the Federal Police and the different State Police in Argentina. These edicts, widely used and expanded by the military dictatorships in Argentina, did not guarantee any sense of justice to those trapped by them. According to Gastón Chillier, lawyer for the Center of Legal and Social Studies in Buenos Aires (CELS in Spanish), these edicts have five characteristics that he summarizes as follows: '[a] In its great majority [those edicts] were dictated by the Head of Federal Police, legitimized to do so by conforming to the decree No. 32,265 the military government of 1932, which was ratified, then, by Law No. 13.030 of 1947; [b] The contravention figures mostly used described personal characteristics – instead of behaviors – that

sex workers because they could work only in specified places – now
they could be monitored and controlled. Nonetheless, it gave Roman
Catholics and Evangelicals more arguments to enhance their battle in
favour of a 'morality' for the citizens of Buenos Aires, as the designation of
liberated zones for commercial sex (called *zonas rojas*[18]) meant trouble for
the neighbourhoods in those areas. Accordingly, it caused protests from
these neighbourhoods, and some religious communities joined them in
the *moral crusade*. Some parishes distributed leaflets in these neighbourhoods, and even the Roman Catholic Auxiliary Bishop of Buenos Aires at
that time celebrated mass in protest against the presence of transgender as
well as female sex workers in the Palermo neighbourhood.[19] About 500
people gathered from the area to attend the mass. The position of religious institutions was made evidently clear, especially since many people
in Argentina equate being transgender with *prostitution*. Thus, it pain-
fully revealed the tensions between transgender sex workers and female
sex workers who competed for better treatment as sex workers. Both
claimed they should be treated as human beings with rights and privi-
leges. On analysing this, Lohana Berkins states,

affected certain groups of people based on their social condition, their sexual
orientation or their age; [c] All the procedure for application of these norms was in
charge of the police agency: detainment, harvesting of proof and, consequently,
judgment of the detainee; [d] The detained person could not exert the right of
defense; and the minimum guarantees of the due process were not fulfilled either.
The edict did not establish the presence of a lawyer; it did not demand minimum
element of proof for a sentence, and the proof could not be controlled by the
detainee; etc.; [and, e] Although the possibility existed of exerting the judicial control, actually it became an illusory practice because there was little time to appeal
and because there were different mechanisms articulated to forbid that right to the
detainee' (Gaston Chillier, 'La sanción de un código de convivencia urbana:
Causas y efectos de la eliminación de las detenciones arbitrarias por parte de la
Policía Federal'. Lecture presented at the seminar *The Police Reforms in
Argentina*, Buenos Aires: Centro de Estudios Legales y Sociales (CELS), 1–2
December 1998, pp. 2–3).

18 *Zonas rojas* literally means 'hot' or 'red' zones and it is a term used to define
liberated zones within the city where some legislation would or would not apply.

19 Cf. 'Misa en Palermo contra la oferta de sexo en la calle', in *Clarín*, 29 June
1998, http://www.clarin.com/diario/1998/06/29/e-0380id.htm (accessed 15 August
2006). Palermo was one of the designated *zonas rojas* in Buenos Aires.

There is an automatic association of the term transgender with prostitution. There is the belief that each of us one day took the decision to go into the 'red district' (*zona rojo*), and that that decision was taken while sitting in a comfortable armchair. And by the way, this is a middle-class type of belief, because many of us do not have armchairs. This type of thinking is too simplistic and tends to obscure the difficult and different personal journeys that each of us has had and still needs to confront. Moreover, I would like to show how, when our rights are violated because of prostitution or any other situation, we are confronted with a certain categorization of human rights. In this it becomes evident who are the people who deserve to be defended or not. Let us be frank in this: it is not the same when a march is organized for an adolescent who has been assassinated, someone whose innocence is not in doubt, as when we demand justice for our 110 transvestites who have been killed. Let us agree that we are dealing with different values when we denounce the cruelty and the arbitrariness of the incarceration, torture and/or assassination (of transvestites). And the same can be said when we need to demand in the name of justice the cases of violations of the rights of our female comrades.[20]

The generalizing discourse of equating *transgender to prostitution* produced an erosion of rights and human dignity with consequent unavoidable stigmatization. Furthermore, if prostitution is defined as an illegal activity, then those who take part in such activity are deprived of their access to rights in society. In the midst of this discussion over legislation, lives, body/ies, identities, are trapped within this discursive determination. Religion is an important element in determining the boundaries and results of this discourse.

Going deeper into the religious realm, it is important to note that Christianity has *body/ies* and *human dignity* at the core of the doctrine of incarnation. For all its drama against certain matters related to the discourse on body/ies and sexuality, the Church's pre-eminent dogma deals with the trans/formation of the divine into a human body. Therefore, it makes God in Jesus a glorified transgender person!

---

20 Berkins, 'Eternamente Atrapadas', pp. 20–1. Translation mine.

While Christian churches emphasize the fact that God incarnated in Jesus to save all humanity, the reality is that some humans are more worthy than others of that salvation. Beyond the nice statements in religious declarations and constitutions as well as in seminary classroom discussions about the mystery of incarnation, when it comes to daily life, transgender and intersex people are completely ostracized from that incarnation and, therefore, from salvation. It is easy for most Christian churches – although there are a few exceptions – to see transgender and intersex people as having a *disease* that has to be *cured* or *corrected*, but the idea of giving transgender and intersex persons a unique identity and dignity within the human community does not make sense to them. Without classifying and making a hierarchy of these performativities of gender and sexuality, what supports these traditional perceptions is the negative view propounded by the heteropatriarchal system which only sees body/ies divided into female and male, a clear-cut divide that does not do justice to the life of transgender and intersex people. Therefore, mainstream churches have also incorporated this into their understanding of ethics, morality and biblical/theological interpretations, ruling universal understandings of body/ies, gender and sexuality that do not reflect the varied experiences of human sexuality.

But is it possible not to relate transgender and intersex people to prostitution as Argentinian society regularly does? Can they be treated in a different way? I am afraid the answer is 'No'. In Gramscian terms, churches and schools are places where the dominant ideology in society, coming from a heteropatriarchal system, is reproduced and passed on. In Argentina, Roman Catholicism and, in a minor way, right-wing evangelical churches, still equate transgender and intersex people with prostitution, which may not always be the case for other countries, especially for non-western countries.

A view that encourages and welcomes the richness of life of transgender and intersex people is very rare. The theologian Barb Greve reflects upon his life journey in relation to this. In his sermon 'Courage from Necessity' he shares a story from his childhood as follows,

I've known my gender since I was in kindergarten. I figured it out at the same time I learned that I was to spend the better part of my life on rocky terrain. I remember the day when our teacher asked us to draw a picture of what we were going to be when we grew up. Without hesitation I began drawing a picture of my future self. I had no doubt that I would grow up to be a minister and so I drew a picture of myself preaching a sermon from my congregation's pulpit. Because church was a formal affair, I drew myself wearing my best suit. As my teacher walked around the classroom he congratulated each of the students on both our career choice and artwork. When he arrived at my place he took a quick look at my picture and asked me whom I had drawn. As I sat there in my pretty purple dress, I explained that the person in the drawing was me. He told me that, 'I was wrong. I wouldn't grow up to be a man, only boys could do that.' I left school that day confused and with a deep understanding that I was different than the other students in my class. While my teacher was telling me that I couldn't grow up to be a guy I was absolutely sure that I would.[21]

This dilemma is shared also by gays, lesbians and bisexuals when they are asked questions, especially as teenagers, that imply or assume overt heterosexuality – such as 'Will you have a girlfriend?' or 'Will you marry a Christian boy?' Greve's experience is doubly important as he is open enough in his sermon, on the one hand, to describe how deeply this affected him while growing up as a girl not comfortable with that fact, and, on the other hand, to offer us a testimony from his childhood. Sadly, educators, parents and ministers, just to name a few, are generally not adequately prepared to answer questions related to being transgender or intersex. Some cannot comprehend these situations, as the testimony of Greve illustrates very well. Nevertheless, he is able to reflect on this matter much further and challenge the attached expectations of gender dichotomy:

---

21 Barb Greve, *Courage from Necessity*, sermon preached at the Church for the Fellowship of All People, Unitarian Universalist Church, San Francisco, 3 June 2006, pp. 1–2.

Unfortunately, society's need to define, dichotomize, and limit gender sacrifices the real life experience of people like me. Rather than trust us to identify our own gender, society tries to force us into one of two options: man or woman. For me to do that would mean denying a large piece of who I am. When transgender folks are strong enough to refuse the dichotomy of gender, we are still forced to buy into a continuum that puts two options on opposing ends with us 'transitioning' between the two: I was a man, now I'm becoming a woman or you identified me as a woman, but now I'm creating the man I've always known I am. Is it so hard to imagine that there are more than these 2 fixed points at this intersection? What if there is a different road coming into the middle for each gender? What if some folks always stay where they started, others transition between 2 or 3 or more of these roads, some live in the middle of that intersection where it all comes together, and still others don't live anywhere near the intersection?[22]

In this quotation, Greve touches on one of the basic problems that transgender and intersex people have to face: the *female/male* dichotomy as a mechanism of segregation. In this respect, the so-called *transition* that transgender people face while seeking body modification is read within the heteronormative pattern as a way to normalize the *deviant body* of transgender people. In other words, a *wrong body* gets assimilated into a *right female or male body*. Here we see a notorious act of body fascism from the heteropatriarchal system, a fact that has embedded all areas of daily life and social institutions.

Mauro Cabral, one of the most important of transgender and intersex community activists and scholars – along with Lohana Berkins – in Argentina, has analysed this situation. In his reflections given at a meeting of the United Nations Commission on Human Rights, Cabral says,

In Argentina for example, one can not be declared a transgender man unless one is attracted to women; in other words, all trans men must be

22 Greve, *Courage from Necessity*, p. 2.

first lesbians (based on their biological sex) and then heterosexual (based on their chosen gender). However, not all trans people identify themselves in such a way.[23]

In other words, the process of normalization from the hetero-patriarchal system moulds and rules the performativity of transgender and intersex body/ies, most of the time forcing them to live out a life that does not represent them. The term used to describe this experience from the transgender and intersex people's experience is 'passing'. In most cases, the process of normalization is a painful experience that implies the erosion of difference.[24] The manifold experiences of transgender and intersex people are occluded. Leslie Feinberg summarizes the concerns of transgender and intersex people as follows:

We are a movement of masculine females and feminine males, cross-dressers, transsexual men and women, intersexuals born on the anatomical sweep between female and male, gender-blenders, many other sex and gender-variant people, and our significant others. All told, we expand understanding of how many ways there are to be a human being. Our lives are proof that sex and gender are much more

23 Sophie Zhang, 'Gender Rights are Human Rights', report on the Discussion Panel on Trangender/Intersex Issues at the 65th Session of the Commission on Human Rights of the United Nations, 13 April 2005, http://www.ngochr.org/view/index.php?basic_entity'DOCUMENT&list_ids'545 (accessed 18 August 2006).

24 I am aware that this issue is very problematic. I base my statement following Shapiro, who, talking about transsexuals, affirms: 'The efforts of transsexuals to achieve normal gender status involve them in what is generally referred to as "passing." Since the term "passing" carries the connotation of being accepted for something one is not, it is important to consider the complexities that arise when this term is applied to what transsexuals are doing. First of all, transsexuals commonly believe that it is when they are trying to play the role of their anatomical sex, as opposed to their subjectively experienced gender, that they are trying to pass as something they are not. The way they frequently put this is to say that they feel they are "masquerading" as a man or a woman. At the same time, transsexuals must work hard at passing in their new gender status, however more authentic they may themselves believe to be' (Shapiro, 'Transsexualism', p. 256).

complex than a delivery room doctor's glance at genitals can determine, more variegated than pink or blue birth caps. We are oppressed for not fitting those narrow social norms. . . . If you are a trans person, you face horrendous social punishments – from institutionalization to gang rape, from beatings to denial of child visitation. This oppression is faced, in varying degrees, by all who march under the banner of trans liberation. This brutalization and degradation strips us of what we could achieve with our individual lifetimes.[25]

Feinberg and Creve in the United States, Berkins and Cabral in Argentina, along with many other people around the globe all have in common the painful daily experience of dealing with a world that does not understand them, a world that rules and polices their lives to fit into a narrow binary of gender and sexuality.

The same could be seen in the film we are analysing in this section, and little Ludovic has to face it. In scene 24, 'Downsized', we see how the family gives up in their attempts to make 'Ludovic's fantasy' go away. But it also shows the final public statement of the neighbourhood. In this scene, we see Ludovic waking up with stomach cramps. According to her/his sister Zoe, menstruation produces stomach cramps, but it happily marks the moment that someone becomes a 'real woman'. Therefore, Ludovic thinks this is the moment that s/he turns into a 'real girl'. Happy with the 'news', Ludovic runs downstairs where the rest of the family is. Shouting that her/his menstruation has started, Ludovic only finds terrible 'news'. Her/his father is kneeling on the ground, crying while her/his mother is consoling him. Behind them, on the garage door there is a graffiti that reads 'Bent boys out'. Hearing the 'good news' of Ludovic, the mother takes her/him violently inside the house while the father remains outside still crying. This is the most dramatic switch in the film as Ludovic is about to discover the most astonishing news.

Inside the house, Ludovic is crying and asking the mother why 'bent things' must go. Hesitating, the mother gathers energy to finally state that

25 Leslie Feinberg, *Trans Liberation: Beyond Pink or Blue* (Boston: Beacon Press, 1998), pp. 5–6.

'bent' is used to describe negatively someone like her/him, a boy who likes boys. Immediately after that, the mother proceeds to cut Ludovic's girlish long hair to a boyish looking haircut. Finally, Ludovic is confronted with the cruel reality of the world where s/he lives. No matter how much s/he could dream, this world will not accept her/his dreams. The haircut marks the transition moment where Ludovic will be recognized by everyone as a boy. The explanation about God's role in her/his life, and God's authority to change what is wrong/bad into good does not work any more. It is the end of Ludovic's agency over her/his body to begin the normalization of society, of what is mandated and what is expected of her/him. Coming to this point in the film, I still refuse to address Ludovic as a *he* or a *she*. Somehow, those categories, marked by centuries of heteropatriarchal taxonomies of decency, do not fit the painful, complex and yet rich world of Ludovic. But Ludovic has to face issues of religious faith, the isolation from society and, in many aspects, a family that does not accept her/him but imposes onto her/him an exogenous identity. Ludovic has to learn how to perform a *passing* as an/*other* imposed by family and society that does not agree with her/his feelings and identity.

What is really striking in the film is the gap between Ludovic's beliefs and her/his parents/neighbours. In the middle of that disparity, God is occluded and restrained from daily life by assuming the impositions of society. Evidently, the message of the gospel is not a message of exclusion/discrimination but of love and acceptance. But that is a point not noticed by the adult world ruled by a crude heteropatriarchal ideology. In the end, even Ludovic disbelieves everything. In that world, and possibly even in the realm of religious faith, neither Ludovic nor transgender and intersex people have a place because it is a world dominated by body fascism coming from a compulsory heteropatriarchal system. In that world God has become an idol and has been imprisoned in the dungeons of heteropatriarchalism. God also has to learn how to perform a *passing* that would fit into the narrow dichotomy of decent *heterosexualism*.

How can the message of Jesus be recovered amidst this situation? I believe we need to revisit the traditions of Christianity regarding body/ies with other eyes in order to reclaim its liberating message. However, this is not an easy process, either. All Christian traditions are the result of particular historical and geographical moments. Over the years, many layers of new elements are added to those traditions, enhancing them and making them more complex and, at the same time, distorting or sacralizing them. The result is a corpus static and exogenous to the original background, making body/ies a territory where *normalization* from dogmas took place. If the original background of Christian traditions was in itself a particular answer to a particular context for a particular time and not universal, the evolution of Christian traditions in regard to body/ies became universal and normatively narrow. However, this corpus, which we have inherited along with the transmission of the Christian faith, has moulded and continues moulding Christian visions of body/ies, gender and sexuality. Furthermore, it has been applied to different contexts during different times expecting those new contexts to adapt themselves to that exogenous corpus of Christian traditions. That is a colonial performativity that keeps captive the new contexts, body/ies, genders and sexualities. Therefore, we need to queer and decolonize those traditions from their colonial heteropatriarchal clothes, stripping them in order to reach their *true* body.

I propose to go back to the Christological/incarnational concerns as a way to retrieve the Christian message beyond its wrapping. By revisiting these concerns I believe we will be able to move further on an *indecent theology* that would contribute to the liberation of body/ies in relation to the transgender and intersex experiences.

Incarnating human body/ies

The second century of the Christian era marked the point of inflection where the unstable interpretations of Jesus' message and his movement began to explode into a myriad of possibilities and practices that could no longer be kept together. All sorts of doctrines as well as all kinds of disputes and battles are found among the multiple sectors of an ever be/coming Christianity in formation and constant reshaping. If the apostolic period, that is the immediate time after Jesus' death and resurrection, is plagued by missionary movements aiming to spread the new message to every land, that time is also embedded in the intermixing of different strains of models of Jesus' following. For example, in Acts 15 we see the early Church dealing with the case of the anointing of gentiles by the Holy Spirit and the questions about gentiles following Jewish traditions, especially circumcision. The council of the apostles and church leaders gathered in AD 49 to recognize that for gentiles, following Jesus could not be moulded after the set of requirements that was asked of those with Jewish ancestry. The decision of the council was not to require circumcision for gentile converts. In doing this, the *plurality* – if the word is appropriate at that time – of Jesus' movement under the leadership of the apostles is clearly evident.

If the council in Jerusalem in AD 49 ended with a peaceful decision to embrace the assemblies of the gentiles, it may have turned out differently in other Christian communities. In Paul's recounting of the events when Peter goes to Antioch, the dispute between them reflects the dissimilar political agendas among the various sectors of the Christian movement. It is in Galatians 2.11–16 where Paul decisively expresses his opposition to Peter's perspective on the circumcision issue in relation to the gentiles.[26]

Given these events, it is logical to expect that at the turn of the second century, the growing and sometimes opposite interpretations of the Christian communities about the content of Jesus' message would collide with each other. A major dispute is related to the body of Jesus and the

---

26 Although not in the scope of this chapter, the mentioned passage has been problematic for interpretation due to the use of the name 'Cephas' instead of 'Peter'. In John 1.42 Jesus calls Peter 'Cephas'. For many centuries, Bible scholars and church historians have debated whether the 'Cephas' throughout the New Testament is the same as Peter the apostle. The first in-depth study on this was done by Jean Hardouin, a Jesuit priest in the France of the seventeenth century. While the debate still remains, this chapter wants to emphasize the tensions already present in the scriptures among the apostles and among the Christian communities. For a better understanding of Hardouin's thorough study, see James M. Scott, 'A Question of Identity: Is Cephas the Same Person as Peter?', *Journal of Biblical Studies* 3.3 (October 2003), pp. 1–20.

incarnation. This dispute began with Cerinthus in Asia Minor around AD 100, who opposed John the Apostle's views about the incarnation of the *logos*, denying the union between the *logos* and the flesh of Jesus.[27] Others, such as the Docetists – from the Greek word *dokein* which means 'apparition' – would deny the existence of the flesh of Jesus completely, arguing that Jesus was simply a spirit.[28]

The consequences of interpretations such as those mentioned above threatened not only the historicity of Jesus, but also the main elements of the Christian faith: incarnation, death and resurrection and, consequently, salvation. I do not want to go into details here about the specifics of the Christological positions in Antioch and Alexandria and all the disputes that occurred from the second century to the fourth century, which would be another interesting analysis for another article. However, we must affirm that it was the Cappadocian Fathers (Gregory of Nyssa, Gregory of Nazianzus, and Basil of Caesarea) along with Athanasius of Alexandria who developed the official interpretation of Jesus Christ, the incarnation and salvation process. Their contributions eroded the doctrines of other theologians, later condemned by the emerging Christian orthodoxy. From the beginning of the second century until the mid-sixteenth century, all sectors of Christianity were embedded in Trinitarian and Christological discussions. The Councils of Nicaea (325), Constantinople (381) and Chalcedon (451) saw the full development and definition of almost all core doctrines of Christianity that continue to this day. However, after those ecumenical councils there were still revisions and oppositions to these dogmas. New interpretations continue to come

---

27 See G. L. Carey, 'Cerinto (ca. 100)', in *Diccionario de Historia de la Iglesia*, ed. Wilton M. Nelson (Miami, Fla.: Caribe, 1989), p. 233.

28 See G. W. Grogan, 'Docetismo', in *Diccionario de Historia de la Iglesia*, ed. Wilton M. Nelson (Miami, Fla.: Caribe, 1989), pp. 351–2. The First Epistle of John has a notorious emphasis on the 'flesh' of Jesus against what 'false prophets' would affirm. For example, the First Epistle of John states: 'Beloved, do not believe every spirit, but test the spirits to see whether they are from God; for many *false prophets* have gone out into the world. By this you know the Spirit of God: every spirit that confesses that Jesus Christ has come in the *flesh* is from God, and every spirit that does not confess Jesus is not from God' (1 John 4.1–3, emphasis mine).

out. Almost in every moment of the histories of Christianity, theologians and churches have revisited those discussions.[29]

In general terms, the Christological discussion was not resolved with the decisions of the Council of Chalcedon. But it defined a *via media* in the following terms: in taking previous theologians, the Council would understand the union of the *logos* in Jesus as *communicatio idiomatum*.[30] Besides, the incarnation of Christ can be understood as the *kenosis* (self-emptying abiding) of God operated by the power of the Holy Spirit. In other words, the *immanent Trinity* manifested in creation as *economic Trinity*.[31] At the same time, the resurrection of Christ is the beginning of

29 Take for example the famous work of Anselm, *Cur Deus Homo* (Why God was Made Human Being), written in the eleventh century, which revisits the classical Christological questions but adds the still traditional understanding of the Atonement. For a complete translation into English of this work, see St Anselm, *Proslogium; Monologium; An Appendix in Behalf of the Fool by Gaunilon; and Cur Deus Homo*, trans. Sidney Norton Deane (La Salle, Ill.: Open Court, 1958), pp. 171–288.

30 The expression *communicatio idiomatum* comes from the writing of Pope Leo, *Tome to Flavian*, through which Pope Leo intervenes in the *Eastern* Churches' theological disputes. 'Although Leo does not mention "deification," he admits its essential theological presupposition. Finally, there is in Leo's text a clear concept of communicatio idiomatum, the very thing that was the stumbling block for all the "nestorianizing" theologians of Antioch: the unity of person makes it possible to say that "the Son of God died" (*unitatem personae in utranque intelligendam Filius Dei crucifixus dicitur et sepultus*), without the divine nature losing its natural impassibility. This was precisely the point on which Cyril had fought against Nestorius: God, without ceasing to be God, made human nature his own to this point of mortality' (John Meyendorff, *Christ in Eastern Christian Thought* (New York: St Vladimir's Seminary Press, 1975), p. 25).

31 See Philippians 2.6–11. Karl Rahner defines both terms in what is known in systematic theology as 'The Rahnerian *Grundaxiom*': 'The "economic" Trinity is the "immanent", and the "immanent" Trinity is the "economic" Trinity.' We understand as 'Economic Trinity' the 'self-communication' of the Trinitarian God in the 'person of Christ and the activity of the Holy Spirit' in the economy of salvation. We call 'Immanent Trinity' the 'inner' life of God, the 'self-relatedness of Father, Son and Spirit' (Karl Rahner, *The Trinity* (London: Burns & Oates, 1970), p. 220. See also Catherine Mowry LaCugna, *God for Us: The Trinity and Christian Life* (San Francisco: HarperSanFrancisco, 1991), p. 2; Jürgen Moltmann, *The Spirit of Life: A Universal Affirmation* (Minneapolis: Fortress

his process of returning (*apokatastasis*)[32] to unity with God. Therefore, *theosis/theopoiesis* (or the process of *divinization/deification*)[33] is also the materialization of the *apokatastasis* of humanity and all creation returning to God after the event of the incarnation of Christ. As God has chosen creation as God's indwelling place, this represents the ultimate union of divinity and creatureliness. This could not be possible without the theological reflection of the Cappadocian Fathers, especially Gregory of Nazianzus. He made this very important statement:

> If someone believes in Him as man without human reason, such a one definitely lacks reason, and is not worthy of salvation. *Because what He has not assumed, has not been saved, because He has saved what He has also assumed to his divinity.* If only the half of Adam fell down, then it is possible that what Christ assumes and saves is alone the half. But if the whole of his nature fell down, it is necessary that the whole of

---

Press, 1992), p. 151; and Guillermo Hansen, 'La concepción trinitaria de Dios en los orígenes de la teología de la liberación: el aporte de Juan Luis Segundo', *Cuadernos de Teología* 16.1–2 (1997), p. 47).

32 The term *apokatastasis* [αποκαταστασις] is taken from Origen and his cyclic worldview in relation to soteriology (see Origen, *Commento al Vangelo di Giovanini: A cura di Eugenio Corsini* (Turin: Unione Tipografico-Editrice Torinese, 1968), pp. 143–4, note 27). For him, humanity and creation have fallen from God in a process that he calls *kenosis*, already present in the thought of St Paul in the second chapter of his Epistle to the Philippians. The process of returning to God is called *apokatastasis*, and is related to soteriology, because it represents, for Origen, the ultimate salvation for all creatures (F. L. Cross, ed. *The Oxford Dictionary of the Christian Church* (London: Oxford University Press, 1957), p. 67. See also Angelo Di Berardino, ed. *Diccionario Patrístico y de la Antigüedad Tardía* (Salamanca: Sígueme, 1998), pp. 168–9). Origen bases this doctrine on 1 Corinthians 15.23–26 (see Di Berardino, *Diccionario Patrístico*, pp. 164–5).

33 'The word "theosis" is the transliteration of a Greek word meaning "deification" (being made God)' (Robert V. Rakestraw, 'Becoming Like God: An Evangelical Doctrine of Theosis', *Journal of the Evangelical Theological Society* 40.2 (June 1997), p. 260). Take for example the words of Origen against Celsus in his argument about the incarnation of Christ in the Virgin Mary: 'human and divine began to be woven together, so that by prolonged fellowship with divinity, human nature might become divine' (Origen, *Contra Celsum* 1.35, trans. H. E. Chadwick (Cambridge: Cambridge University Press, 1965), p. 34).

it would be united to the totality of the Generated in order to be saved as a whole.[34]

In this statement, the basic argument of the incarnation is laid out: 'Because what He has not assumed has not been saved, because He has saved what He has also assumed to his divinity.' This statement has tremendous consequences for a liberating understanding of body/ies as the indwelling place for God, along with the whole of creation.[35] However, this has not been the case. If the original context of this affirmation was soteriological 'good news', it soon became its opposite as Christianity would elaborate a complex corpus of traditions. At the end, this same statement would be less important than a spiritual(ized) vision of body/ies that has been policed and constructed in a way that has de-

34 Gregory of Nazianzus, *Epistle 101*, Migne, PG 37, pp. 181–4, emphasis added. This statement transcends previous positions of other patristic writers, but still it will not be able totally to erase the gap between Jesus' body and human body in terms of sexuality. For example, the position of Clement of Alexandria would remain, reinterpreted and adequate to different times and contexts. On this, Brown states: 'Through the Incarnation of Christ, the Highest God had reached down to make even the body capable of transformation. In admitting this possibility, Clement implied that the stable environment posited by pagan thought, an intractable body and a social order adjusted to its unchanging needs, might burst from its ancient bounds. Sexual renunciation might lead the Christian to transform the body and, in transforming the body, to break with the discreet discipline of the ancient city' (Peter Brown, *The Body and Society: Men, Women and Sexual Renunciation in Early Christianity* (New York: Columbia University Press, 1988), p. 31).

35 The Hebrew scriptures contain a similar understanding in the image of the *Shekinah*. The notion of the *Shekinah* of God is the way to understand how God accompanies and has a communion with humanity in their suffering, as the experience of the Exodus reveals to us. Jürgen Moltmann says of the *Shekinah*: 'We become sensitive to the *Shekinah* in us, and equally sensitive to the *Shekinah* in other people and in all other creatures. We expect the mystical union of the *Shekinah* with God in every true encounter. That is why we long for the love in which we forget ourselves and at the same time find ourselves. We encounter every other created being in the expectation of meeting God. For we have discovered that in these other people and these other creatures God waits for our love, and for the homecoming of his *Shekinah*' (Moltmann, *Spirit*, pp. 50–51.)

incarnated them. In the West, the union of incarnation to a philosophy with Aristotelian flavour would produce the understandings of body/ies as a dangerous place, a trap for the spirit, and a matter of censorship. Finally, it has be/come a place for painful exclusion of transgender and intersex people. For example, this was the position of the desert tradition passed on to the monastic tradition, which provided a diligent policing of body/ies in the ascetic ideal, not denying their existence but negating the possibilities for the development of a positive theology of body/ies.[36]

Although the topic is complex, its evolution took many centuries. The constant battle against spiritual(izing) movements forced orthodoxy to see body/ies as a dangerous place. From the affirmation of Irenaeus of Lyon: 'because the body has come from the earth, it is impossible that it could be saved,'[37] many theologians would maintain the importance of the incarnation of Christ for soteriology along with a negative under-standing of human body/ies. This duality, later institutionalized in the West, would produce even the diminishing of the doctrine of the incar-nation by moving its focus to a mere preparation for the really important issue: the cross as the most important moment in the life and ministry of Jesus Christ. By doing this, the door for body fascism within Christianity was opened, as the cross also opens the door for the acceptance of body punishment as God's will. From that moment on, body/ies would be obsessively policed, controlled, corrected, normalized in order to

---

36 On this Brown states that 'In the desert tradition, vigilant attention to the body enjoyed an almost oppressive prominence. Yet to describe ascetic thought as "dualist" and as motivated by hatred of the body, is to miss its most novel and its most poignant aspect. Seldom, in ancient thought, had the body been seen as more deeply implicated in the transformation of the soul; and never was it made to bear so heavy a burden. For the Desert Fathers, the body was not an irrelevant part of the human person, that could, as it were, be "put in brackets." . . . Theologians of ascetic background, throughout the fourth and fifth centuries, would not have pursued with such ferocious intellectual energy the problems raised by the Incarnation of Christ, and the consequent joining of human and divine in one single human person, if this joining had not been sensed by them as a haunting emblem of the enigmatic joining of body and soul within themselves. Hence the double aspect of ascetic literature' (Brown, *Body and Society*, pp. 235–6).

37 Irenaeus of Lyon, *Adversus Haereses* 5.27.9.

achieve heavenly salvation . . . Body/ies went into the prisons of Christianity, all in the name of salvation and morality. Returning to the body of Christ is an act of freedom for the creation that Christ embodied, as facing the issue of the incarnation is, consequently, a political act towards the dismantling of politics that have imprisoned body/ies.[38]

If Gregory of Nazianzus' statement was liberating news for human body/ies in relation to the divine through the incarnation of Christ, the subsequent history of theological thought in terms of body/ies has remained negative towards them. For that reason, is there any hope for transgender and intersex people within Christianity?

Body/ies matter

What matters to us here is whether the affirmation of the Cappadocian Father Gregory of Nazianzus, which summarizes the doctrine of the incarnation, would apply when we look at the experience of transgender and intersex people in relation to their body/ies. This concern also has implications for soteriology (salvation), as the question raised by the feminist theologian Rosemary Radford Ruether cunningly addresses: 'Can a male saviour save women?'[39] This has broader implications for

---

38 Ward also argues in the same direction when analysing the sexual and queer language behind the notion of the *Body of Christ*: 'there are good theological reasons for this reflexivity – to wit, being so implicated is to participate in the unfolding of the Godhead with respect to creation. To accept, reflect upon and work within the cultural politics of any one time and place is an incarnational act itself, the constitution then of the body of Christ. As such theologians reflecting upon the embodiment of Jesus Christ help to raise the question of the politics of embodiment itself. In doing this those politics become not simply a cultural but a theological issue' (Graham Ward, 'On the Politics of Embodiment and the Mystery of All Flesh', in Marcella Althaus-Reid and Lisa Isherwood, eds, *The Sexual Theologian: Essays on Sex, God and Politics* (London: T & T Clark, 2004), p. 84).

39 See Rosemary Radford Ruether, *Sexism and God-Talk: Toward a Feminist Theology* (Boston: Beacon Press, 1983), ch. 5. Feminist theologians have seriously taken into account the Shekinah/Sophia/Wisdom images of the Hebrew Bible to read Christ and posterior Christology. See Ruether, *Sexism and God-Talk,*

body/ies. The fact is that the incarnation of Christ is difficult to assume if we tie the whole process of salvation to Jesus' maleness. Therefore, we need to queer this doctrine in order to unpack its relevance for the life and body/ies of transgender and intersex people. We must not forget that notions of gender, performances of sexuality, power and order are intrinsically related to the incarnation, and conditioned by culture, political environment, economic relations, historical events and social processes. Furthermore, according to Peter Brown, the way these notions are performed has an intrinsically direct impact in the way that societies construct those notions.[40] Christian churches are part of every society and, therefore, must evaluate their part regarding the issue at stake.

As already said, Christians tend to perceive transgender and intersex people in a binary opposition of *good/bad* that does not always allow for

---

pp. 54–61, where she explains the term *Sophia*/Wisdom and *Shekinah*; Elisabeth Schüssler-Fiorenza, *In Memory of Her: A Feminist Theological Reconstruction of Christian Origins* (New York: Crossroad, 1994/2000), pp. 130–40; Elisabeth Schüssler-Fiorenza, *Jesus: Miriam's Child, Sophia's Prophet: Critical Issues in Feminist Christology* (New York: Continuum, 1999), especially chs 5 and 6; and Elizabeth Johnson, *She Who Is: The Mystery of God in Feminist Theological Discourse* (New York: Crossroad, 2000), especially chs 7–9. They are not alone in this as Orthodox theologians have followed similar paths. See Sergei Bulgakov, *Sophia, the Wisdom of God: An Outline of Sophiology* (Hudson, NY: Lindisfarne Press, 1993), especially ch. 2; the thoughts of Vladimir Solovyov (1853–1900) and Dmitry Merenzhkovsky, whose work is analysed by Michael Aksionov Meerson, *The Trinity of Love in Modern Russian Theology: The Love Paradigm and the Retrieval of Western Medieval Love Mysticism in Modern Russian Trinitarian Thought from Solovyov to Bulgakov* (Quincy, Ill.: Franciscan Press, 1998), especially chs 2 and 5; and Pavel Florensky, whose work is analysed by Robert Slesinski, in *Pavel Florensky: A Metaphysics of Love* (New York: St Vladimir's Seminary Press, 1984), especially chs 7 and 8.

40 According to Brown, whose study focuses on the early Christian Church period, 'A thing of the natural world, the body was expected to speak of its own needs in an ancient, authoritative voice. It was only prudent to listen at times. The tolerance that was extended to the body in late classical times was based on a sense that the antithesis to the animal world, the city, was so strong that, once made, the claims of the city were inexorable. The family and the city determined the degree to which the results of the body's connection with the natural world was acceptable in organized society' (Brown, *Body and Society*, p. 45).

appreciating the complexity of their lives and experiences. When it comes to the performance of identity based on a gender display that does not match with the 'biological' sex – and taking into account that by saying this we are regrouping many different experiences in a single term – or when someone transits from one point to another in their sexuality, again maybe never landing on the other side of the assumed male/female polarity, churches are mainly not able to affirm those experiences. Issues related to strictly economic or social issues are worth fighting for; however, those related to body/ies, gender, and performances of sexuality are on unstable ground and, therefore, hard to fight for. The few churches who would take a definite stand on these are looked upon by mainstream/traditional denominations as *not-serious/not-correct churches*.

However, in a vacuum, economic matters are divorced from social issues, and gender issues divorced from theological statements, politics or geography. In reality, the truth is that they all intertwine in various ways making it complex to divorce one from the other/s. For example, a transgender male-to-female person in Argentina, who injects used aeroplane oil into her breast to increase its size – because she has no money to go to a clinic and pay for surgery that would implant silicones in her breast – is not worthy of churches' attention. Will they raise their voice and seek justice for this transgender person? Is this person less worthy than another transgender male-to-female person in California who has the resources to undergo a complete breast implant treatment as part of the gender change procedures and have periodical follow-up visits with her doctors? I believe that economy makes a world of difference in these two cases. Some privileged transgender persons have access not only to specialized treatments but also to a sanitized and safe environment. Whatever the motivations are for these two different individuals to modify their bodies, the result will always highlight the intricate network of decisions based on economic resources, social access to medical care, family support, geographic locations, and so on.[41]

---

41 This issue is connected to many others. We could also wonder how a transgendered dancer or female 'im/personator' crosses the boundaries of heteronormative gender/sexual categories and carries with her/him the fetish of capitalist production for physical satisfaction of her/his audience or of her/his personal life.

Christianity cannot afford – and actually should never do it – to privilege one person over the other, or to refuse both because those persons do not fit narrow understandings of body/ies, gender and sexuality. Transgender and intersex people are telling us that the incarnation of Christ is not just a servant of heteropatriarchal taxonomy, but a cosmic event that embraces multiple and distinct beings into the divine. The option of God to incarnate *a* human body is not trivial but a sublime act to dignify the beauty of *every single* human body, whether they are straight, transgender, intersex, poor, Latina/o, and so on. In Jesus, God made a distinct act of divine power and opened up a world, a divine world, to all the creation. This is what Gregory of Nazianzus, I believe, was trying to say to Gnostics and Orthodox: 'You should not decide whose body/ies are going to be saved because the logos incarnated the whole of humanity!' Therefore, we should not use that sublime act to punish those who do not fit into a binary narrow reading of the incarnation as 'Jesus the straight, white, middle-class, able, fit body' but as Jesus the multiple human body/ies! This is the core of the Christian doctrine and we bastardize that doctrine every time we use it to segregate people that we think should not fit into our own fantasy of the cosmic event of the incarnation.

Body/ies do change, are fluid, and are modified for different reasons, and those reasons are never defined in clear-cut personal/social ways. They are, most of the time, an intricate mix of both, in different degrees or categories. As theologians, how can we take those degrees or categories in a way that would render liberation to those whose body/ies are be/coming modified? I believe, in part, that this is related to the extent of our participation in policing networks of body fascism and social (hetero)normativity. We need to ask ourselves: Do we honestly accept a trans/gender person or an intersex person in our communities, activities, churches, panels, classes or advocacy? Or are we just being polite when we say so? To what extent do we participate in liberation, oppression, indifference, (in)tolerance, and so on, without questioning that participation? As we saw in the analysis of the film *Ma Vie en Rose*, we ask: How do we deal with the family of a transgender or intersex person? The theologian Barb Greve raises this question in relation to the issue of *transition*. On relating an experience with a female co-worker from his denomination, Greve tells,

> She asked, 'How is your transition going?' – How <u>deep</u> into the soul does this reminder that one's life is lived as a specimen for others reach? Perhaps it is meant as a friendly question, such as 'how are you?' or 'how is your family?' But it digs deeper. Is it truly meant as a friendly question, asked by someone who is or is becoming an ally? Or is it more asked out of entitled curiosity? Does it matter that my transition lasted a week or less – that my 'transition' is less about me than it is about you. I suspect you assume that I am transsexual, not transgender and as such you also assume I will change my body and name.[42]

I believe this has a lot to do with the way we perceive the other/s, especially the way their lives, gender, sexualities and body/ies are constructed. On this, Judith Butler in her book *Bodies that Matter* analyses how body/ies are socially constructed and materialized. She begins with a thought-provoking proposal toward understanding how materializing/materialization happens.

> What I would propose . . . is a return to the notion of matter, not as site or surface, but as a process of materialization that stabilizes over time to produce the effect of boundary, fixity, and surface we call matter. That matter is always materialized has, I think, to be thought in relation to the productive and, indeed, materializing effects of regulatory power in the Foucaultian sense.[43]

To better understand how this is done, she also defines *construction* as *reiteration of norms*.

---

42 Barb Greve, 'Transformation', sermon preached at the chapel of Starr King School for the Ministry (SKSM), The Graduate Theological Union (GTU) (Berkeley, Calif., 2 May 2006), p. 2.

43 Butler, *Bodies*, pp. 9–10.

Crucially, then, construction is neither a single act nor a causal process initiated by a subject and culminating in a set of fixed effects. Construction not only takes place *in* time, but is itself a temporal process which operates through the reiteration of norms; sex is both produced and destabilized in the course of this reiteration.[44]

In other words, following her argument shows that body/ies are also constructed by the reiteration of norms that produce the understanding of those body/ies here and now. In analysing the issue further, she states,

The forming of a subject requires an identification with the normative phantasm of 'sex,' and this identification takes place through a repudiation which produces a domain of abjection, a repudiation without which the subject cannot emerge. . . . Further, the materialization of a given sex will centrally concern the regulation of identificatory practices such that the identification with the abjection of sex will be persistently disavowed.[45]

Following Butler's line of thought, she also specifies that,

The forming, crafting, bearing, circulation, signification of that sexed body will not be a set of actions performed in compliance with the law; on the contrary, they will be a set of actions mobilized by the law, the citational accumulation and dissimulation of the law that produces material effects, the lived necessity of those effects as well as the lived contestation of that necessity.[46]

In this way, following Lacan and the formation of the 'I', Butler arrives at the relationship between *materiality* and *identity*:

The process of that sedimentation or what might be called *materialization* will be a kind of citationality, the acquisition of being through

---

44 Butler, *Bodies*, p. 10.
45 Butler, *Bodies*, p. 3.
46 Butler, *Bodies*, p. 12.

the citing of power, a citing that establishes an originary complicity with power in the formation of the 'I'.[47]

If Butler is correct, we cannot separate the display of identities from their connection to body/ies. In other words, our body/ies are necessary for the way we display/deploy ourselves in the world. But these body/ies are not constrained to fixed/static performativities. Rather, they vary according to manifold experiences that will also modify the way identities are constructed. It is interplay and a performativity that allow for power from the heteropatriarchal system to mould those identities, but following Foucault again, it simultaneously allows for disruptions and resistance to those heteronormativities. To remember this is important in order to open up spaces for the reception of the experiences of transgender and intersex people.

Furthermore, if it is true that Christianity plays a role in the construction of normativities that do not allow people such as transgender and intersex people to be themselves and be accepted within churches as such, then the liberating step is to confront those normativities, their discourse, and their colonial activities. In order to do this, it is necessary to bring back the liberationist message of Gregory of Nazianzus in relation to the incarnation. As the Christian Bible reads, 'in Christ God was reconciling the whole world',[48] which implies that the incarnation is not only the starting point where God and the creation join through Jesus Christ, but also an entry point to the possibility to argue in favour of transgender and intersex people within the Christian faith. The heteropatriarchal basement of those normativities within Christianity falls by itself when confronted with the liberating message of the incarnation. Transgender and intersex people, among other/s are witness of the multiple layered experiences of gender and sexuality. Within Christianity, we cannot occlude that fact any more. They tell us about a whole universe of multiple worlds contained in the word 'body/ies'. They invite us to celebrate the diversity of God's creation of humanity as it is, not as

47 Butler, *Bodies*, p. 15, emphasis in the original.
48 2 Corinthians 5.19a.

we think it should be. Recovering the doctrine of the incarnation from its prison implies opening it up to a dialogue and relationship with many different and yet very rich experiences of life, being transgender and intersex precious voices to that dialogue.

Conclusion

Throughout this article I have focused on the life experience of transgender and intersex people, especially in relation to their exclusion from society and Christian churches due to a narrow body fascism coming from the heteropatriarchal system. This body fascism is an instrument to regulate their body/ies in a male/female dichotomy that does not allow for their experiences to reveal themselves. Consequently, this body fascism is a root for colonization and oppression of the experience, lives and body/ies of transgender and intersex people as it fits one model of being human that does not reflect the varied experiences of human body/ies, gender and sexuality.

By analysing the film *Ma Vie en Rose*, we are witnesses to the struggles of transgender and intersex people from their childhood. Growing up in adverse situations permanently marks/hurts those who have suffered the consequences of a heteropatriarchal regime. Liberation is an issue at stake that cannot wait within the context of discourses but has to permeate the common understanding of body/ies, gender and performances of sexuality.

Drawing on the doctrine of the incarnation as defined by Gregory of Nazianzus we rediscovered that Christian theology does not support a regime of colonization without betraying its roots. In other words, when allowing and being an ally to a heteropatriarchal system, Christianity has left the core of its faith and embraced an exogenous ideology that is injustice. Transgender and intersex people, among others, have been witnesses to this injustice.

The need for an *indecent theology* that not only values but also encourages the lives, experiences and contributions to humanity of transgender and intersex people is an urgent matter as has been shown in this article.

Several theologians are dedicating their whole life and work for the sub/version of structures of dominance that police, punish and outcast transgender and intersex people, their body/ies and their experiences. Body fascism is one of the mechanisms to be dismantled in order to achieve liberation. By doing this, God's image and the doctrine of the incarnation will be also liberated from their heteropatriarchal prison.

The ultimate recognition of transgender and intersex people is when the divine incarnates their experiences and the faithful can express this in their belief. Here language has a great part in acknowledging/denying those experiences of gender and performances of sexuality. Is it possible for God to be *GodtoGoddess* or *GoddesstoGod*? How about a God that is in *transition* but never becoming one or the other? Can God be one with this people and remain a God for heterosexual people? If the doctrine of incarnation is accurate and implies not only relationality of the divine with the creation but also the embodiment of God into the creation, then God is the God of transgender and intersex people as well as gays, cross-dressers, bisexuals, heterosexual people and the like. A theology that denies this reality is in fact a pseudo-spiritualism that colonizes by functioning as what Marx called 'opium of the people'. In this case, the images of God and Christ that come from this colonial religion are idols that segregate people whether in churches or in societies. Despite the predominance of these heterocolonial visions, the fact remains that by confessing belief in the doctrine of incarnation, we abide by a cosmic process through which God embodies all the creation, including those who we want to segregate from God's love.

Throughout this article I have conveyed two messages. On the one hand, that the life and richness of experiences of transgender and intersex people is an important voice for Christian churches to hear, as well as the locus of God's embracing love beyond the power of institutionalized Christianity; on the other hand, a message to mainstream Christian churches that their interpretations of Christian doctrines are not definitive, that they are oppressive when universalized and when they are used to cast out people based on discriminatory criteria. In this way, I am not advocating for assimilation of transgender and intersex people into mainstream Christianity. Rather, I am advocating for the recognition of every human life as being important and valuable beyond narrow dictums from heteronormativity. Christian churches are responsible for playing their part in this in order not to collaborate with injustice and discrimination. Ultimately, God's will to interact with humanity and the whole creation is that, God's will, and neither Christian churches nor social orders could ever twist God's will. Therefore God also trans/forms herself/himself/Godself in order to reach the whole of creation. Related to this, a beautiful poem comes to mind, written by Onaldo Alves Pereira from Brazil entitled *God is Transgender*.[49] I reproduce this poem with the hope that transgender and intersex people, their body/ies and their experience can be reunited again with God when we contemplate the marvellous work of God's creation. By acknowledging this we also hope that liberation and justice will shine through the love of a God who calls for transgender and intersex people to be also one with the divine.

> God is transgender
> Brings on Godself the contraries,
> Dresses the brightness of the night
> Hides him/herself in sunlight
>
> In high heels
> Shakes with pleasure,
> Sparkling out lamé
> Everywhere s/he passes
> Don't you see the stars?
>
> Change the wig
> For another show
> From the green of the mounts
> Takes away the colours of autumn
> And then, all in white,
> Sleepy rests.

49 Onaldo Alves Pereira, 'Deus é Travesti' (Comunidad Asha, Goiânia, Brazil), http://brasil.indymedia.org/pt/red/2003/08/259943.shtml (accessed 7 July 2006), translation mine.

Raye

ITEM CHARGED

Waiting,
Until the corners
Are available again.

And transgender God closes and shakes.

References

Airaksinen, T. (1995), *The Philosophy of the Marquis de Sade*, London: Routledge.

Althaus-Reid, M. (2003), *The Queer God*, London: Routledge.

Althaus-Reid, M. and L. Isherwood, eds (2004), *The Sexual Theologian: Essays on Sex, God and Politics*, London: T & T Clark.

Alves Pereira, O., 'Deus é Travesti' (Comunidad Asha, Goiânia, Brazil); http://brasil.indymedia.org/pt/red/2003/08/259943.shtml (accessed 7 July 2006).

Anselm of Canterbury (1958), *Proslogium; Monologium; An Appendix in Behalf of the Fool by Gaunilon; and Cur Deus Homo*, trans. Sidney Norton Deane, La Salle, Ill.: Open Court.

Ash, J. and E. Wilson (1992), *Chic Thrills: A Fashion Reader*, London: Pandora.

Bakhtin, M. (1984), *Rabelais and His World*, trans. Helen Iswolsky, Bloomington: Indiana University Press.

Balasuriya, T. (1988), *The Eucharist and Human Liberation*, London: SPCK.

Balsamo, A. (1996), 'Forms of Technological Embodiment: Reading the Body in Contemporary Culture', in M. Featherstone and R. Burrows, eds, *Cyberspace, Cyberbodies, Cyberpunk: Cultures of Technological Embodiment*, London: Sage, pp. 215–37.

Barthes, R. ([1967] 1990), *The Fashion System*, trans M. Ward and R. Howard, Berkeley: University of California Press.

Barthes, R. (1977), *Sade, Fourier, Loyola*, trans. R. Miller, London: Jonathan Cape.

Beauvoir, S. de ([1949] 1972), *The Second Sex*, trans. H. M. Parshley, Harmondsworth: Penguin.

Benthien, C. ([1999] 2002), *Skin: On the Cultural Border between Self and the World*, New York: Columbia University Press, chs 3–6.

Berkins, L. (2004), 'Eternamente Atrapadas por el Sexo', in J. Fernández, M. D'Uva and P. Viturro, eds, *Cuerpos Ineludibles: Un Dialogo a Partir de las Sexualidades en América Latina*, Buenos Aires: Ediciones Ají de Pollo, pp. 19–24.

'Body Fascism: Another Form of Discrimination?', *Sportsteacher*, 25 February 2005; http://www.sportsteacher.co.uk/news/editorial/01autF_bodyfascism.html (accessed 4 May 2006).

'Body Modification', in *Wikipedia: The Free Encyclopedia*; http://en.wikipedia.org/wiki/Body_modification (accessed 4 May 2006).

Boenke, M., ed. (2003), *Trans Forming Families: Real Stories About Transgendered Loved Ones*, 2nd edn, Hardy, Va.: Oak Knoll Press.

Bolin, A. (1992), 'Vandalized Vanity: Feminine Physiques Betrayed and Portrayed', in F. Mascia-Lees and P. Sharpe, eds, *Tattoo, Torture, Adornment and Disfigurement: The Denaturalization of the Body in Culture and Text*, Albany: SUNY Press, pp. 79–99.

Bordo, S. (1993), *Unbearable Weight: Feminism, Western Culture, and the Body*, Berkeley: University of California Press, 1993.

Bronfen, E. (1992), *Death, Femininity and the Aesthetic*, Manchester: Manchester University Press.

Brookes, R. (1992), 'Fashion Photography: The Double-Page Spread: Helmut Newton, Guy Bourdin and Deborah Turbeville', in J. Ash and E. Wilson, eds (1992), *Chic Thrills: A Fashion Reader*, London: Pandora, pp. 17–24.

Brown, P. (1988), *The Body and Society: Men, Women and Sexual Renunciation in Early Christianity*, New York: Columbia University Press.

Bulgakov, S. (1993), *Sophia, the Wisdom of God: An Outline of Sophiology*, Hudson, NY: Lindisfarne Press.

Buss, D. and D. Herman (2003), *Globalizing Family Values: The Christian Right in International Politics*, Minneapolis: University of Minnesota Press.

Butler, J. (1990), *Gender Trouble: Feminism and the Subversion of Identity*, London and New York: Routledge.

Butler, J. (1993), *Bodies that Matter: On the Discursive Limits of 'Sex'*, London: Routledge.

Cameron, D. and E. Frazer (1987), *The Lust to Kill*, New York: New York University Press.

Caputi, J. (1992), 'On Psychic Activism: Feminist Mythmaking', in C. Larrington, ed., *The Feminist Companion to Mythology*, London: Pandora Press, pp. 425–40.

Caputi, J. (1993), *Gossips, Gorgons and Crones: The Fates of the Earth*, Santa Fe, New Mexico: Bear & Company.

Carter, A. (1979), *The Sadeian Woman*, London: Virago.

Chasseguet-Smirgel, J. (1985), *Creativity and Perversion*, London: Free Association Books.

Chernin, K. (1983), *Womansize: The Tyranny of Slenderness*, London: The Woman's Press.

Chillier, G. (1998), 'La sanción de un código de convivencia urbana: Causas y efectos de la eliminación de las detenciones arbitrarias por parte de la Policía Federal', lecture presented at the seminar *The Police Reforms in Argentina*, Buenos Aires: Centro de Estudios Legales y Sociales (CELS), 1–2 December.

Christ, C. ([1972] 1992), 'Why Women Need the Goddess: Phenomeno-logical, Psychological and Political Reflections', in C. Christ and J. Plaskow, eds, *Womanspirit Rising: A Feminist Reader in Religion*, San Francisco: HarperCollins, pp. 273–87.

Christ, C. (1997), *Rebirth of the Goddess: Finding Meaning in Feminist Spirituality*, New York: Addison Wesley.

Clack. B. (2001) 'Sade: Forgiveness and Truth in a Desacralised Universe', *Literature and Theology* 15.3, pp. 262–75.

Clack, B. (2002), *Sex and Death: A Reappraisal of Human Mortality*, Cambridge: Polity.

Colebrook, C., (2003), *Gender*, Basingstoke: Palgrave Macmillan.

Coles, F. (1994), 'Feminine Charms and Outrageous Arms', *Trouble & Strife* 29/30.

Craik, J. (1994), *The Face of Fashion*, London: Routledge.

Cross, F. L., ed. (1957), *The Oxford Dictionary of the Christian Church*, London: Oxford University Press.

Daly, M. (1984), *Pure Lust: Elemental Feminist Philosophy*, London: The Women's Press.

Daly, M. (1991), *Gyn/Ecology: The Metaethics of Radical Feminism*, London: The Women's Press.

Daly, M. (1993), *Outercourse: The Be-Dazzling Voyage*, London: The Women's Press.

Davis, K. (1995), *Reshaping the Female Body: The Dilemma of Cosmetic Surgery*, London: Methuen.

De la Haye, A. (1997), *The Cutting Edge: Fifty Years of British Fashion 1947–1997*, London: V&A.

Di Berardino, A., ed. (1998), *Diccionario Patrístico y de la Antigüedad Tardía*, Salamanca: Sígueme.

Douglas, M. (2002), *Purity and Danger: An Analysis of Concepts of Pollution and Taboo*, London: Routledge.

Dworkin, A. (1981), *Pornography: Men Possessing Women*, London: Women's Press.

Ebersole, L. and R. Peabody, eds, *Mondo Barbie: An Anthology of Fiction and Poetry*, New York: St Martin's Press.

Ensler, E. (2004), *The Good Body*, London: William Heinemann.

Epstein, J. and K. Straub, eds, (1991), *Body Guards: The Cultural Politics of Gender Ambiguity*, London: Routledge.

Erikson, E. (1968), *Identity: Youth in Crisis*, London: Faber & Faber.

Falk, P. (1994), *The Consuming Body*, London: Sage.

Feinberg, L. (1998), *Trans Liberation: Beyond Pink or Blue*, Boston: Beacon Press.

Fernández, J., M. D'Uva and P. Viturro, eds, (2004), *Cuerpos Ineludibles: Un Dialogo a Partir de las Sexualidades en América Latina*, Buenos Aires: Ediciones Ají de Pollo.

Fiedler, L. (1978), *Freaks: Myths and Images of the Secret Self*, New York: Simon & Schuster.

Foucault, M. (1982), *Discipline and Punish: The Birth of the Prison*, trans. A. Sheridan, London: Penguin.

Foucault, M. (1984), 'Nietzsche, Genealogy, History', in P. Rabinow, ed., *The Foucault Reader*, London: Penguin, pp. 76-100.

'Frequently Asked Questions: What is Intersex?' *Intersex Society of North America*; http://www.isna.org/faq/what_is_intersex (accessed 4 May 2006).

Freud, S. (1905), 'Three Essays on Sexuality', in *Standard Edition of the Works of Sigmund Freud* (hereafter, *SE*), vol. 7, trans. J. Strachey, London: Vintage, pp. 125-245.

Freud, S. (1911), 'Formulations on the Two Principles of Mental Functioning', *SE* 12, trans. J. Strachey, London: Vintage, pp. 213-38.

Freud, S. (1919), 'The "Uncanny"', *SE* 17, trans. J. Strachey, London: Vintage, pp. 218-56.

Freud, S. (1937), 'Analysis Terminable and Interminable', *SE* 23, pp. 216-53.

Gallop, J. (1982), *Feminism and Psychoanalysis*, Basingstoke: Macmillan.

Gallop, J. (1995), 'Sade, Mother and Other Women', in D. B. Allison, M. S. Roberts and A. S. Weiss, eds, *Sade and the Narrative of Transgression*, Cambridge: Cambridge University Press, pp. 122-41.

Gear, N. (1963), *The Divine Demon: A Portrait of the Marquis de Sade*, London: Frederick Muller.

Gerhardt, S. (2004), *Why Love Matters: How Affection Shapes a Baby's Brain*, London: Routledge.

Gilroy, S. (1989), 'The EmBodyment of Power: Gender and Physical Activity', *Leisure Studies* 8, pp. 163–71.

Glasser, M. (1979), 'Some Aspects of the Role of Aggression in the Perversions', in I. Rosen, ed. *Sexual Deviations*, Oxford: Oxford University Press, pp. 278–305.

Golding, S., ed. (1997), *The Eight Technologies of Otherness*, London: Routledge.

Gregory of Nazianzus (1862), *Epistle 101*, Migne, PG 37, pp. 181–4.

Greve, B. (2006), 'Transformation', sermon preached at the chapel of Starr King School for the Ministry (SKSM), The Graduate Theological Union (GTU), Berkeley, Calif., 2 May.

Greve, B. (2006), *Courage from Necessity*, sermon preached at Church for the Fellowship of All People, Unitarian Universalist Church, San Francisco, Calif., 3 June.

Griffiths, M. (2004), *Born Again Bodies: Flesh and Spirit in American Christianity*, Berkeley, Calif., University of California Press.

Grosz, E. (1994), *Volatile Bodies: Toward a Corporeal Feminism*, Bloomington, Ind.: Indiana University Press.

Hansen, G. (1997), 'La concepción trinitaria de Dios en los orígenes de la teología de la liberación: el aporte de Juan Luis Segundo', *Cuadernos de Teología* 16.1–2, pp. 43–67.

Heywood, L. (1998), *Bodymakers: A Cultural Anatomy of Women's Bodybuilding*, New Brunswick, NJ: Rutgers University Press.

Hollander, A. (1993), 'Accounting for Fashion', *Raritan* 13.2, pp. 121–32.

Holy Bible. New Revised Standard Version, Oxford: Oxford University Press, 1977.

Hume, D. ([1779] 1947), *Dialogues Concerning Natural Religion*, Indianapolis: Bobbs-Merrill.

Hurley, K. (1996), *The Gothic Body: Sexuality, Materialism and Degeneration at the Fin de Siècle*, Cambridge: Cambridge University Press.

Irenaeus of Lyon, (1996), *Adversus Haereses* 5.27.9, in *Ante-Nicene Fathers*, vol. 1, ed. A. Roberts and J. Donaldson, Grand Rapids: Eerdmans.

Isherwood, L. (2006), *The Power of Erotic Celibacy*, London: T & T Clark.

Isherwood, L. (2008), *The Fat Jesus*, London: Darton, Longman & Todd.

Isherwood, L. and E. Stuart, eds (1998), *Introducing Body Theology*, Sheffield: Sheffield Academic Press.

Jantzen, G. (1998), *Becoming Divine: Towards a Feminist Philosophy of Religion*, Manchester: Manchester University Press.

Johnson, E. (2000), *She Who Is: The Mystery of God in Feminist Theological Discourse*, New York: Crossroad.

Jung, S. (2004), *Food for Life: The Spirituality and Ethics of Eating*, Minneapolis, Fortress Press.

King, P. and R. Steiner, eds (1990), *The Freud–Klein Controversies 1941–45*, London: Routledge.

Klein, M. ([1921] 1975), 'The Development of a Child', in *The Writings of Melanie Klein*, vol. 1: *Love, Guilt and Reparation*, London: Hogarth Press, pp. 4–13.

Klein, M. (1926), 'Infant Analysis', *International Journal of Psycho-Analysis* 7, pp. 31–63.

Klein, M. ([1932] 1997), *The Psycho-Analysis of Children*, London: Vintage.

Klein, M. ([1935] 1975), 'A Contribution to the Psychogenesis of Manic-Depressive States', in *The Writings of Melanie Klein*, vol. 1: *Love, Guilt and Reparation*, London: Hogarth Press, pp. 236–89.

Klein, M. ([1936] 1975), 'Weaning', in *The Writings of Melanie Klein*, vol. 1: *Love, Guilt and Reparation*, London: Hogarth Press, pp. 290–305.

Klein, M. (1946), 'Notes on Some Schizoid Mechanisms', in *The Writings of Melanie Klein*, vol. 3: *Envy and Gratitude and Other Works*, London: Hogarth Press, pp. 292–320.

Kristeva, J. ([1977] 2002), 'Stabat Mater', in M. Joy, K. O'Grady and J. L. Poxon, eds, *French Feminists on Religion: A Reader*, London: Routledge, pp. 112–38.

Kristeva, J. (2001), *Melanie Klein*, trans. R. Guberman, New York: Columbia University Press.

Lacan, J. (1977), *Ecrits*, trans. A. Sheridan, New York: Norton.

Lacan, J. and the École Freudienne (1982), *Feminine Sexuality*, ed. J. Mitchell and J. Rose, trans. J. Rose, London: Macmillan.

LaCugna, C. M. (1991), *God for Us: The Trinity and Christian Life*, San Francisco: Harper San Francisco.

Laplanche, J. and J. B. Pontalis ([1964] 2003), 'Fantasy and the Origins of Sexuality', in R. Steiner, ed., *Unconscious Phantasy*, London: Karnac Books, pp. 107–43.

LeBesco, K. (2004), *Revolting Bodies? The Struggle to Redefine Fat Identity*,

Boston, Mass.: University of Massachusetts Press.

Lenskyj, H. (1986), *Out of Bounds: Women, Sport and Sexuality*, Toronto: Women's Press.

Lowe, M. R. (1998), *Women of Steel: Female Bodybuilders and the Struggle for Self-Definition*, New York: New York University Press.

Ma Vie en Rose (1997), dir. Alain Berliner, DVD, Sony Pictures.

Ma Vie en Rose (official web page), http://www.sonyclassics.com/mavieenrose (accessed 5 May 2006).

Maffesoli, M. (1996), *The Time of the Tribes: The Decline of Individualism in Mass Society*, London: Sage.

McNay, L. (1991), 'The Foucauldian Body and the Exclusion of Experience', *Hypatia* 6.3, pp. 126–39.

Meerson, M. A., (1998), *The Trinity of Love in Modern Russian Theology: The Love Paradigm and the Retrieval of Western Medieval Love Mysticism in Modern Russian Trinitarian Thought from Solovyov to Bulgakov*, Quincy, Ill.: Franciscan Press.

Merleau-Ponty, M. (1964), *The Primacy of Perception*, ed. J. M. Edie, Evanston, Ill.: Northwestern University Press.

Meyendorff, J. (1975), *Christ in Eastern Christian Thought*, New York: St Vladimir's Seminary Press.

Milton, J., C. Polmear and J. Fabricius (2004), *A Short Introduction to Psychoanalysis*, London: Sage.

'Misa en Palermo contra la oferta de sexo en la calle', *Clarín*, 29 June 1998; http://www.clarin.com/diario/1998/06/29/e-03801d.htm (accessed 15 August 2006).

Mitchell, J. (2003), *Siblings*, Cambridge: Polity Press.

Mollenkott, V. R. (2001), *Omnigender: A Trans-Religious Approach*, Cleveland, Ohio: Pilgrim Press.

Moltmann, J. (1992), *The Spirit of Life: A Universal Affirmation*, Minneapolis: Fortress Press.

Moore, S. (1996), *God's Gym*, London and New York: Routledge.

Moore, T. (1990), *Dark Eros: The Imagination of Sadism*, Dallas, Tex.: Spring.

Nelson, W. M., ed. (1989), *Diccionario de Historia de la Iglesia*, Miami: Caribe.

Orbach, S. (1993), *Hunger Strike*, Penguin.

Origen (1965), *Contra Celsum*, trans. H. E. Chadwick, Cambridge: Cambridge University Press.

Origen (1968), *Commento al Vangelo di Giovanini: A cura di Eugenio Corsini*, Turin: Unione Tipografico-Editrice Torinese.

Paglia, C. (1991), *Sexual Personae*, Harmondsworth: Penguin.

Peterson, S. (1996), 'Freaking Feminism: *The Life and Loves of a She-Devil* and *Nights at the Circus* as Narrative Freak Shows', in R. G. Thomson, ed., *Freakery: Cultural Spectacles of the Extraordinary Body*, New York: New York University Press.

Phillips, J. and L. Stonebridge (1998), *Reading Melanie Klein*, London: Routledge.

Poovey, M. (1995), *Making a Social Body*, Chicago: University of Chicago Press.

Rahner, K. (1970), *The Trinity*, London: Burns & Oates.

Rakestraw, R. V. (1997), 'Becoming Like God: An Evangelical Doctrine of Theosis', *Journal of the Evangelical Theological Society* 40.2, pp. 257–69.

Raphael, M. (1996), *Thealogy and Embodiment: The Post-Patriarchal Reconstruction of Female Sacrality*, Sheffield: Sheffield Academic Press.

Raphael, M. (2000), *Introducing Thealogy: Discourse on the Goddess*, Cleveland, Ohio: Pilgrim Press.

Reid-Bowen, P. (2007), *Goddess as Nature: Towards a Philosophical Thealogy*, Aldershot: Ashgate.

Rich, A. (1977), *Of Woman Born*, London: Virago.

Ruether, R. R. (1983), *Sexism and God-Talk: Toward a Feminist Theology*, Boston: Beacon Press.

Russo, M. (1994), *The Female Grotesque: Risk, Excess, and Modernity*, London: Routledge.

Scarry, E. (1985), *The Body in Pain*, Oxford: Oxford University Press.

Schussler-Fiorenza, E. (1999), *Jesus: Miriam's Child, Sophia's Prophet: Critical Issues in Feminist Christology*, New York: Continuum.

Schussler-Fiorenza, E. (2000), *In Memory of Her: A Feminist Theological Reconstruction of Christian Origins*, New York: Crossroad.

Scott, J. M. (2003), 'A Question of Identity: Is Cephas the Same Person as Peter?' *Journal of Biblical Studies* 3.3, pp. 1–20.

Seid, R. (1994), 'Too Close to the Bone: The Historical Context For Women's Obsession with Slenderness', in P. Fallon, M. Katzman and S. Wooley, eds, *Feminist Perspectives on Eating Disorders*, New York: Guilford Press, pp. 3–16.

Shapiro, J. (1991), 'Transsexualism: Reflections on the Persistence of Gender and the Mutability of Sex', in J. Epstein and K. Straub, eds, *Body Guards: The Cultural Politics of Gender Ambiguity*, London: Routledge, pp. 248–79.

Showalter, E. (1990), *Sexual Anarchy: Gender and Culture at the Fin de Siècle*, London: Viking.

Shute, J. (1992), *Life-Size*, London: Minerva.

Silver, A. K. (2002), *Victorian Literature and the Anorexic Body*, Cambridge: Cambridge University Press.

Slesinski, R. (1984), *Pavel Florensky: A Metaphysics of Love*, New York: St Vladimir's Seminary Press.

Stewart, S. (1993), *On Longing: Narratives of the Miniature, the Gigantic, the Souvenir, the Collection*, Durham, NC: Duke University Press.

Tannen, D. (1994), *Gender and Discourse*, Oxford: Oxford University Press.

Tanner, L. (1994), *Intimate Violence: Reading Rape and Torture in Twentieth-Century Fiction*, Bloomington: Indiana University Press.

Thomson, R. G., ed. (1996), *Freakery: Cultural Spectacles of the Extra-ordinary Body*, New York: New York University Press.

Truth, Sojourner (1997), 'Ain't I a Woman?', in K. Conboy, N. Medina and S. Stanbury, eds, *Writing on the Body: Female Embodiment and Feminist Theory*, New York: Columbia University Press, pp. 231-2.

Ward, G. (2004), 'On the Politics of Embodiment and the Mystery of All Flesh', in M. Althaus-Reid and L. Isherwood, eds, *The Sexual Theologian: Essays on Sex, God and Politics*, London: T & T Clark, pp. 71–85.

Warner, M. (1994), *From the Beast to the Blonde: On Fairy Tales and their Tellers*, London: Chatto & Windus.

Weldon, F. (1983), *The Life and Loves of a She Devil*, London: Sceptre.

Welsh, L. (2002), *The Cutting Room*, Edinburgh: Canongate.

West, V. [Beth Westbrook] (2003), 'Secret Identity', in Mary Boenke, ed., *Trans Forming Families: Real Stories About Transgendered Loved Ones*, 2nd edn, Hardy, Va.: Oak Knoll Press, p. 20.

Wigley, M. (1992), 'Untitled: The Housing of Gender', in B. Colomina, ed., *Sexuality and Space*, New York: Princeton Architectural Press, pp. 327–89.

Wolf, N. (1991), *The Beauty Myth*, London: Vintage.

Wolf, N. (1994), 'Hunger', in P. Fallon, M. Katzman and S. Wooley, eds, *Feminist Perspectives on Eating Disorders*, New York: Guilford Press, pp. 94–111.

Wood, C. (1981), *The Pre-Raphaelites*, London: Weidenfeld & Nicolson.

Yarborough, M. *'Ma Vie en Rose*: Transgender, the Child and the Family', http://village.fortunecity.com/carnival/383/ludovic.htm (accessed 5 May 2006).

Zhang, S. 'Gender Rights are Human Rights', report on the *Discussion Panel on Trangender/Intersex Issues* at the 65th Session of the Commission on Human Rights of the United Nations (13 April 2005), http://www.ngochr.org/view/index.php?basic_entity'DOCUMENT&list_ids'545 (accessed 18 August 2006).

6

Uses and Abuses of Power in the Shoah and the Silent Genocide of Abused Women[1]

VICTORIA ROLLINS

And a sword will pierce your heart.[2]

Crimes of male violences against women as abuses of power are based beyond biology, hormones, or conditioning as a choice of behaviour or action, using power over women through abuse as violence, both individually and systemically. Hearn states that violence, from abusive men interviewed, is perceived with ambivalence, as 'understood as a major, maybe the prime form of power', yet simultaneously viewed as 'inappropriate, unfair, and at times illegal'. Terms of 'violence against women' and 'domestic violence' cover a myriad of crimes as international human rights violations done to women by men who perceive their wives and partners as different from, meaning inferior, 'the other',[3] an otherness as being diminished, deficient and unworthy of human value. Individual women, devalued, controlled, dominated and abused face further

---

1 This article, with similar and new text, originates out of a published thesis, 'Violence Against Women and the Role of the Church', Exeter University, 2005.

2 Luke 2.35.

3 Jeff Hearn, *The Violences of Men: How Men Talk About and How Agencies Respond to Men's Violence to Women* (London: Sage, 2000); Elizabeth Johnson, *She Who Is: The Mystery of God in Feminist Theological Discourse* (New York: Crossroad, 2001), pp. 24–5.

oppression from institutions such as the Church[4] and other agencies within societal hierarchies competing for their own dominating power and control.

The epidemic of violence against women and the battering of wives is as significant to our cultures as and within the civil rights movements beyond personal issues of domestic terror, reaching wide dimensions of human rights violations destroying the marital vows[5] and ultimately the marriage, the family and, most often, the woman's life itself. Atrocities committed against women, of beatings and sexual assaults, injuries and murders committed within relationships dominated and destroyed by men doing male violences, are found within the supposed sanctity of marriage against wives, as well as witch-hunts, rape camps, practices of genital mutilation, pornographic practices, stonings, gang rapes, suti, foot-binding, 'honour' killings, and female infanticide. As battered women trapped in unresponsive communities, expressed in pen and ink by those interned in the Polish community found beside the imploring Hebrew prayer, 'Hear, Oh Israel, Hear our cry!':

'No God in Lodz.'[6]

Suffering from evil: the power of male violences

I am arguing that violence against women worldwide is an abuse, an enormous sin and misuse of power, comprising a genocide of crimes in

---

4 Discussion of 'Church' referencing denominational tenants is beyond the scope of this present writing, but 'Church' is intended by this author as representing both the collective embodiment of Christian churches on an ecumenical level and the embodiment of those individuals professing to hold and practice of those Christians gathered in both corporate formal and informal dimensions within the wider community.

5 Mitzi N. Eilts, 'Saving the Family: When is a Covenant Broken?', in Carol J. Adams, and Marie M. Fortune, eds, *Violence Against Women and Children: A Christian Theological Sourcebook* (New York: Continuum, 1996), p. 448.

6 Josef Kownjer, untitled sheet, pen and ink, Poland, catalogue 82, in Glenn Sujo, *Legacies of Silence: The Visual Arts and Holocaust Memory*, Imperial War Museum Exhibition (London: Philip Wilson, 2001), pp. 64, 118.

its own right within and beyond research within past and present genocidal histories, as an integral, real and pervasive occurrence of such horrific events against women, who exist in many ways as ignored, unrecognized and silenced prisoners of 'regular' and daily war throughout most societies in history. Women from church and cultural histories[7] existing in still acculturated male entitlement and domination, seen as parasites, appendages, or objects to men[8] through the sin of sexism and the sinful interpretation of wives as subhuman imperfections, are still subjugated to a husband's male authority, control, humiliations, and male violences – abused women leading endangered lives with similar consequences to Shoah victims, hostages, and prisoners of war.

I urge the Church to require governments to condemn the everyday genocide of women, yet, as in the Shoah, why does the Church most often fail to speak out against these crimes against women forming its own genocide, fail to hold men accountable for choosing to do violences against women and still fail to speak up for empowerment and provision for battered women? Calling for leadership and naming the 'extent of the violence against women even in Christian communities' as shocking, the leader of the World Council of Churches Raiser identified the most important issue of the decade of the 1990s as 'violence against women in church and society':

> this situation constitutes a fundamental ethical and social challenge that could well be compared to the challenge of racism and its impact on the ecumenical movement of the 1970's.[9]

---

7 '. . . women . . . converted to Christianity, they have been forced to realize through baptism they had jumped from the culturally traditional "frying pan" into the Christian "fire" . . . in the vast majority of cases, they did not experience any improvement in their role as a woman, retaining their servile function'. Anne Suchalla, 'Like a Rolling Stone', in *It's Time to Talk About It: Violence against Women in Culture, Society and the Church* (Wuppertal: United Evangelical Mission, 2001), p. 9.

8 Pamela Cooper-White, *The Cry of Tamar: The Church's Response to Violence Against Women* (Minneapolis: Fortress Press, 1986), p. 262.

9 Konrad Raiser, WCC General Secretary, cited by Aruna Gnanadason, *No Longer a Secret: The Church and Violence against Women*, Risk Book Series (Geneva: World Council of Churches, 1997), p. 81.

This article draws attention to the diverse and damaging particularities of battered women's oppressions done by men through violence, domination and control within myriad forms of abuses paralleling but not in competitive ranking with the enormity of the evil known as the Shoah.[10] As in the Shoah, the abuse of women worldwide, comprising a genocide in its own right, encompasses varied and particular nuances within countries as 'holocaust', yet simultaneously holding similarities of imprisonment, humiliation, torture, punishment, injury, displacement, and killings all melded into one inadequate and neutralizing, sanitizing term absenting moral agency as 'domestic violence'. The rooting of the Shoah in dominant, patriarchal values of unequal power through acculturated prevailing norms and control as viewed by Raphael[11] bears remarkable similarity to the harsh realities identified by feminist research and feminist liberation theologies recognizing the hierarchical organization of the Church, whose leadership (despite its reference as the 'Bride of Christ' and as 'she')[12] has established male control of language, space and function as church life in patriarchal thought and social organization of domination[13] permeating and infused with culture, whereby:

men are distinguished from women by their commitment to do violence rather than be victimized by it.[14]

---

10 The term Shoah, as distinguished from holocaust, including for example the people of black history, Cambodia, East Timor, Native Americans, is used here with specific reference to what is most known as the Holocaust or persecution of the Jews, with six million men, women and children killed, as well as vast numbers of gypsies, political dissidents, the handicapped, Jehovah's Witnesses, during the reign of Nazi Germany.

11 Melissa Raphael, *The Female Face of God in Auschwitz: A Jewish Feminist Theology of the Holocaust* (London: Routledge, 2003), p. 110.

12 Ephesians 5.23–32; 2 Corinthians 11.2.

13 Lynn N. Rhodes and Kathleen M. Black, 'Church History', in Letty M. Russell and J. Shannon Clarkson, eds, *Dictionary of Feminist Theologies* (London: Mowbray, 1996), p. 46.

14 Andrea Dworkin, *Pornography* (New York: Perigree, 1981), p. 53, cited by Andy Smith, 'The Crucified Ones: Pornography of the Cross', in Carol J. Adams and Marie M. Fortune, eds, *Violence Against Women and Children: A Christian Theological Sourcebook* (New York: Continuum, 1996), p. 384.

As in the inscribed voices of Holocaust victims and expressed Holocaust survivors where memory important to a people's redemption and freedom as in the historic Exodus must not be just recollection but 'reactualization',[15] the voices of international genocide refugees as battered wives and all abused women spoken for still today speak out of our own abused bodies, hearts, minds and souls of pain, violations, sufferings, betrayals, losses, hope – for some, survival, and for some, finding our groundings of empowerment in the divine incarnation of our relational lives.[16] Still we lament the incalculable destruction of lives, talents and compassions sacrificed in inestimable numbers of women annihilated throughout the centuries in diminished, devalued, choiceless and terrifying existences,[17] who received neither safety, validation, nor flourishing unto death.

Connected with the theological human/divine split, similar patriarchal, prevailing, enculturated binaries of male/female, public/private, good/bad allow for stereotyping and power abuses of domination and control within people, groups and individuals sanctioned by church teaching the submission of women within marriage particularly[18] – and coupled with women absented from histories including the Shoah keep the door wide open for violence against women in patriarchal paradise on earth. A man is safest in his home, while a woman is least safe there, especially if she is married,[19] the use and abuses of power as acceptable men's

---

15 Yosef H. Yerushalmi, *Zohar, Jewish History and Jewish Memory* (Seattle and London: University of Washington Press, 1982), p. 44, n. 28, cited in Sujo, *Legacies of Silence*, p. 27 (p. 114, n. 27).

16 Carter Heyward, 'Empowerment', in Lisa Isherwood and Dorothea McEwan, eds, *An A to Z of Feminist Theology* (Sheffield: Sheffield Academic Press, 1996), p. 52.

17 Mary F. Belensky, Blythe M. Clinchy, Nancy R. Goldberger and Jill M. Tarule, *Women's Ways of Knowing* (New York: Basic Books, 1986), referenced by Mary Grey, *Redeeming the Dream: Feminism, Redemption and the Christian Tradition* (London: SPCK, 1999), p. 158 (p. 202, n. 10).

18 Grace M. Jantzen, *Power, Gender, and Mysticism* (Cambridge: Cambridge University Press, 1995, 2000), pp. 1, 22–3.

19 Jeff Hearn, *The Violences of Men: How Men Talk About and How Agencies Respond to Men's Violence to Women* (London: Sage, 2000), p. 4.

violences permeating our cultures in hierarchical dualisms of glorified dominant/submissive, male/female practices undergirding oppressions of women as partners and wives destroy ironically for both men and women our desires, capacities for compassion, and our need for intimacy and love.

As in the Shoah, components of violence against women beyond domination and control include being 'targets of repeated aggression and forced internment',[20] impoverishment and dehumanization;[21] characteristics festering in the disgrace and humiliation of the culture within the Weimar Republic post-First World War[22] as in today's 'shame-based' cultures.[23] Nelson names social violence as 'a sexually transmitted disease' rooted in masculine identities.[24] Hearn's research identifying male fear of sexual inadequacies and aggression linked with sanctioned male power through violence to control and dominate[25] joins church teaching blaming women (as Eve) as were the Jews for killing Jesus,[26] with lethal outcomes for women as for Jews. Experiences of women's powerlessness in the home and workplace today from being silenced, disrespected,

20 Glenn Sujo, 'Ghetto', in Sujo, *Legacies of Silence*, p. 64; Lee Ann Hoff, *Battered Women as Survivors* (London: Routledge, 1990), pp. 42, 44, 198.

21 Elisabeth Schussler Fiorenza, 'Ties That Bind: Domestic Violence Against Women', in Mary J. Mananzan *et al.*, eds, *Women Resisting Violence: Spirituality for Life* (Maryknoll: Orbis, 1996), pp. 42-3.

22 Frank H. Littel, 'The German Churches in the Third Reich', in Carol Rittner, Stephen Smith and Irena Steinfeldt, eds, *The Holocaust and the Christian World* (New York: Continuum, 2000), p. 44.

23 Robert Albers, *Shame: A Faith Perspective* (Binghamton: Haworth, 1995), p. 139 (p. 172, nn. 14-15) cited by Nancy Nason-Clark, *The Battered Wife: How Christian Churches Confront Family Violence* (Louisville: Westminster John Knox Press, 1996), pp. 52-3.

24 James Nelson, 'Male Sexuality and the Fragile Planet', in Stephen B. Boyd, W. Merle Longwood and Mark W. Muesse, eds, *Redeeming Men: Religion and Masculinities* (Louisville: Westminster John Knox Press, 1996), p. 274.

25 Hearn, *The Violences of Men*, pp. 15, 37.

26 Margaret Shepherd, 'Journey to Poland: Remembrance and Reconciliation: A Personal Reflection', in Rittner, Smith and Steinfeldt, *The Holocaust and the Christian World*, p. 197; and Iiii Tertullian, referencing Genesis 3.16, cited by Karen Armstrong, *The End of Silence: Women and Priesthood* (London: Fourth Estate, 1993), pp. 54-5.

patronized, infantilized, and made invisible while enduring the crimes of male violences bear resemblance to those expressed by genocide survivors experiencing control, domination, intimidation, humiliation and assaults by those in power within refugee and war-torn conditions of camps, ghettos and internments[27] across ethnic, racial, religious and national lines.

The evil of the concentration camp locates in the behaviours and actions, emphasized as chosen, as ordinariness of the majority of its initiators and implementers and the enjoyment of power beyond explanations of defined abnormality, fanaticism, sadism or even standard explanations of the instinctive 'evil within', 'shadow', or reversion to a 'natural' bestial state.[28] Todorov rather in lamenting the actions of the guards and leaders like Hoss names the use of their power over victims – confusing power as 'good, or as the one holding it'[29] – as for battered wives and all victims of physical and sexual assault powerless to our assailants' control. Suppressing compassion in seeing 'softness as weakness',[30] Hoss's strength meant 'hard, pitiless', who, not satisfied with just leaving them, murdered the women inmates chosen and no doubt forced to be his mistress in Auschwitz when finished with them.[31] These Nazi patriarchal masculine norms and behaviours remain valorized today as:

doing violence, . . . more importantly, enjoying dominance, establish a man's credentials as a masculine male.[32]

---

27 Aids F. Santos, *Violence Against Women in Times of War and Peace*, Gender, Reproductive Health, and Development Monograph (Quezon City: University of Philippines Centre for Women's Studies, and Ford Foundation, 2001), pp. 2–3.

28 Tzvetan Todorov, *Facing the Extreme: Moral Life in the Concentration Camps*, trans. Arthur Denner and Abigail Pollack (London: Orion, 1996), pp. 121, 126, 140.

29 Todorov, *Facing the Extreme*, p. 169.

30 Rudolph Hoss, *Le commandant d'Auschwitz parle* (Paris: Maspero, 1979), cited by Todorov, *Facing the Extreme*, pp. 171–2.

31 Hoss, cited by Todorov, *Facing the Extreme*, p. 172.

32 Marvin M. Ellison, *Erotic Justice: A Liberating Ethic of Sexuality* (Louisville: Westminster John Knox Press, 1996), p. 103.

Linked with Raphael, Chicago's research indeed identifies the prevalence of men seeking power over each other, women and children, animals and the earth as values of worth in patriarchal order which built the grounds for the holocaust.[33] Still today bringing 'real advantages to many people',[34] the promoted and sanctioned patriarchal use of force by men choosing to do male violences carries stated or unstated but assumed norms of control, making power through violence today definitive to conforming masculinity, escalating from the individual battered wife and rape victim to a sustained genocide against women. These acculturated norms are based upon a man's perceived entitlement to possessiveness and jealousy, expectations of women doing 'women's work', men's sense of 'right' to punish their women and:

> the importance of maintaining or exercising their position of authority.[35]

Silencing, silence and the male creation of death by murder

We are still waiting for such leadership from the Church in 2007. Failing to mention that many women encounter racism as well as sexism and abusive male partners, it is still shocking for those of us on the receiving end of such male violences coming out of the shock of trauma from abusive men, especially husbands and significant, 'intimate' partners, to accept that, despite daily newspaper reports and an important, everyday steady stream of reporting violence against women, people are still 'shocked'. Required as post-Holocaust theologies is a paradigm shift acknowledging the significance and meaning of the evil of these crimes – repeat, this requires a paradigm shift acknowledging the significance and

---

33 Judy Chicago, *Holocaust Project*, p. 10, cited by Raphael, *The Female Face of God in Auschwitz*, p. 40 (p. 176, n. 91).

34 James Gilligan, *Preventing Violence* (London: Thames & Hudson, 2001), p. 25.

35 R. Emerson Dobash and Russell P. Dobash, *Violence Against Wives* (London: Free Press, 1979), pp. 98–106.

the enormity of the evil of these crimes of male violences upon women, informing a new world vision in theological, Christian practice. Such new and re-visioned reference accepting zero tolerance for male violences formed as a lens of expression and interpretation from the experiential oppressions of abused women could and should create liberating space for empowerment, non-violence and societal transformation of humanity – male and female.

This enables embodied, transformative theologies representing hope and resurrected, new life as well as experiential, embodied lives of mourning, outrage, vulnerability and risk still left on the cross. Drawings and paintings left as legacies and testimonies of Nazi brutalities testifying to the copious amounts of suffering and near-death states in those being murdered by the Shoah,[36] as well as those enduring, stand shoulder to shoulder with the experiential brutalities depicted by women's suffering, hope and strength who have survived abuses from men doing violences found in the shirts inscribed and designed by families and friends of those women murdered by the men that supposedly 'loved' them the most in *The Clothesline Project, Manchester Mosaic*,[37] and the *Christas*[38] of recent times. Speaking to the unspeakable horrors but also of the relationship between captive and captor, hard work, the need for spiritual as well as physical nourishment, trust given and trust betrayed, the endurance of pain, the holding together of sanity, and loss,[39] they speak also of the primacy of life and both the fragility and the strength of the human spirit. Women depicted in Holocaust paintings hold in day-to-day tension the uncertainty of survival with grief and anger from violence.

---

36 Glenn Sujo, 'Legacies of Silence', in *Legacies of Silence*, p. 74.

37 *The Clothesline Project*, visual display of T-shirts designed by survivors of violence against women, Baptist Church chapter, Manchester, England, and chapters in the USA; *The Manchester Mosaic*, embroidered patchwork panels made by women suffering from being abused by men, first displayed at an ecumenical service in Manchester, England, 1993.

38 '*Christa*', Edwina Sandys, sculpture of crucified woman; *The Bosnian Christa*, Winchester, England.

39 Sujo, *Legacies of Silence*, p. 74.

inflicted by dominators in common with battered women, demonstrating the life-embodied range in possibilities, from

> resilience, earthbound strength . . . and cries of rebirth [to] atrocity and a generation's end.[40]

As 'domestics' still may be omitted from crime lists and battered women excluded from certain medical, employment and housing policies today, women and women's experiences are omitted from written records including the Bible and history books in number and nuance: 52 per cent of the research on Jewish women in wartime Poland 'went missing';[41] patriarchy shares with many dictatorships the ability to control, limit, filter and interpret available information, decreeing only men's experience as normative, thus ensuring its power.[42] Still often in determined survivorship, women's need to be recorded as expressed by one woman's struggle depicted in mundane but life-affirming tasks to stay alive in Auschwitz-Birkenau and be heard declared to her interned friend:

> If you live to leave this hell, make your drawings and tell the world about us. We want to be among the living, at least on paper . . . an extraordinary force that carried me to survival.[43]

The persecution, torture and elimination of millions of political and religious dissidents, gypsies, Jehovah's Witnesses, homosexuals and the handicapped as well as two-thirds of Europe's Jews and one-third of

---

40 Kathe Kollwitz, 'Die Mutter', and Max Slevogt, 'The Mothers from the Suite ... (Gesichte)', cited in Sujo, *Legacies of Silence*, p. 23.

41 Gershon Bacon, 'The Missing 52 Percent Research on Jewish Women in Interwar Poland and Its Implications for Holocaust Studies', in Dalia Ofer and Lenore J. Weitzman, eds, *Women in the Holocaust* (London: Yale University Press, and Binghampton: Vailballou Press, 1998), p. 55.

42 Dale Spender, 'Modern Feminist Theories: Reinventing Rebellion', in Dale Spender, ed., *Feminist Theories: Three Centuries of Key Women Thinkers* (London: Women's Press, 1983), p. 369.

43 Halina Olomucki, cited by Sujo, *Legacies of Silence*, p. 76.

the world's Jewish population[44] by Nazi leaders and workers wielding power abuses through control and violence were couched in religious-sanctioned efforts to rebuild a war-torn nation under the guise of patriotism. So also the maleness of power and control dominant in world cultures negated from recognition covers the enormity of its own evil as violence against women in the guise of success, achievement, competition, tradition, 'progress' and development. Aspects of human distance from holiness, including theological doctrines of the breach by Adam and Eve with God relating a transcendent God of terror as recorded in the writings of P – suggesting separation through degrees of impurity versus holiness, root suffering and evil as part of the human condition and separate gender in differing holiness through the shedding of blood.[45]

Yet scriptural tradition is located also in sufferings within the experiential trauma of the times including the exile and the forming identities of those seeking understanding of the nature of and closeness to God as faith. Those whose experience of exile included sufferings of oppression and displacement may have had to develop a strong individual identity and faith differing from a distant God whose own holiness emanated from hierarchical priestly castes and differing worship practices between temple and synagogue limiting human interaction and inclusion. Perhaps the purification laws even then, while hierarchical and separating, provided an active way for the traumatized to find explanation and purpose to the suffering they endured through a connection to a God of compassion and care beyond a remote temple worship interpreted and enacted solely through priests.[46] The quest for holiness despite active suffering for the exiled may indeed have contributed to the historical development of human rights and the sanctity of human life within a faith

44 John K. Roth *et al.*, *The Holocaust Chronicle: A History in Words and Pictures* (Lincolnwood: Publications International, 2000), cited in John K. Roth, *Holocaust Politics* (Louisville: Westminster John Knox Press, 2001), pp. 71–2 (p. 302, n. 7).

45 Karen Armstrong, *The End of Silence: Women and Priesthood* (London: Fourth Estate, 1993), pp. 31–6.

46 Armstrong, *The End of Silence*, p. 32.

belief based on inner spirituality and, above all, compassion. Both the devaluing of women and the negation of the divine power in creation in female form by the Church now acculturated in societies have sanctioned the sacrifice of women to the power of male violences, allowed men to abdicate responsibility by negating accountability for their crimes, and upheld the male valorization in Mayland's term in chilling similarity to Nazi, Aryan tradition as the three 'p's':

purity, property, and power.[47]

The Christian church tradition, by currently deleting the perceived 'other' as abused women from pastoral mention and recognition during liturgies of regular services, deletes abused women from value to share 'Christian' care and love – as were the Jews and all designated as sub-humans by Nazi devaluation and abuse then absented from most prevailing church liturgies including prayers and Christian consciousness. Shoah churches avoiding conflict, similar to individuals, churches and agencies avoiding getting involved in domestic conflict, do and did so by blaming and shaming victims of the Shoah, as abused women and single mothers were/are blamed for many social evils.[48] A woman's bodily sanctity as a man's prerogative to so violate, understood as paralleling the desecration of temples in the Shoah (*Kristallnacht*) and mosques in Bosnia,[49] and in prevailing male privilege and domination by authority and marital rule, does little justice for women in the Church and beyond, left vulnerable, injured and without a voice. This exclusion from pastoral prayer reflects the continuing unstated acceptance of women's inferior

47 Jean Mayland, *et al.*, eds, *Time for Action: Sexual Abuse, the Churches and a New Dawn for Survivors* (London: Churches Together in Britain and Ireland, 2001), p. 119.

48 Victoria Barnett, 'The Role of the Churches: Compliance and Confrontation', in Rittner, Smith and Steinfeldt, eds, *The Holocaust and the Christian World*, p. 55.

49 Roth, *Holocaust Politics*, pp. 262–3 and Michael A. Sells, *The Bridge Betrayed: Religion and Genocide in Bosnia* (Berkeley: University of California Press, 1996, 1998), pp. 76–7.

status within the Church, within the home and beyond, as expressed by Arad, speaking out against the Church's failure to protect the Jews:

> in the Soviet territories the extermination of the Jews by the Nazis was a known fact and was witnessed by the local population . . . It should be stressed that by remaining passive the population actually helped the Germans, because at that time the rescue of the Jews demanded active help.[50]

As identities and relational strengths of battered wives irritate and threaten abusing and jealous husbands, belittling and objecting to kindnesses and nurturing directed to others including children, Vardy and Arliss suggest the ability as strength of the Jews to maintain a strong and unique identity may be seen as a factor contributing to their being scapegoated by the Nazis.[51] Yet kindness named by Frank and Hillesum during the Shoah was seen as essential for the creation of a new order through the divinely sparked purposes[52] discerned by each of us through the calling within our own hearts in responsive actions of non-violent and just relating. Battered wives who survive, even temporarily, the attempts of our husbands to annihilate and extinguish the divine spark within us re-consecrate as healing, *tikkun*, violated bodies and desecrated homes as sacred space in renewing relationality[53] through an embodied resistance to the demonic profane violating our hearts, minds, souls and bodies through such encountered male violences as in the camps.

---

50 Yizhak Arad, 'The Christian Churches and the Persecution of Jews in the Occupied Territories of the Soviet Union', in Rittner, Smith and Steinfeldt, eds, *The Holocaust and the Christian World*, pp. 110–11.

51 Peter Vardy and Julie Arliss, *A Thinker's Guide to Evil* (London: HarperCollins Religious, 1992), p. 105.

52 Etty Hillesum, cited by Rachel F. Brenner, *Writing as Resistance: Four Women Confronting the Holocaust: Edith Stein, Simone Weil, Anne Frank, Etty Hillesum* (University Park, PA: Pennsylvania State University Press, 1997), p. 16, referenced in Raphael, *The Female Face of God*, p. 152 (p. 202, n. 87).

53 Raphael, *The Female Face of God*, p. 148 ('*tikkun atzmi*: the redemptive healing of the self; *tikkun olam*: the redemptive healing of the world'), in Raphael, *Select Glossary*, p. 206.

Tortured in private prisons known as our homes, aid for battered women has begun, as in the Shoah, at the grassroots level first by individuals or small groups of people responding in moral agency including now organized refugee workers, Women's Aid, Refuge, and the National Coalition for Battered Women, who have worked tirelessly even to shift battered women into governmental welfare inclusion as categories of 'homeless' and 'refugee'.[54] So also did compassion and sanctuary for some of the Jews and persecuted minorities during the Holocaust often come from within the grassroots resistance movement establishing refuges (for example, in France), and safe houses near the Polish ghettos,[55] embodied by individuals such as Slaschta and lay and religious women. These courageous but all too few people crossed social, political and cultural boundaries at personal risk by moving against the established hierarchies, church, state and societal, prevailing in order to honour and practise the sanctity of life.[56] Yet as for battered women, many POW survivors of Buchenwald, most now bearing physical and emotional scars, found indifference and disbelief of their devastating ordeals when expressed:

> And the cruel thing is that nobody has ever wanted to know, nor even really believed our story when we attempted to retell some of the more dramatic events. Such indifference I am certain has only made us all the more bitter and frustrated, and somewhat bitter of authority who should have taken our welfare to heart.[57]

54 Vivien Johnson, *The Last Resort: A Woman's Refuge* (New York: Penguin Books, 1981), p. 1.

55 Sujo, *Legacies of Silence*, p. 62.

56 Jessica A. Sheetz-Nguyen, 'Transcending Boundaries: Hungarian Roman Catholic Women and the "Persecuted Ones"', in Omer Bartov and Phyllis Mack, eds, *Genocide and Religion in the Twentieth Century* (New York: Berghahn Books, 2001), pp. 222–35.

57 Letter, Park Chapman, POW survivor, Buchenwald, to Gunther, Hull, 1 December 1941, *FRUS*, 1941, vol. II, pp. 876–7, cited by Mitchell G. Bard, *Forgotten Victims: The Abandonment of Americans in Hitler's Camps* (Boulder: Westview Press, 1994), pp. 109–10 (p. 144, n. 19).

Struggle for survival or extinction

As a Shoah survivor who suffered the separation from and subsequent loss of his family, Braham identifies the importance of teaching the occurrence of the Shoah as the culmination of horror with a loss of moral integrity when humanity eliminates belief in the sanctity of human life;[58] the same belief in the sanctity of life I am arguing which is denigrated, violated and eliminated in man's choices to use the power of violence to control, own, objectify, dehumanize and do male violences against women through male entitlement. One must ask: as Roth gives a church mandate to eliminate all which counters the sanctity of life in the face of evil in creed and praxis,[59] I must ask: are women allowed yet to be understood as made as human, let alone divine, and allowed to live?

Women of the Shoah found leadership defying expected roles in 'rebellious circles'[60] as battered wives are often deemed 'rebellious'. Women's efforts to resist the power of evil suffering through the active, courageous, and hard decision-making work done during the Nazi pogroms, struggling to pack under strict orders, complete and collect required lists and documents, and suffering through encounters with officials including the Gestapo in order to help their families stay put, file papers and orders, relocate, flee or even rescue their husbands from camp deportation to avoid the pain of being separated forever from loved ones,[61] are resistance efforts similar to the work required of battered wives dodging abusive husbands. As today, resistance given against the oppressors in varied hues of prayer, and even uttered in a curse of one's tormentors during the Shoah, in similar ways expresses the experiences,

---

58 Randolph Braham, 'Epilogue', in Survivors of the Shoah Visual History Foundation, *The Last Days* (film by Steven Spielberg and James Moll) (London: Seven Dials, 2000), p. 237.

59 Roth, *Holocaust Politics*, pp. 4, 194, 197f.

60 Yehuda Bauer, 'Gisi Fleischmann', in Ofer and Weitzman, *Women in the Holocaust*, pp. 6, 254.

61 Marion Kaplan, 'Jewish Women in Nazi Germany', in Ofer and Weitzman, *Women in the Holocaust*, pp. 46–8.

frustrations and varying gyrations expected of battered wives in resistance to abusive husbands, risking further assaults and revictimizations.[62]

Today's sad news of women targeted by ex-husbands and boyfriends, stalked, assaulted and/or murdered, encounter intentional, planned targeting by abusive men in similar 'selection' to those preyed upon and violated by members of the Nazi regime.[63] Although battered wives are not asked to work in gas chambers,[64] they also face economic and employment decisions for survival, even more heightened for mothers, propelling them towards limited, difficult, demeaning and even dangerous employment opportunities;[65] yes, including for some working time shifts of greater vulnerability from husbands' stalking and attacks. As in the selection of the Shoah, battered wives are judged by men and women in power and by cultural standards of beauty as well as accepted issues of ability, dress code, age, and even victimization in accessing both help and employment.[66] Sexual assaults used to defile, shame and break spirits of prisoners of war representing the rooting of shame with violence and defiled selfhood rightfully bring public voices of outrage and

---

62 Yehuda Bauer, *History of the Holocaust* (New York, 1982), pp. 210–11, referenced in Robert S. Wistrich, *Hitler and the Holocaust* (London: Weidenfield & Nicolson, 2001), p. 231 (p. 297, n. 49).

63 Goldenberg recounts the heroic actions of women of Birkenau whose determination to avoid both rape and separation from their loved ones as part of the selection process risked being shot and killed, with similar coping skills necessary as for battered wives. Judith M. Isaacson, *Seed of Sarah: Memoirs of a Survivor* (Chicago: University of Illinois Press, 1990), p. 85, referenced by Goldenberg, 'Memoirs of Auschwitz Survivors', in Ofer and Weitzman, *Women in the Holocaust*, p. 334 (p. 338, n. 22).

64 I condemn the systemic, planned and ruthless construction of gas chambers and burial pits conducted by the Nazi policy of the Final Solution: it is a Jewish proverb which states that 'Whoever saves one life, it is as if they had saved the whole world.' Eva Fleischner, 'The Memory of Goodness', in Rittner, Smith and Steinfeldt, *The Holocaust and the Christian World*, p. 158.

65 Dalia Ofer, 'Gender in Ghetto Diaries and Testimonies', in Ofer and Weitzman, *Women in the Holocaust*, p. 162.

66 'Their long, shapeless, dark dresses could make them appear older than they were and so more likely than secularized women to be selected by the SS for immediate death rather than slave labour.' Raphael, *The Female Face of God in Auschwitz*, p. 173, n. 27.

accountability, but wives and women selected, used and abused as 'bagged' property through marriage and/or 'capture' (or marriage as capture) as in-house prisoners of war becoming 24–hour 'comfort stations' in 'peace' as prize-winning trophies of husbands do not receive similar public support.[67]

Women, as official 'comforters' and/or battered wives, similar to the heinous treatment of Jews, have been seen for our purpose enslaved in serving men wielding power, and, after work-goals are finished, careers established and/or experimentations accomplished, discarded and/or exterminated in dramatic and/or subtle ways.[68] As for Shoah victims, battered women's existences find 'security in direct proportion to our labour productivity',[69] entrapped in a climate set by political-economic forces in patriarchal marriages.[70] Personal and positional power by male partners along constructions of gender and sexism used over women through socially sanctioned personal choice to use domination, force, aggression and violence, bears ominous parallels to Todorov's expression of the guard's power of one person over another and the 'enjoyment' of exercising it.[71] Indeed beyond bringing pleasure, he states, more affirmation of one's power comes through seeing another's displeasure, culminating in:

> To cause the death of another is to have irrefutable proof of my power over him.[72]

---

67 'Sexual abuse is experienced by many abused women but may not be easily disclosed because of intense feelings of embarrassment and shame.' Jacqelyn C. Campbell, *Empowering Survivors of Abuse* (Thousand Oaks and London: Sage, 1998), p. 178.

68 Women assigned the role of 'comforters', a biblical word for the Holy Spirit, best officially illustrated by those in 'comfort' stations and rape 'camps' designed during wartimes. 'Sexual Slavery', in Jonathan F. Vance, ed., *Encyclopedia of Prisoners of War and Internment* (Santa Barbara: ABC-CLIO, 2000), pp. 268–9.

69 Sujo, *Legacies of Silence*, p. 64.

70 Hoff, *Battered Women as Survivors*, p. 231.

71 Tzetan Todorov, *Facing the Extreme: Moral Life in the Concentration Camps*, trans. Arthur Denner and Abigail Pollack (London: Orion, 2000), p. 180.

72 Todorov, *Facing the Extreme*, p. 180.

It is disheartening to accept Power's research noting America's poor record of response to many genocides; disheartening further is the conclusion that it may indeed bear testimony to a political system which is ruthlessly effective in allowing such genocides to rage on.[73] Identified by Power as the greatest challenge to passive indifference regarding nationally recognized genocides are the voices of those refusing to remain silent, as for voices raised against violence against women, stating what is required, I am arguing in both interrelated arenas, is to honour the existing good but challenge a system and a system's use of power that works all too well in negative ways.[74] Hebrew scriptures and the writings of Isaiah suggest that those exiled in life may not always be led back, but God will move forward with them.[75] Shared between Jewish and Christian tradition is the understanding of human involvement and response as divine revelation.[76]

Battered women being told most often to shut up by both abusive husbands, courtrooms, churches and 'communities' worldwide, bearing labels for truth-telling as 'troublemakers, home wreckers, man-haters, liars or crazy, hysterical women'[77] throughout history gather strength in history with the persisting but all too few protesters against the Nazis leading up to the Second World War in newspapers and public meetings labelled as 'the Screamers',[78] sad to say who then slid into 'the blissful peace of ignorance and non-involvement'[79] when met with indifference and non-hearing – history and destiny indeed becoming written upon our bodies.[80] As for many instances in the Shoah, the divine is found for battered women beyond voices viewed as 'background noises' when

73 Samantha Power, *A Problem from Hell* (London: HarperCollins, 2002), p. xxi.

74 Power, *A Problem from Hell*, p. xxi.

75 Barry Webb, *The Message of Isaiah* (London: Intervarsity Press, 1996), pp. 225f.

76 Sujo, *Legacies of Silence*, p. 22.

77 Cooper-White, *The Cry of Tamar*, pp. 49–52.

78 Arthur Koestler, cited by Power, *A Problem from Hell*, p. 515, n. 4.

79 Koestler, cited by Power, *A Problem from Hell*, p. 515.

80 Lisa Isherwood and Elizabeth Stuart, *Introducing Body Theology* (Sheffield: Sheffield Academic Press, 1998), p. 22.

offering day-to-day care when nothing is left to give but the self, the self that may soon cease to be.[81]

The words of Hearn's interviewed, abusing men naming violent actions experienced as powerlessness, a powerlessness 'relative to their expectations of entitled more power or as their taken for granted "all-powerfulness"'[82] have an important and serious bearing upon the impact of church teaching and beyond sanctioning male domination and the way men may see themselves in relation to an omnipotent God. Raphael, in attributing qualities of caring to both 'the male and female of Israel', nevertheless counters holocaustal theologies of God's absence with the immanent divine found in acts of witness and caring during the Shoah linking feminine, maternal attributes of God found in Hebrew Scripture.[83] These attributes and images of the divine are all too often disused in regular Christian liturgies,[84] disabling both men and women from being able to call upon a more rich, balanced and indeed more fair portrayal of gender relating the divine in their own personal faith development.

As intended and chosen behaviours to use the power of evil in violences over another human both in the Shoah and in the genocide of abused women, the luminous is indeed blocked on earth yet its blockage from within the relational embodiment can neither destroy its subsequent power found in battered women's non-violent responses and testimony to such evil nor block its power of those risking a compassionate and caring response as witness to such crimes as in the Shoah. As articulated in Shoah survivors' memoirs in response to suffering, God was searched within the family, friends or group one belonged to, while even for some Shoah victims, as for battered women, such groups and even

---

81 Raphael, *The Female Face of God in Auschwitz*, p. 113.

82 Hearn, *The Violences of Men*, p. 215.

83 Raphael, *The Female Face of God in Auschwitz*, p. 10.

84 Virginia Mollenkot, *The Divine Feminine: Biblical Imagery of God as Female* (New York: Crossroad, 1993), pp. 5–6, and Marjorie Proctor-Smith, '"Reorganizing Victimization": The Intersection Between Liturgy and Domestic Violence', in Adams and Fortune, *Violence Against Women*, p. 430.

family members became a hindrance and obstacle to safety and empowerment.[85] Battered wives resisting in non-violent agency, finding choices out of 'non-choices' through determined placement of strength and hope within hopelessness, parallel Tichauer's choice among so few allowed her in Auschwitz-Birkenau:

> To fight and be beaten with batons is part of the program designed for our annihilation. I decide that day that I will never fight to eat, that I will never lift a hand to beat anyone.[86]

Refugee status of battered women

Destroyed by our husbands' violences is the actual, spiritual and archetypal sense of 'home'.[87] Beyond people, battered women experience loss of connection, rootedness, history, place, jobs, community and creativity, as 'being placed in God's *is* of creation',[88] embodied as loss of self, links with family members, disruption of traditions, with extra difficulties for single mothers. Male violences against women have created significant problems in particular with Britain's housing crisis and America's homeless.[89] The international, global village of today has produced an

---

85 Raphael, *The Female Face of God in Auschwitz*, p. 39.

86 Eva Tichauer, *I Was # 20832 At Auschwitz*, trans. Colette Levy and Nicki Rensten (London: Vallentine Mitchell, 2000), p. 29.

87 'All the women in Slepak's research describe the move to the ghetto as the greatest disaster for them . . . Others had stayed in refugee centers for weeks and feared becoming homeless again.' 'B and D, subscript #1', cited in Emmanuel Ringelblum, *Last Writings*, vol. II (Jerusalem: Yad Vashem, 1992), p. 179, by Ofer, 'Gender in Ghetto Diaries and Testimonies' in Ofer and Weitzman, *Women in the Holocaust*, p. 152 (p. 166, n. 36).

88 Vitor Westhelle, 'Creation Motifs in the Search for Vital Space', in Susan B. Thistlethwaite and Mary P. Engel, eds, *Lift Every Voice: Constructing Christian Theologies from the Underside* (Maryknoll: Orbis, 1998), p. 151.

89 'Violent relationships are fueling Britain's housing crisis as more and more people flee the family home in fear of attacks by a partner or a parent.' Jamie Doward, 'Homeless crisis fuelled by domestic violence', *The Observer*, 17 August 2003, p. 11.

alarming commonality despite differing cultures in the broken bodies, hearts, lives and silences of abused women living similar endangerment in the painful realities of suffering from the power choices of violent men resulting in damaged, compromised and/or extinguished potentialities of women's lives. Battered women coming out of abusive marriages and relationships indeed need the same services as those coming out of war zones, from shelter, medical and legal care, and financial aid to employ-ment/re-employment, rehousing and new community reintegration, often as Shoah refugees 'forever on the move'.[90]

Destroyed, diminished or extinguished by our husbands' violences are relationships with loved ones. As in the Shoah, forced, painful sepa-rations from children and loved ones evidenced by courtroom affidavits, including expressions by women in 'ordinary' cities and towns and from women as recent genocide refugees,[91] include at times coping with the threats and/or actualities of further trauma witnessing to the abuse and/or killing of children, family members, friends; even as sacrificial.[92] Rape, beating and torture are power choices used alike in bedrooms of 'civi-lized' towns, war-torn villages and refugee camps worldwide today by husbands and soldiers, with the risks and actualities of pregnancy com-pounding women's status, options, requirements and choices amid the choicelessness of being victimized as in the Final Solution. Recognizing that women's lives, even if they survive male violences, will never be the same,[93] battered women share with Shoah survivors a sense of internal

---

90 Sujo, 'Precursors', in Sujo, *Legacies of Silence*, p. 26.

91 Mary Robinson, speaking as the UN Commissioner for Human Rights, in Santos, *Violence Against Women in Times of War and Peace*, p. 1.

92 While mothers are cited in numerous texts as sacrificing themselves for children, husbands, parents, and siblings, the cruelty of the regime also forced mothers to give up their children to save their own lives and perhaps their husbands and other relatives: 'Nazi cruelty and brutality toward women were mentioned in many diaries as a symbol of ultimate barbarity.' Ofer, 'Gender in Ghetto Diaries and Testimonies', in Ofer and Weitzman, *Women in the Holocaust*, pp. 162–3.

93 Lisa Isherwood, 'Heaven or Hell? Twin Souls, Broken Bones', *Feminist Theology Journal*, 11.2 (January 2003), p. 215.

death bringing irrevocable changes from sustained trauma. As a battered wife expressed:

I stayed there (in the marriage) until I died inside.[94]

Remaining in marriages or seeking divorces after years of violent physical, sexual, psychological, verbal and spiritual assaults and torture from husbands also comprise a similar shattering of life as for Shoah victims in the loss of cultural placement and identity within the desecrated sacred bonds of marriage – sacred union embodying what had been hoped to be safe in relationality and in home and personal space of mutual and abundant life now desecrated of personhood and of being human literally to our breath, bones, blood and sinew as well as souls. This shattering of our lives comprises a violation and death not only of the present but also of the future, of self and of self-in-relation with and in the divine. As Gnanadason identifies as special the targeting of women for bearing the brunt of the world's injustices today upon women and children,[95] so also:

the abuse of mothers and children left speechless even the longtime witnesses of Nazi cruelty.[96]

The power of religious symbolism, especially Christian, influenced the creation of the Shoah and still influences the ongoing genocide of women by church doctrines, liturgies and practices which sanction, promote and ignore violence done to the oppressed, especially as women assaulted by men doing power in male violences. These ongoing crimes and injustices against women and children call out in response for women's remembrance and expression as prophetic action, justice-

---

94 Battered woman survivor, cited by Vivien Johnson, *The Last Resort: A Woman's Refuge* (Harmondsworth: Penguin, 1981), p. 107.

95 Aruna Gnanadason, *No Longer a Secret: The Church and Violence Against Women*, Risk Book Series (Geneva: World Council of Churches, 1997), p. 5.

96 Ofer, 'Gender in Ghetto Diaries and Testimonies', in Ofer and Weitzman, *Women in the Holocaust*, p. 163.

seeking and societal transformation as required for Holocaust remembrance. Keeping God's commandments in one's heart (Deuteronomy 6), as yet a crucial commandment calls for identity, integrity and witness for Christians embodying the great commandments to love God and love your neighbour as yourself[97] – a biblical commandment now immortalized in inscription on the wall of the US Holocaust Memorial Museum near the eternal flame and the soil deposited from the Nazi death camps.[98]

The continuance throughout the world of blood shed from women's mutilated and maimed bodies, 'Listen, your ("sister's") brother's blood is crying out to me from the ground',[99] and women's lives extinguished by those we loved by actions of non-equal partners in 'loving relationships' violates biblical commandments including the Christian Great Commandment, breaks the marital vows to honour and cherish one another, and denigrates the baptismal vows to respect and honour the dignity of all peoples. Even the Nazi acquisition and turning of the swastika symbol, once an ancient Sanskrit symbolic for 'su', meaning good, and 'asti' still used, representing well-being for some world religions,[100] into a recognized symbol for evil is not dissimilar to the perversion of the cross as the acceptable load for wives to bear in beatings, rapes and subjugation to husbands unto death for woman's sinfulness. These vastly accumulated crimes of male violences require the same, searing question to be asked of accountability from violent men and Christians as witnesses inscribed at the Holocaust Memorial first found the Bible, placing Christian responsibility for the Holocaust in: 'What have you done?'[101] Are women, as Jews became, excluded from Christian personhood, placed outside the realm of societal moral obligation, ethical

---

97 Matthew 22.37–39.

98 'Keep these words that I command you close to your heart.' Deuteronomy 6, cited by John K. Roth, 'What Does The Holocaust Have To Do With Christianity?', in Rittner, Smith and Steinfeldt, *The Holocaust and the Christian World*, pp. 7–8.

99 Genesis 4.10.

100 Brent Jarvie, 'It's the True Meaning of Swastika', *London Metro*, 26 April 2006.

101 Genesis 4.10; Roth, 'What Does The Holocaust Have To Do With Christianity?', p. 6.

Christian duties, compassionate care? Should the parable of the Good Samaritan be taught with the caveat:

> For men only beaten and robbed; not for women beaten, raped, tortured, and robbed of safety, human rights, dignity, family, personhood, kind interactions, health, equality, and strength, financial security, pursuit of happiness, partnership, life in abundance, choice, and/or life itself?

Unblocking the divine through just power-sharing

As after the Shoah, any theologies must be rooted in this truth and lived out as a practical as well as theoretical, embodied, believed and practised theology.[102] As Soelle, Cargas and Roth rightfully call Christian theology in repentance (metanoia) or *teshuvah*[103] to an integrity of praxis in solidarity with respect for the human dignity, faith and flourishing of all Jews and to root out all 'latent anti-Judaism' and Antisemitism from Christian tradition and practice, so Christian theologies must also come into an integrity of solidarity with all abused women to dismantle male domination and the use of power through violence named and accounted for as sins of injustice and oppression opposing gospel tradition of authentic love in discipleship, non-hierarchical relationship and re-imaged servanthood – not 'controlled and dominated in order to serve the male of the species'[104] – freeing men as well as women.

Articulating the presence and compassionate agency of women to God and humanity as holiness despite invisibility of women from both

---

102 Sidney G. Hall, *Christian Anti-Semitism and Paul's Theology* (Minneapolis: Fortress Press, 1993), cited in Rittner, Smith and Steinfeldt, *The Holocaust and the Christian World*, p. 212.

103 '"*teshuvah*": an act of repentance . . . Cardinal Cassidy noted the need for the whole Church to make an act of repentance for its role in preparing the way for and in perpetrating, through so many of its members, the Shoah.' Cardinal Edward Cassidy, cited by Eugene J. Fisher, 'How Have the Churches Responded to the Holocaust?' in the 1995 statement upon the 50th anniversary of Auschwitz, in Rittner, Smith and Steinfeldt, *The Holocaust and the Christian World*, p. 181.

the image of the human and the divine of traditional sacred celebration, Raphael integrates the divine mystery of the sacred with the restoration of presence of relationship and caring between God, humanity and each other as embodied in acts of seeing the suffering of others and in washing, caring touch, and covering of embodied selves and others while maintaining family traditions in Auschwitz[105] – sanctification as best possible to counteract the evil actions designed to destroy and obliterate.[106] In similar acts of caring for self, children, and indeed husbands of the sacred within a marital partnership, battered wives keep alive the divine spark in protest, protection and moral agency against the power to denigrate life through choices of male violences against women and children. Understood within this required paradigm shift is the recognition of the covenantal break of marriage and the family not in a woman's speaking out and/or leaving for safety and protection but in the choices of husbands to do male violences.[107]

It is to recognize the divine in the human resistance and responses to evil wherever encountered – to resist defiling the face of God by compromising one's personal integrity by choosing retaliation, vengeance, and hatred is to choose life despite evil and death, including our own murder or suicide. The failure by societies and many individuals to see salvation as individual acts of life-giving risk and the giving of tender care and attention in providing protection for the Jews of the Shoah and victims of past and present genocides, and the failure of the Church and beyond to see salvation as protection, empowerment and new life for battered

---

104 Anne Suchalla, 'Like a Rolling Stone', in Suchalla, *It's Time to Talk About It: Violence against Women in Culture, Society, and the Church*, p. 8.

105 Raphael posits the divine in the images of the bent woman offering covering, care, washing, as the Shekinah, as a maternal, womb-like embodiment against the image of the Holy found in the valorization of masculine power: 'For a woman to see, touch, cover . . . to be present as positioning one to the other . . . women's holding . . . the other from death back into the slender possibility of life.' Raphael, *The Female Face of God in Auschwitz*, pp. 5–6, 23–9.

106 Raphael, *The Female Face of God in Auschwitz*, p. 7.

107 Mitzi Eilts, 'When is the Marital Covenant Broken?', in Adams and Fortune, *Violence Against Women*, p. 448.

wives and therefore for all community members in responsibility to one another by the Church, is indeed a matter of life and death.[108]

A moral stance requires personal risk beyond mere words, even at cost to personal benefit despite dehumanizing treatment by those wielding power as evil over another extended even unto the stranger. This kind of moral action can give a sense of personal, unmitigated joy[109] found in simple acts of kindness, one human being to another, or in maintaining one's integrity despite risk as in the Shoah of 'marching out of time'[110] and for a battered woman in risking to assert oneself and/or protect children, family, friends and even caseworkers against an oppressive husband. Todorov suggests no separation between the ordinary and 'heroic' virtues of courage and generosity.[111] The courageous, steadfast witness of faith given by the Jehovah's Witnesses during the Shoah bearing purple triangles leading to family separation, imprisonment, torture and murder as for the Jews is seldom mentioned in mainline Churches, but should stand as a benchmark of Christian compassion; embodied also in battered women who refuse to submit personal integrity and faith including non-violent values and care speaking out against violent husbands and those all too few who risk as in the Shoah responding in life-affirming, relational empowerment. As exiled people of Hebrew scriptures, Shoah victims and battered women cry out:

Our bones are dry, our thread of life is snapped, our web is severed from the loom.[112]

---

108 '. . . to protect the needy.' Nechama Tec, 'A Glimmer of Light', in Rittner, Smith and Steinfeldt, *The Holocaust and the Christian World*, p. 154.

109 Todorov, *Facing the Extreme*, pp. 291, 295.

110 Todorov, *Facing the Extreme*, pp. 291, 295.

111 Todorov, *Facing the Extreme*, p. 295.

112 Ezekiel 37.11–14: In opposition to the images of Israel as a violated and rejected woman as punishment for the sins of Israel (see Lamentations 1.9: 'Her uncleanness clings to her skirts, no one to comfort her'; Jeremiah 13.22: 'It is because of your great iniquity that your skirts are lifted up, Your limbs exposed'; as well as Ezekiel and Hosea), Raphael states the divine is found in the caring for the violated, abused, desecrated bodies instead. Raphael, *The Female Face of God in Auschwitz*, p. 141, quoting Ezekiel 16.4–10.

Feminist liberation theologies of justice-making parallel post-Holocaust Christian theologies such as Roth placing 'a hunger and thirst for righteousness', a justice, as a power stronger than the despair resulting from the Holocaust bringing 'light, the light of every human life', love, and life beyond history and within history 'as sources of hope that set people free to resist injustice and to show compassion'.[113] Human love holding greater power than death in the face of human atrocities of evil and human violence such as Auschwitz and the ongoing genocide of women – carved on the bodies and memories of survivors as well as victims created not in tenderness of just relationship but in heaps of discarded, abandoned human life with its desecrated power of potential in divine spark, witness and authentic love.

The numinous of God found in the compassion within the gatherings of Auschwitz[114] as in the huddled survivors in battered women's shelters, refugee camps, kitchen tables, guest rooms and/or lounge floors stands as testimony to enable God not as absent in the world but to counter those whose choices to inflict power through male violences in the world reject the divine. In similar ways, such gatherings manifest the absent or present numinous in the community response of the Church and beyond for abused women, choosing to create a space for or casting out of the divine from the world once again. These actions parallel the image and embodiment of battered wives being cast out, or cast aside, by the power of our husbands' violences in a way similar to Hagar's expulsion to the desert.[115]

In conclusion, I must ask as in the Shoah whether it is indeed still possible to 'do theology' facing the reality of the enormity of the atrocities of these crimes against women – crimes against God. If still possible, theology must undergo a social and theological paradigm shift to address the enormity of worldwide, sanctioned violence against women as male violences of power. The Church needs to teach its communities that

---

113 Roth, *Holocaust Politics*, pp. 210–11, citing John 1: 'The Word became flesh and dwelt among us.'

114 Raphael, *The Female Image of God in Auschwitz*, p. 74.

115 Genesis 16.1–16; 21.9–21.

authentic, non-violent love instead as the power of justice-making in respecting the theological sanctity of life and in life in abundance are neither just abstract virtues nor finite commodities in need of being hoarded, controlled, separated out and possessed for those in powerful status. They are generated in a power of an infinite Love which increases by being given away, shared and passed on in passionate and compassionate caring for God, self and one another expressed within the individual and collective experiences of survivors.[116] What better place for the Church to begin teaching and practising theologies with the power of non-violent mutuality and justice-making as authentic love to prevent genocides than in forming, enabling and practising non-hierarchical relating most exemplified in partnerships of non-violent intimacy, compassion and respect in all encounters but manifest most especially in marriage. Guillebaud's witness of faith through the evils of the Rwandan genocide with its human atrocities speaks to inform also the pervasive genocide of male violences against women:

> They often used to say at the foot of the cross there is level ground, with no room for anything that divides.[117]

Shoah victims who worked and were beaten and humiliated unto death, awaiting 'level ground' in appropriate community response, found no God in the humanity they encountered except for within their own community of victims. The Church of the Shoah experienced as an unresponsive or re-victimizing Church with its veneered silence is still found today by abused women, condemned by its own Ecumenical Decade in Solidarity with Women as:

---

116 Of the Ravensbruck women who 'tasted death' and survived, Ronowicz states: 'One-quarter are crippled for life.' Doris Ronowicz, trans., *Beyond Human Endurance: The Ravensbruck Women Tell Their Story* (Warsaw: Interprosp, 1970), front jacket quotation.

117 Meg Guillebaud, *Rwanda: The Land God Forgot: Revival, Genocide and Hope* (London: Monarch Books, 2002), p. 71.

a sign of moral failure and . . . biblical and theological legitimizations of this violence call into question the very authority and power of the church as a moral community.[118]

Battered women worldwide who hold audacious hope searching and striving for a space of enablement and empowerment in a suspicious, doubting and re-victimizing world are placed at further risk – risk of inescapable abuse from violent husbands and ex-husbands, inescapable re-victimization, imprisonment and/or disempowerment in our own homes and courts, shackled in our new 'communities' – all await being murdered in violent episodic killings and/or in slow deaths of wasted potentialities, talents, hopes, dreams and callings. As for all too many Shoah victims, for all too many battered women:

There is no tomorrow.[119]

---

118 Gnanadason, *No Longer a Secret: The Church and Violence Against Women*, p. 77.

119 Saying from Botswana, cited by Suchalla, *It's Time to Talk About It: Violence against Women in Culture, Society, and the Church*, p. 4.

7

Biblically Slicing Women

JANET WOOTTON

Women are of very little account, for the most part, in the narratives of the Hebrew scriptures. There are notable exceptions, but generally they are definable as the *Wives, Harlots and Concubines* of Alice Laffey's imaginative book title,[1] with the addition of mothers, daughters and, perhaps, victims.

The women in this article are marked by their death, or by their victimization in relation to death. In three of the four major stories, the body is also mutilated: butchered, burnt or eaten by dogs. Two are incidental victims of violence and war; two are protagonists who lose the battle. Their fate interacts with their gender in different ways. Jephthah's daughter is an almost random victim. Her gender does not influence her death, though it does influence her response and the way the narrative treats the story. The concubine who is raped to death is, in fact, a second choice. The mob first demands the Levite himself. Nevertheless, the host and the Levite seem to hold women of such little account that they can be offered up to the mob in his stead.

The other women involved in this farcical tragedy are entirely expendable. The only concern is the provision of wives for the truncated tribe of Benjamin. The women are treated utterly shamefully, less than pawns in this nonsense-game.

Jezebel and Athaliah are, in contrast, powerful and independent women. As such, they are vilified within the narratives that tell their stories. Jezebel typifies the foreign seductress, luring Israel away from the

---

1 Alice Laffey, *Wives, Harlots and Concubines: The Old Testament in Feminist Perspective* (London: SPCK, 1990).

true worship of Yahweh and, perhaps, creating the circumstances in which a queen in her own right, Athaliah, can seize power and retain it for a substantial period. Both die violently as the conservative forces of Yahwistic purity regain control after a long struggle. Their crime is not just that they were Baal-worshippers, but that they were powerful, intelligent and independent women.

Tragically, the stories are not alien to our own times, but show how human violence is so often written on women's bodies.

The Levite's concubine

It is not easy to cut up a corpse. To cut a woman's body into twelve pieces would present quite a challenge. This is literally butchery – that is how archaeologists identify cannibalism. If human remains show the signs of skilled butchery, rather than the random injuries inflicted in war, then the humans have been eaten.

But I am not talking about cannibalism, but something equally deliberate and brutal. This act of butchery takes place during the decline of the political system in the Hebrew scriptures described by the term 'Judges' and before the establishment of the monarchy in Israel. The situation is described a couple of times in the words: 'At that time, there was no king in Israel, and everyone was a law to himself.'[2]

During this lawless time, a young woman is gang-raped to death, and her dismembered body is used, as it were, as a communication, to bring about the justice which is no longer readily available. The butchery of the body is not the crime, but an attempt to find a solution. The horrible act of savagery is just part of a story in which a community tears itself apart, with appalling violence, particularly against women.

The couple at the centre of the story are a Levite and his concubine, or wife. Levites did not have tribal rights to territory, but could serve as priests to households (see Judges 17.7–13). They were classified with widows, orphans and foreigners in lists of needy people who were

---

2 E.g. Judges 17.6; 21.25.

worthy of support (e.g. Deuteronomy 16.11, 14). This is not like the stories in the main body of the book of Judges, where national heroes rise up and save the day, bringing the people back to Yahweh. In the decay of that political system, we are dealing with people of no account. Indeed, there is no mention of God at all in the narrative of the small events that lead up to the rape of the concubine.

The Levite comes across as a hesitant and ineffectual man. He is not a successful husband. His concubine runs home to her father, and it is four months before he sets out, accompanied by one servant, to appeal to her to come home. The language is touching – he does not ride in and seize her back, like property. He appeals to her affections (19.3).

He cannot even manage his departure from her father's house, but yields to the pressure to stay till evening, then overnight, and then till evening the next day. In common with many indecisive people, he can only bring himself to a decision when it is really too late, and he leaves at sundown.

The poverty and frailty of his entourage is stressed again, as he sets out into the dangerous night, with his servant, his concubine and the two donkeys. The narrative refers several times to the ending of the day, with a sense of gathering danger. The Levite's weakness is evident in the servant's initiative in suggesting that they stay in Jebus, and he makes the fateful decision to try to reach somewhere where they will be among Israelites.

The narrative sees him sitting forlornly in the town square when the sun actually sets, until eventually someone invites him into his house. No doubt the woman was better off in her father's house than travelling with this feckless man.

These chapters may well have been added to the book of Judges from other sources, but their present position invites comparison with the heroic action and derring-do of a Jephthah or a Gideon – or a Deborah.

It is not surprising, then, that the mob comes in the night, demanding a bit of fun with this unattractive stranger. Have they seen him sitting in the square, vaguely hoping for hospitality? Have they noted that it is the 'old man' who has taken him in? For they do not regard him as a man, their equal, to join in their evening entertainment, or even have a fight with. They want to bugger him. They want to commit the ultimate act of violence and humiliation against a man, to rape him, to pierce his body.

This is not an argument about homosexuality, but a desire to commit violence. He is a stranger. He is a derisory figure. And they want to humiliate him.

While there are obvious parallels with Genesis 19, this story is different. The rescue of Lot and his family is an act of God. It is a story full of action and drama, very different from this drab little scene. Most notably, of course, in the earlier story, the angels effect a dramatic rescue from the mob, pulling Lot back into the house and blinding the crowd with dazzling light, affording precious moments for Lot to get his people together and flee in the nick of time. The offer to send the women out to be raped is overtaken by events.

But not here. The host half-heartedly offers his virgin daughter, as Lot does, but it is the concubine who is actually bodily delivered to the mob. She is the one who is pierced again and again.

This part of the story is sickening enough. What cuts to the heart is the plethora of similar stories from war zones throughout history and up to the present day. Until very recently, rape as part of war was either hidden, or seen as a natural part of the violence: 'part of a soldier's proof of masculinity and success, a tangible reward for services rendered'.[3] But the cost to the women is only now being told, in books and television documentaries, where the dead eyes of women who were gang-raped in the aftermath of war, maybe sixty years ago, speak even more eloquently than their words about the kind of living death their piercing condemned them to.

The concubine, who had taken the bold decision to return to her father's house, and had presumably made the journey quite safely, found herself once more in the feeble hands of the man who would turn her over to destruction to save his own life.

---

3 S. Brownmiller, *Against Our Will: Men, Women and Rape* (New York: Simon & Schuster, 1975), p. 33, quoted in Alice Bach, 'Re-reading the Body Politic: Women, Violence and Judges 21', in Athalya Brenner, ed., *Judges: A Feminist Companion to the Bible* (Sheffield: Sheffield Academic Press, 1999), pp. 143-59, p. 154.

The act of butchery is still to come. When the Levite gets up after his night's sleep, the narrative suggests that he is not expecting to see his concubine again, but there she is, lying with her hands on the threshold – stretched out in her last attempt to regain safety, but with no angelic hands to pull her inside the door as they had Lot.

The Masoretic text is not clear whether she is dead at this point, or whether the Levite kills her. His version of the story paints them both as victims: 'They intended to murder me. They raped my concubine to death' (20.5–6). Apart from setting out to find the woman, this act of butchery is the Levite's first decisive act in the whole story. The despicable man suddenly finds his balls. This violent murder requires revenge.

In a parody of the Judges' calls to action, the Levite calls the whole assembly together. Deborah issued the call to war and marched with Barak at the head of a 10,000-strong army. Gideon called the people to war when, under the power of the Spirit of Yahweh, he sounded the trumpet and sent out messengers to rally the troops. The cause was victory over the enemies of Israel, and a return to the God of Israel.

The Levite sends out messy bits of concubine. The cause is vengeance for an act which is actually the Levite's fault. And it leads not to a victory of Israel's enemies, but to bloody civil war. It also makes a 'man' out of the Levite. Ilse Müllner comments on the butchery, 'Through this act of semiotization, the body of the woman is desexualized, perfectly and repulsively. With this act of violence, the Levite affirms his solidarity with the attackers at the level of sexual difference and, in so doing, reaffirms his masculinity.'[4]

When his 'masculinity' might have offered protection to the concubine, in this patriarchal society, he was vacillating and weak. He couldn't even find her somewhere to stay. When he was threatened with feminization and humiliation through rape, he threw her to the mob. Only now does he assert his masculinity by reinforcing his difference from the woman, and calling on the solidarity of the men of Israel.

---

4 Ilse Müllner, 'Lethal Differences: Sexual Violence as Violence against Others in Judges 19', in Brenner, *Judges*, pp. 126–42, p. 141.

The women of Gibeah, Jabesh Gilead and Shiloh

And only now does Yahweh get involved. In the narrative's present setting, the story seems like a re-enactment of the old days. The whole community is roused to action. They call together the great assembly in the presence of Yahweh, and vow a horrible vengeance on Gibeah.

And they get their vengeance. Gibeah is destroyed, along with the tribe of Benjamin, to which it belongs. Most of the men are killed in battle, but – here is the bitter irony – *all* the women are slaughtered. The women of Gibeah, who may have listened with horror behind closed doors to the baying of the mob (or – admittedly – may have egged their menfolk on), are slaughtered.

Pause for a moment, to consider this brutal extermination. Recently, a report on the *Today* programme on BBC Radio 4 so moved the listeners that the producers were overwhelmed by emails asking what they could do to help. It was an interview with a woman from a village which had come under attack from the Interahamwe. She spoke of appalling violence, in which every member of her family had been killed, and she had suffered terrible torture.

All she wanted, she said, was for the Interahamwe to go back over the border to Rwanda, so that she could live in peace in her village. She had done nothing. Her peaceful life was brutally, utterly shattered by the actions of people she did not know, over whom she had no influence or control, and who thought of her as a dog.

These are the horrors captured in one short verse – Judges 20.48. It is just a postscript to the battle, which is told in vivid detail. Oh yes, and after that, they went back into the territory and put every living thing to the sword.

There follows a descent into farce. Like almost every abuser, the men, once their bloodlust has subsided, feel sorry. What have they done? The language denies their palpable responsibility: 'a tribe has been amputated from Israel', they say – as if unaware how this could have happened (21.6). Later, it is 'Yahweh has made a breach in Israel' (21.15)!

The problem is that, if the tribe of Benjamin is to be regenerated, they actually *need* women. The violent rape of the concubine – dehumanizing and destructive – has brought about a situation in which women are needed as breeding machines, to be pierced, impregnated and to provide a future for the lost tribe. They are a commodity, which apparently the other tribes have in abundance.

The farcical element lies in a vow, taken by the Israelite men, in their raging thirst for revenge. They vowed before Yahweh not only to destroy Benjamin, but, in order to prevent the tribe's regeneration, not to give their daughters to the Benjaminites in marriage. This is the dilemma. Now that the thirst for revenge has been satisfied, their hasty vow stands in the way of restoration.

What to do? The first solution is to seek out a tribal group that did not take part in the oath. Even in the heyday of the judges, not every tribe answered the call to battle. This is known from the condemnation of those who stayed away. The great triumphal song of Deborah lists the champions and heroes that followed their leader into battle, but is scathing of Reuben, Gilead and Dan, who stayed behind (Judges 5.13–17). But now, in a parody of the days of greatness, the Israelites need to find some renegades, who didn't sign up to the grand heroic task of destroying Benjamin, so that they can undermine their original purpose by offering their daughters. The culprit turns out to be Jabesh in Gilead.

But they are not asked to offer their daughters. Instead the Israelites embark on another act of senseless slaughter, destroying the whole population of Jabesh in Gilead, but this time saving the unmarried women of marriageable age. Chillingly, we are told that there are four hundred – and that this is not enough. Another community has been wiped out. Four hundred young women have had their families and towns destroyed in front of their eyes, and it is not enough. Four hundred would surely be enough to begin the regeneration of a tribe, but it seems that the abusers are deep into repentance and regret now.

Their next solution is simply utterly ridiculous and abhorrent. The dehumanizing and demeaning of women has one last twist. It would seem as though any humiliation of women is worthwhile to save face for the men – except that the narrative gives no sign of even appreciating that humiliation is taking place. It is blind to the outrage of what is happening.

At an annual festival, at Shiloh, at which the eligible young women will gather, the men of the tribes of Israel give permission to the Benjaminites to seize and carry off as many women as they need. This does not count as giving them in marriage, and so preserves the letter of the vow, though patently not the spirit.

The daughter of Jephthah

There are many similarities between the story of the Levite and his concubine and that of an earlier and more typical judge over Israel. The call to lead Israel erupts into the life of Jephthah and, presumably, his family quite unexpectedly. He is living in exile, having been driven out by his father's legitimate sons because he is the son of a prostitute and has no place in the inheritance. Like the Levite, therefore, he has no inheritance, no land rights in Israel.

Like the Levite, he therefore comes into the community as a stranger. But he is no shrinking violet, cowering in the marketplace till someone will take him in. The Israelites have come to him in humiliation, to ask him to lead them against a new enemy. Jephthah can dictate his own terms for readmission to the community. He comes from a position of strength. This is not a man who has to trail after the womenfolk in his life and persuade them to come back to him, nor, would we think, is he a man who would fail in the protection of his family. In fact, as in the case of most of the other judges, we would not expect to hear about his family at all.

Except that he too, in the heat of battle lust, makes a vow to God. If he is granted victory, he will sacrifice to God the first thing that greets him on his return to his house. Of course, when he returns, he is greeted with festivity suitable to the returning hero, and at the head of the procession, dancing to the sound of tambourines, is his beloved daughter, his only child.

Like the Israelites following the destruction of Gibeah, Jephthah is faced by the dilemma of a ridiculous vow, whose consequences, in this instance unforeseen, but surely foreseeable, are intolerable.

Like the women at Shiloh Jephthah's daughter takes part in a festival with her unmarried friends. And, as in the later instance, the festival is a parody of what should presumably have been a celebration of fertility and youth. The women of Shiloh are intended as sacrifices to the blood-lust and comical repentance of the warring tribes. Jephthah's daughter is about to become a literal human sacrifice, because of the blood-lust and tragic repentance of her father.

It is suggested that the annual festival mentioned in Judges 11.40 as the commemoration of Jephthah's daughter may be the forerunner of the feast from which the Benjaminites were invited to steal the Israelite women away.

The difference is that she is shown to be shockingly and strangely compliant. The women of Gibeah, Jabesh and Shiloh have no choice. They are variously slaughtered, offered and seized while they remain mute in the narrative. Jephthah's daughter dances, hears and speaks. She comes out to meet her father on his return from battle. When she learns of the oath, she immediately reassures him, reminding him that the vow 'worked'; he achieved his victory. From this point on, she lays down the timetable, and, at the end of her time of freedom, returns to face the completion of the vow.

The narrative does not record the moment of death, and there are arguments that the vow was not, in fact, carried out. But the simplest interpretation of the narrative is that Jephthah's daughter was sacrificed as a burnt offering, killed, most likely by having her throat cut, then burnt entirely, so that the pleasing scent reached the nostrils of God in heaven (see e.g. Exodus 29.38–42). Despite stringent warnings against human sacrifice in Israel, the oath taken in war, a man's bargain with the warrior God, the Lord of Hosts, was more powerful, even when it caused injustice, anguish and destruction.

Where was Yahweh in this? As with the story of the Levite and his concubine, this story cries out for comparison with a similar situation whose outcome is totally different. In Genesis 22, Abraham is called on to sacrifice his only child, the son of the promise, Isaac. In this instance, Isaac remains totally unaware until, presumably, he is bound and the knife is out. He does not heroically comply, as Jephthah's daughter does.

In each case, no question of disobedience or demurral is raised. The sacrifice is prepared. But in the case of Abraham's only child, Yahweh dramatically intervenes at the very last moment. Abraham's hand is stayed; his child does not die. Why, in the two parallel narratives, does Jephthah's notional obedience not count for as much? Why does Yahweh allow Jephthah's abominable and illegal murder of his daughter, while he prevents Abraham from sacrificing his son?

Jezebel

The story of the Levite and his concubine is topped and tailed with the statement that these were lawless and leaderless times: there was no king in Israel and everyone did what he wanted. Some have seen a similar message in the story of Jephthah, a later spin, perhaps, to indicate that pre-monarchic Israel lacked the innate stability and security of the monarchy.

It is hard to judge between the two political systems, so far as they affected the lives of women. Indeed, it is almost impossible to know what the lives of ordinary women were like.

One new element under the monarchy, as Israel came to have more of an international presence as a nation, was extra-Israelite intermarriage, and the introduction of foreign customs, including foreign religious customs, through the presence of foreign women in the royal harem. Solomon was very much a modernizer. He took Israel into the international arena of his time, and among his reportedly seven hundred wives and three hundred concubines were women from the many cultures of the day (1 Kings 11.1–3).

With typical Deuteronomistic puritanism, the narrator at this point condemns the presence of the foreign women. Intermarriage in any case is forbidden (v. 2) and its prohibition is borne out by the fact that Solomon himself is tempted to turn away from his pure faith by their presence.

It is here that the interpretation and symbol of the foreign woman as wicked temptress begins to take shape. This horrible and destructive image will worm its way into prophecy and song; it will be used to describe humanity in its relationship to God – the unfaithful woman and her faithful but retributive Lord; the racial purity laws of Ezra and Nehemiah will be built on the same gyno-xenophobia and disgust at intermarriage; Jesus will encounter the same prejudice and learn to over-come it, but a visionary on the Island of Paphos will give it apocalyptic status in the person of the Great Whore of Babylon.

The archetype of the image in the period of the monarchy is Jezebel, wife of Ahab, and a woman of considerable power – which only adds to her vilification. From Medea to EastEnders, the worst thing a woman can be is powerful. Jezebel is introduced with Ahab at the beginning of his reign, and her influence over him and within Israel continues through the narrative.

She imports the cult of Baal into Israel, and maintains a large religious establishment of 450 prophets, who 'eat at her table' (1 Kings 19). The contest between these and Elijah on Mount Carmel can be seen as a con-test not between Elijah and Ahab, but between Elijah and Jezebel.[5] It is her threat to kill Elijah that drives him to flight, though his prophecy about her will eventually come true and his political successor, Jehu, will bring about her death.

After Ahab's death in battle, Jezebel remains in power as Queen Mother, the mother of the next two kings of Israel (the northern king-dom). Extraordinarily, Ahaziah is condemned for following the example of his father *and mother* (1 Kings 22.53) and following the cult of Baal. His successor to the throne of Israel, Jehoram, is likewise compared with his father and mother (2 Kings 3.2). Jezebel's influence is still powerful, and even extends to the southern kingdom of Judah through the marriage of one of Ahab's daughters (though not necessarily Jezebel's daughter), Athaliah, to Jehoram of Judah.

But opposition was rising too. Elijah's followers, Elisha, Hazael and Jehu work to bring about the downfall of the house of Ahab and all the descendants of his hated father, Omri. Anointed secretly and proclaimed king by his loyal followers, Jehu begins a campaign of destruction against

---

5 Phyllis Trible, 'The Odd Couple: Elijah and Jezebel', in Christina Büchmann and Celina Spiegel, eds, *Out of the Garden: Women Writers on the Bible* (New York: Fawcett Columbine, 1994).

the Omride kings and their families. The narrative proceeds at breakneck speed, matching the legendary speed of Jehu's chariot. Jehoram is slaughtered because of the 'prostitutions and countless sorceries' of his mother Jezebel (2 Kings 9.22–4), as is the tainted Ahaziah, king of Judah, husband of Athaliah.

And then the two real protagonists come face to face: Jehu, representing the ideology of Elijah, and Jezebel, and the narrative slows in pace, relishing the wicked queen's come-uppance. Famously, Jezebel appears at the window of her palace dressed and decked like the woman of substance that she is, and with a taunt for Jehu. She has fought a long battle for supremacy, and, for the most part, enjoyed power. Now the narrator shows her meeting death with courage and defiance.

Her own attendants turn against her and throw her down from the window to her death. What happens to her body? Remember, the concubine was butchered and Jephthah's daughter was burnt as a pleasing odour for God. Jezebel is eaten by the dogs, while Jehu enjoys a meal and a drink. The 'accursed woman' (2 Kings 9.34) is destroyed. There will be no trace left of her, and therefore no focus for any revolt by those loyal to her.

Following this pause, the narrative picks up pace again, with the massacre of both the royal households of Israel and Judah. This leaves one descendant of Omri and Ahab, untouched by the slaughter of the royal princes, in a position to seize power, the daughter of Ahab and wife of Ahaziah, Athaliah.

Athaliah

It is tempting to wonder what relationship existed between those two powerful women. Jezebel gained the most powerful position that a woman in a patriarchal monarchy could possibly attain to. She made the absolute most of the power behind the throne, as wife and mother of kings. She maintained her own religious establishment, and incidents such as Naboth's vineyard (1 Kings 21.1–16) show that she had political clout and could manipulate the legislature as well.

Would she have been pleased that Athaliah not only subverted the patriarchal monarchy, but, for a short time, overturned it? Was Athaliah inspired and educated by Jezebel's example so that, when the opportunity came, she was confident and ruthless enough to seize it? Is it possible that part of Jezebel's legacy was a disruption of male supremacy sufficient for the establishment of a female monarch?

Certainly, the fear of powerful women, evidenced in reactions to feminism in our own time, is that, somehow, they will fatally disrupt the status quo. Look, for example, at Ahasuerus' reaction to Vashti's independence in the book of Esther: 'Queen Vashti has wronged not only the king but also all the officers-of-state and all the peoples inhabiting the provinces of King Ahasuerus. The queen's conduct will soon become known to all the women, who will adopt a contemptuous attitude towards their own husbands. They will say, "King Ahasuerus himself commanded Queen Vashti to appear before him and she did not come." Before the day is out, the wives of the Persian and Median officers-of-state will be telling everyone of the king's officers-of-state what they have heard about the queen's behaviour; and that will mean contempt and anger all round' (Esther 1.16–19). I have quoted at length, since this describes exactly the kind of paranoia that is stirred by independent action on the part of women.

Her reign is narrated extremely briefly in both the Kings and Chronicles accounts, though it lasted six years. To be fair, the same is true of her grandfather Omri. But in Athaliah's case even the normal introduction and ending to kings' reigns is withheld. It would be wonderful to know what this woman ruler accomplished in Judah during those six years. Chronicles condemns her for despoiling the Temple and diverting its revenue to the Baal cult (2 Chronicles 24.6–7). This is not unlikely, given her ancestry. And yet, there must have been more!

The period of the only woman judge over Israel is narrated with barely a comment on her gender in Judges 4, and with a ringing endorsement in the poetic Judges 5. We know that Deborah restored peace and prosperity, and re-established trade. Normal life, which had been disrupted by enemy incursions, was possible once more (Judges 5.10–11).

But we have no way of knowing Athaliah's achievements or failures, or how Judah fared under her leadership. It seems that she was better accepted among the people of the city than those of the rural communities, judging by reactions to her death (2 Kings 11.20). The leaders of the plot to overthrow her are the Temple priesthood, joined either by foreign mercenaries or by Levites drawn in from the rest of Judah, depending on whether you follow Kings or Chronicles.

But the narrators of Kings and Chronicles are only interested in her accession and overthrow. Unknown to Athaliah, an infant male successor, Ahaziah's son, has been saved from the slaughter of the royal house. When he is around seven years old, a coup is carefully arranged and successfully carried out, so successfully that Athaliah has no inkling of what is happening till the child has been proclaimed king in the Temple. Too late, she learns what the shouting is all about, and she is taken off to be killed in the palace. There is no mention of what happened to her body.

Women are by no means the only victims in these stories. The body count in this article is enormous, from the destruction of Gibeah and Jabesh Gilead to the slaughter of Baal-worshippers and royal princes. The narratives occur at highly unstable times. Nor are the women entirely innocent of bloodshed. Jezebel is perfectly capable of murder, and Athaliah comes to the throne by destroying the rest of the royal household (although, puzzlingly, Jehu has already done this, thus creating the conditions by which she can seize power).

But the narratives do demonstrate a wildly asymmetric relationship between men and women, exacerbated by Yahweh's inexplicable silence, or alignment with male soldiers and priests. In this ancient, patriarchal culture, women are expendable in weakness and dangerous in strength. In either case, their lives and their bodies are forfeit.

If this were simply a set of stories about an ancient, patriarchal society, it would be tragic enough. But these stories resonate with the history of the human race right up to the present day. Through genuinely heroic efforts, and remarkable perseverance, women have won the right to be powerful and independent, to have a voice, in many societies. But the old stereotypes still wreak terrible damage.

Women of independence, intelligence and power are still pilloried and feared, and where political systems break down catastrophically, women are still offered up for rape and sacrifice, often in the name of a patriarchal God.

Who can forget the images that came out of Afghanistan under the Taliban, of women cloaked and hidden by threat of mutilation or death, women forbidden any activity or skill that could win them even the most basic dignity or independence? Women and girls, forced into positions of total vulnerability and dependence on fathers, husbands and sons.

Eylem Atakav, writing in *Feminist Theology* about the situation in Turkey, a country which has had a political acceptance of women's rights since 1923, records a poignant conversation with a 68-year-old woman:

I asked her, 'Why did you wait such a long time to start learning how to read and write?' She replied, 'Oh, my father! He did not let me go to school.' 'But, when you got a bit older, what happened?' I said. She answered, 'My brother did not let me learn.' 'Haven't you got married?' I asked. 'I did,' she said. 'But then, my husband did not let me learn how to read and write.' I was amazed with her answers and I could not help but wonder: 'How come you managed to come to these classes now, then?' She answered, with tears cascading from her eyes: 'All three are dead now!'

Where women do find a voice, it is all too often written out of history. I have had the pleasure of editing a book about Free Church Women's Ministry in England and Wales. What comes out in the range of articles and stories is a rich heritage of subversion, social concern, courage, perseverance against mighty odds, which is almost entirely unknown. Why? In large part, because it is a story of women. The official biographies, obituaries and year books do not mention them. Denominational magazines of the time are entirely silent, indeed, some refused to publish articles about women ministers.

And it gets worse. In a terrifying backlash against the advances made by women in recent years, a rising fundamentalist and apocalypticist movement, particularly in the USA, is offering women the chance, like Jephthah's daughter, to sacrifice themselves joyfully, while absolving their menfolk with gentle words: all in the name of the God who remained silent while Jephthah, weeping, slit his daughter's throat, but spoke out to prevent Abraham from doing the same to the son who carried the Promise of God.

Patriarchy is alive and well and living all over the world. These stories from the Bible are not horror tales locked in a mythical past, but examples of what happens to a greater or lesser extent when an asymmetry is permitted to develop between women and men. It is always and ever pernicious.

References

Bach, A. 'Re-reading the Body Politic: Women, Violence and Judges 21', in Athalya Brenner, ed., *Judges: A Feminist Companion to the Bible* (Sheffield: Sheffield Academic Press, 1999), pp. 143–59.

Brenner, A., ed., *Judges: A Feminist Companion to the Bible* (Sheffield: Sheffield Academic Press, 1999).

Büchmann, C. and C. Spiegel, eds, *Out of the Garden: Women Writers on the Bible* (New York: Fawcett Columbine, 1994).

Laffey, A., *Wives, Harlots and Concubines: The Old Testament in Feminist Perspective* (London: SPCK, 1990).

Müllner, I. 'Lethal Differences: Sexual Violence as Violence against Others in Judges 19', in Athalya Brenner, ed., *Judges: A Feminist Companion to the Bible* (Sheffield: Sheffield Academic Press, 1999), pp. 126–42.

Trible, P. 'The Odd Couple: Elijah and Jezebel', in Christina Büchmann and Celina Spiegel, eds, *Out of the Garden: Women Writers on the Bible* (New York: Fawcett Columbine, 1994).

8

Will you Slim for Him or Bake Cakes for the Queen of Heaven?[1]

LISA ISHERWOOD

'It is in part the anxiety of being a woman that devastates the feminine body.'[2]

The 'Slim For Him' and 'Weigh Down' programmes are billion-dollar industries in the USA which extol the religious virtue of being slim and frame fat as sin. This movement is particularly popular with women, and becoming slim for Jesus appears to be almost part of what good Christian womanhood implies in some circles. Of course we should not be too surprised at this, as there have always been women throughout the history of Christianity who have given up eating for Jesus. These programmes would perhaps be less of a concern for me if it was not for the ever increasing number of deaths from anorexia that are sweeping through our world. With 1 in 5 young women affected we are really at crisis point yet the world does not appear to notice. We have young women walking among us whose bones are on display; they have dark shades in their faces, and they walk slowly, only swallow bits of bread and have white spittle on their lips. They move like the living dead of concentration camps, and there is no medical reason for this; they are not stricken with a wasting disorder and they do not live in countries where food is hard to find. Should we be holding crisis talks? The future is

---

1 This article is created from my forthcoming book, *The Fat Jesus* (London: Darton, Longman & Todd, 2008).

2 Simone de Beauvoir, quoted in Kim Chernin, *Womansize: The Tyranny of Slenderness* (London: Women's Press, 1983), p. 66.

being diminished through the death of so many of these bright and able young women – through the suicide of young women. In 2002 a web search revealed 650,000 sites that were to do with eating disorders, 415,000 of which were related to anorexia; they had names such as 'Dying to be Thin', 'Anorexia Nation' and 'Stick Figures'.[3] These sites then, as you can see, were not sites to help people understand and overcome this killer condition but rather to encourage and celebrate this slow suicide. Although, as one site tells us, the successful anorexic is the one that does not die, she is the one who embraces the lifestyle and refers to her condition as 'Ana' or 'Mia' if she is bulimic. These pet names hide a terrible truth which is that emaciated bodies are a lifestyle for millions of young women and girls and one that allows them to be part of a group, indeed to wear the badges. Yes, there are badges, and they are sold on the websites, so the possible death of young people is also serviced by capitalism. The badges read, 'I love my bones', 'Pro Ana', 'Fading Away', 'Starving 4 Perfection', 'Perfect 00 Number', 'Light as a Fairy', 'I want Control'. The website tells us that they also do custom-made charms, key chains, bracelets and necklaces – they also customize photographs for the charms.[4]

It is obvious from the websites that these women and girls can not imagine a life without this eating disorder and they encourage one another with helpful tips about how to deal with the pressure to eat, including how to fool doctors at weigh-ins. People are told if they eat more than 500 calories a day then they should vomit and use laxatives; they are even given tips on how to vomit most effectively. The sites carry inspiring pictures of celebrity anorexics and other pictures of fat women as a warning to people of how they may become if they do not keep to their regimes. It has to be noted that once these sites were discovered in 2002, there was pressure on servers not to provide space. Some responded, but this simply meant that the sites changed server or went more deeply underground with more secretive descriptions. There is ambivalence as to whether they wish others to join or not – some say they

---

3 See www.ohpe.ca

4 See www.italian-charms.com.

would not wish anorexia on their worst enemies while others talk of how to become a good anorexic and advocate it as a worthy way of life. There appears to be an underlying message about being strong and in control which pervades much of the web material.

In truly religious style there are ten commandments for anorexics posted on the websites, called '0Thin Commandments'. The heart of this guide for life is that you can never be too thin, and you have to buy clothes which make you appear as thin as possible. You must understand that being thin is more important than being healthy and 'thou shall not eat without feeling guilty', 'thou shall not eat fattening foods without punishing yourself afterwards' and 'what the scales says is the most important thing'.⁵ A truly religious frame, especially as the outcome of all this, is something that would make the Church Fathers proud: will power and success in controlling the body. These websites, which make perfect sense to those who create them and provide a supportive community, may leave the rest of us a little mystified. As a feminist liberation theologian I find myself asking what has happened that these young women and girls can not imagine their lives without a life-threatening condition? What has happened that they can not engage with their desire and imagination, that these have to be reduced through limiting lifestyles that affect the body and the mind, that make them lethargic, weak and ill? And crucially, what is it in the world that allows so much of this behaviour to go unnoticed – even to be applauded to some extent – and what is it that makes it so hard for our young women to live life in abundance on this planet at this time?

As a body theologian I have some ideas already in answer to this. It is difficult for women to be fully embodied under patriarchy, as has been demonstrated in works relating to sexuality, and it may just be that food is seen as just as physical and sensual, and so to be restricted in women in a way it is not with men. The rhetoric of over-sensual women can, I believe, extend to eating and the enjoyment of food for women. The whole idea of sensuous enjoyment can set off alarm bells in many Christian circles for both sexes. Of course there is a paradox here, since the messianic banquet

5 www.ohpe.ca

which is thought to be at the end for all is heralded through the Eucharist meal shared between believers. Christianity like many religions has in this respect understood the powerful way in which food acts as a language of memory; in celebrating with bread and wine in memory of Christ we are drawing believers into a fully embodied experience. They take into themselves that which they are remembering, and that in turn acts as a series of ongoing memories, their own and those of the generations before them, all of whom shared that same meal with that same memory. Catholics have always believed that a profound change takes place at the Eucharist, not only to the elements themselves but also to those who ingest them; they become drawn into a totality of life that is both public and private. Those who share this table are asked to accept a set of radical values that are in opposition to those of the world and the respectable and established order of things. Those assembled in community around the table are in an act of profound friendship which extends to the whole of the created order. More than the brain is connected here: the whole body is engaged. In the Eucharist food is not just what we do as part of a celebration, it is the core of what it is we are remembering, engaging in – ingesting. I would hate to think that this powerful tool of remembering and embodying could be turned into the ultimate contemporary food ideal, that is to say, heavenly satisfaction and no calories!

Interestingly, the Bible uses food as a sign of many matters of divine importance; it is a sign of love, community and the sacred. This is perfectly in line with the way in which the societies at the time would have understood the significance of food, as we shall see in a moment. For now though the question arises whether, if women are at odds with food through the cultures we have created, are they too at odds with the love, community and sacredness of life itself? If women are not honoured guests at those tables of love, community and the sacred, where are they to find full humanity? Understanding incarnation as I do, then the politics of eating are as important as any other matter – they are a theological issue. Eating, like any other human activity, becomes an incarnational matter too, one that enables or restricts our divine becoming and the glorious explosion of our *dunamis* through our embodied, lived realities. Of course food, who can eat what and when, has always been a matter of religious and cultural significance, and so there seems no better time than now to look at it through feminist incarnational eyes.

In primitive society the act of eating symbolized the partaker being eaten by the community and through sharing food becoming a companion (*com panis*, shared bread), an equal in that society. This simple and basic act then carries historically a great deal of significance – at the heart is a notion of sharing, not exchange, in which subjects are born through the powerful symbolism of food.[6] Perception itself is understood as 'taking in' or 'spitting out' – how we see the world is shaped through this medium. Falk argues that although one became a member of a group self through being eaten by the community and sharing with them, there always remained 'an oral type of self autonomy'[7] – subjectivity and group identity were in harmony through the primitive understanding of food as a symbol. He goes on to argue that with the collapse of the primitive systems, eating changed from an open to a closed activity; from the notion of an eating community to that of a bounded individual eating. He points out that in the nineteenth century, communal eating reappeared as a sign of Utopia. Of course the Christian Church can argue that the eating community never went away within its walls since the eucharistic meal has always been there. There are great symbolic differences between the Roman Catholic and Protestant traditions, in relation to the continued significance of the food shared, which may, I argue, help to explain the outbreak of 'Slim for Him' programmes in Protestant Christianity – a phenomenon that is entirely absent in Roman Catholic circles. Of course this may be as much cultural as it is religious, but then which affects which? Norbert Elias has argued that with the shift from eating community to bounded self there also comes an armouring of the self, a level of control put in place that is not seen in eating communities.[8] This also signals a shift from values lying in the community to a new and imaginary inwardness of emotional experience where value may be found as well as the notion that what is outside may harm this inner

---

6 Pasi Falk, *The Consuming Body* (London: Sage, 1994), p. 20.

7 Falk, *The Consuming Body*, p. 21.

8 Falk, *The Consuming Body*, p. 25.

depth. The shift in understanding of the symbolic nature of food leads to a crucial shift in the place of the individual in relation to others; there is much more emphasis on the bounded self, which in terms of Christian theology can be understood as personal salvation, the relationship between an ethereal God and the self-defined individual. In broader terms this individual sense also disconnects people from the wider community and leaves them vulnerable, indeed primed to be, genocidal consumers by which I mean their bounded selves need things and the cost is not counted – there is no 'eating community' to which they are attached and so only a bounded self to be served.

There is a further shift which may throw some light on this research. Falk suggests that 'the decline of the ritual significance of the meal manifests itself not only in the shift from food to words but also in the informalization of the reciprocal speech acts into conversation in the modern sense of the word'.[9] If we place this alongside Derrida's view that the mouth is highly significant as it signifies an in-between place, a place of both outside and inside, a place where we both find speech and are silenced, then more light may be shed on the differences between Protestant and Roman Catholic meal significance and that relationship to global capitalism and beyond. This may all be far too great a claim, and the research will decide. Protestant theology moves the saving significance from the communal meal to the Word in the book, a speech act, not an embodied act of community, I wonder if it is too much to claim that in such movements as 'Slim for Him', the Word has become informalized as Falk suggests, but to such levels of down-home Godspeak that it becomes gibberish that carries no salvific significance at all. 'You are what you eat', which once carried the power of magical transformations within the eating communities, has now become an individualized soundbite aimed at making us better consumers. The sensual pleasure of the eating community has, as has been suggested, been replaced by a consumer culture trying to satisfy the internal emotional depths that have replaced the community. The power of religious symbolism appears to have been lost, but within certain traditions in Christianity the actions are

9 Falk, *The Consuming Body*, p. 34.

still there – it may then not be too late to transform the people of God back into an eating community, consuming one another in the passionate desire of the divine incarnate. I will explore some of these issues in this article.

The big question is: Who let the skinny girls in?[10]

Skinny girls have not always been welcome at the cultural party, and in religious circles they were at one time almost unknown, a sign of ill omens and scarcity. If we are to believe feminist anthropologists, and I do accept that the jury is out, then there was a time when this ecologically friendly, non-competitive and peaceful relational society existed. It was the time when the divine was imaged as female – but not simply female, rather as a large, fleshy mound of divinity. Among the earliest known depictions of the divine was the Venus of Willendorf, who has mountainous breasts and a vast belly, her hips move round to a huge ass, she is 'a sweeping hill of flesh'.[11] Most such statues show the genitals of these women as huge and genuinely erotic rather than pornographic. Were they fashioned in cultures then where men could face the site of their birth with no fear to their maleness and what part did women play in enabling this? Of course like other fat women since their time they have suffered at the hands of male anthropologists who have considered they had to be pregnant fertility figures because they could simply not be fat goddesses. Here we see the impossibility of divine subjectivity in fat form par excellence even projected back in history. Certainly some of these figures were fertility goddess used in rituals but these 'lovely ladies abounding in the lush landscapes that compose their visions of paradise'[12] also had other functions. The Venus of Laussel has rolls of flesh, curvaceous hips and pendulous breasts, her delicate fingers sit on her

---

10 Eve Ensler, *The Good Body* (London: William Heineman, 2004), p. 20.

11 Richard Klein, 'Fat Beauty', in Jana Braziel and Kathleen LeBesio, *Fatness and Transgression* (Berkeley: University of California Press, 2001), p. 21.

12 Klein, 'Fat Beauty', p. 22.

mountainous belly and her head is turned to suck on what she has in one hand. This is a powerful symbol for women; is it a phallus she has in her hand, or is it the horn of plenty? Can it be transformed from one to the other through women touching their own flesh in the way she touches hers as a sign of the mysterious, powerful beauty that lies within? This divine woman is enfleshed and she rejoices in the horn of plenty – how did we get from here to the skinny Christ, the one who looks emaciated and drawn? What we can see is that with the restriction of the divine female body and its connection to the earth came a restriction of the female body that in turn has led to, or perhaps gone hand in hand with, a philosophy of control of the earth.

But now skinny girls rule, and patriarchal stories are told about the fat girls. As feminist theological method demands, we are going to tell our own stories, beginning with our sisters in sociology who as always provide thought-provoking analysis for theological reflection. One of the most crucial points of information they remind us of is that obesity is not an ahistorical concept, it is like all others rooted in time and place, it is historical, created by the power dynamics of gender, class and race. As a feminist liberation theologian I am well aware that once we name this fact we are some way to undermining the rhetoric. Once we ask about the ideological underpinning of notions of size we begin to move the debate from one of moral weakness, abnormality and pathology on behalf of the fat woman to one of control and power and exclusion on behalf of cultural forces and those who create them. Indeed, the female body has never in human history been viewed as desirable when as 'close to the bone' as it is today. The full-busted, full-bodied, tall, mature woman has been replaced by the anorexic ideal and the worryingly little-girlish waif look that goes with it. What were once viewed as desirable dimples are now called cellulite and are supposed to be a comment on the social if not moral status of the possessor. We have moved from the days when the undergarment industry made inflatable thighs, shoulders and hips for those unfortunate enough to not possess sufficient themselves.[13] Fat is no longer, to the popular mind, viewed as the 'silken layer' that symbolized

---

13 Klein, 'Fat Beauty', p. 2.

strength and energy; it is a sign of social shame and a signal of lack of control.

We appear to be at a time in history when medical advances have made it possible for us in the West to be more optimistic about the fact of embodiment, yet we fail to fully celebrate this new reality. Rather we trivialize our new embodied possibilities through the 'thinness religion which bankrupts us'.[14] It bankrupts us as it makes us despise our bodies because they are not perfect and not indestructible. Where have we heard this before as feminist theologians? Of course the bodies that are despised in this way tend to be female bodies, since man like God is not represented, he represents; he is not gazed at, he gazes; and if he does not like what he sees then culture emerges to please his eye and his psychological needs, to guard his psychic fears – and as always the female body pays the price. In size as in other matters that feminist theologians have turned their gaze to, it seems that we need to move towards a more generous, dignified and realistic way of living in the body, living in harmony with our flesh and not in a battle against it. Of course this may be in danger of giving us a broader (yes, pun intended) world view, and where would patriarchy be then?

Those of us who have been considering matters of embodiment for some time will even by now be hearing some familiar-sounding ideas, the control of women's bodies being one central theme. Seid and others have wondered if the nineteenth-century obsession with controlling female sexuality has been replaced by the desire to control female size in the twentieth and twenty-first centuries.[15] Certainly we can understand that the female body as a signifier of the state of the nation, the culture, the clan, which we now accept as one way in which it is seen, has to be controlled. It has to show that civilization is central to any particular group of people; this is why so many bodily behaviours that are not acceptable in women are tolerated in men, indeed at times almost seen as part of

14 Roberta Seid, 'Too Close to the Bone: The Historical Context for Women's Obsession with Slenderness', in Patricia Fallon, Melanie Katzman and Susan Wooley, eds, *Feminist Perspectives on Eating Disorders* (London: Piatkis, 1999), pp. 3–16, p. 15.
15 Seid, 'Too Close to the Bone', p. 8.

'manly' behaviour, for example belching, spitting and farting. It is the female body that marks the boundaries of a decent society, which is why rape is so common in war, as it breaks down the boundaries and insults and defiles the society, not just the woman, and as such those boundaries have to be policed by patriarchy. The interesting question for feminists today then is why it is the slender, almost anorexic body that signals the edges of a decent society? The 1960s saw Twiggy introduce us to the girl/woman, the body that at 5 foot 7 inches weighed just 5 stone 7 pounds. We have to wonder how this body replaced Marilyn Monroe in her size 16 glory, or before her the rounded bodies of one hundred years ago. We know what has happened, and that is that the ideal body is one that is actually only inhabited by about 5 per cent of the female population, which means that the other 95 per cent feel too fat. It is curious though that this ideal body is in many ways not a female body at all: to be that slender means that all the female secondary sexual characteristics are suppressed; when a person weighs so little there is not much spare for hips, thighs and breasts. This is of course where plastic surgery comes in, and we are given a strange creature, a body that does not have enough natural flesh to signal its femaleness, with large false breasts attached which declare its sexual attractiveness.

Kim Chernin[16] believes there is a direct correlation between the standards set for women's beauty and the desire to control and limit the development of women. She demonstrates this through a survey of the last forty years and the rise of feminist consciousness and the equal rights agenda. Starting in 1960 she reminds us that Marilyn Monroe, all size 16 of her, was the icon of female beauty. This was the decade in which women protested Miss World, since women paraded and were judged by the passive male gaze. It was also the same decade in which anorexia as we know it emerged – there is a debate about whether fasting saints can be understood as modern-day anorexics – and spread very rapidly among those who wished to work in what had been male preserves. In the 1970s bulimia began to be noticed and Weight Watchers opened its

---

16 Kim Chernin, *Womansize: The Tyranny of Slenderness* (London: Women's Press, 1983), p. 97.

doors; it had of course been preceded by diet workshops as early as 1965. In the mid-1970s the 'addict' status of being overweight was set in place through the opening of Overeaters Anonymous, which of course sits well with the psychopathological view of women and weight that was prevalent at that time. Chernin notes that these two very different movements which were competing for the minds and hearts of women, the Women's Movement and the diet industry, had very different languages for women, which she believes highlight social concerns beyond the body.[17] The diet industry spoke of shrinking, contracting, losing, loss, lessening and lightweightness in relation to women and their bodies, while the Women's Movement spoke of large, abundant, powerful, expansive, development, growth, acquiring weight, acquiring gravity and creating wider frames in relation to the lives of women. Interestingly of course women who embraced either of these options were doing so in order to make sense of the world they inhabited, yet the bodily permissions for them could not have been more different. While those entering the Women's Movement were aware that they entered a political struggle, those who joined diet groups had no idea that this is what they also were doing; this was the case as they entered the domain of the body that was highly symbolically charged and understood the body as something to be shaped according to the political ideals of wider society. Of course this makes it appear that the worlds were divided along very clear lines, but the truth may be nearer to the contradiction in the minds of most women. In truth most women are committed to the idea of their own growth and development, while many are also concerned with the notion of full participation in society, whether they are feminists or not; and at the same time our bodies find it all too easy to be obedient to the conventional world, feminist and non-feminist alike. Chernin's focus on the emergence of the diet industry alongside the Women's Movement is very reminiscent of Mary Daly's claim that the worst excesses of gynaecology emerged at the time of First Wave Feminism; that too was a rhetoric of what would be best for women, how the real woman should be and a wider rhetoric about health concerns and so on. We would do well not to

---

17 Chernin, *Womansize*, p. 100.

forget that the removal of the clitoris was medical practice in Britain until 1947; the reasons for its use were to calm women down, to make them less feisty and to rein in their aspirations to have a place in the public domain. Of course I am not suggesting that this was widely used. There were enough women in the world who did not suffer that fate to demonstrate that its use was limited; but that it existed at all as a possibility and for the reasons given is something to think about from the point of view of body politics. The parallels between what Daly and Chernin suggest are striking and of course in both cases women have their bodies cut, shaped and reduced – for those with eyes to see this is no hidden political agenda, although in truth it probably does develop under the weight of much unconscious but deep-seated anxiety about women's bodies.

Our culture still does not embrace the idea of whole and empowered women, and so the stress and contradictory pressure on women is immense. This may help to explain why in an era of feminism we see an abundance of overweight women alongside emaciated bodies. This signals to me that the underlying questions to do with women and bodies have not been addressed even by secular feminism and its invaluable contribution to the body politic. We live in a world where female fat is considered to be expendable flesh, while we add silicone to women's bodies in order to make them sexy. The reality is that female flesh is sexy, and historically there has been a linking of fatness and fertility, which has some medical basis since fat regulates reproduction. Over one-fifth of women who exercise to shape their bodies have menstrual irregularities and diminished fertility; this kind of hormonal imbalance can lead to ovarian cancer and osteoporosis.[18] The battle against female flesh is in so many ways a battle against nature itself, and this will be familiar ground to feminist theologians who have long ago identified the dualism of the fathers as the ground that diminishes us, in this case literally. The medics who join the war are quick to talk of damage and slow to tell the other side of the dieting culture that we are all part of. In India for example even the poorest women eat some 1,400 calories a day, while women in the West on the Hilton Head Diet eat 600 calories fewer than that. This puts them

18 Naomi Wolf, 'Hunger', in Fallon, Katzman and Wooley, pp. 94–111, p. 99.

on a lower calorific intake than was calculated by the Nazi regime to sustain human functioning in concentration camps such as Treblinka. Further, during the war in Holland, emergency rations were released when people lost more than 25 per cent of their body weight. This is particularly worrying when we realize that many average-sized women in the West are actually trying to lose that amount of body weight.[19] Even today the UN Health Organization calculates that daily calorific intake of 1,000 means there is semi-starvation (they do not emphasize any great difference in necessary calorific intake between women and men) and with it many characteristics of famine such as tension, irritability, preoccupation with food and loss of libido. The famine literature provided by a range of agencies identifies these behaviours as signals of crisis; diet industries associate them, as lack of will power on behalf of individuals, with some kind of psychopathology. Further, there is compelling evidence emerging that links dieting with the development of eating disorders, and as we know, these are ravaging the bodies of our young women. Despite the certainty with which we are told fat is unhealthy, the reality is far from certain, and many of the additional factors that we find connected with weight have to be calculated in too, such as poverty, class and race. However, it does appear to be arguable that dieting can cause many of the illnesses we are told it prevents, such as hypertension, high cholesterol and diabetes. There is compelling evidence that those who diet and then regain weight have a much higher mortality rate than those who never lose weight. In addition of course with the mounting anti-fat feeling in the West, fat people are suffering more stress than ever before. This is beginning at an early age with children as young as nine believing they are too fat and indeed actually hating their bodies. We should not be surprised at this body hatred by young girls since they are bombarded with images from the media of models and actresses many of whom are already anorexic and surgically altered. Models are now 23 per cent lighter than average women, whereas a generation ago that differential was 8 per cent. This certainly means that these women are not healthy, and that they create a very unhealthy image for our young girls. In addi-

19 Wolf, 'Hunger', p. 98.

tion to being of less weight than is healthy, they are also airbrushed and computer-altered to enhance their looks. However, people do not take the time to explain to the young that these are not real women at all, they are computer- and surgical-composites of what were once flesh and blood women. They may no longer be real in any meaningful sense, but they nevertheless fuel the body images of the young and the not-so-young, they become the role models, unattainable by real women of feminine beauty, just as the Virgin Mary was the unattainable role model before them. Just as the Virgin created a tension in us that left us vulnerable to the Church and the ways of male-inspired spiritual direction and the mutilation of body and psyche that often ensued, so these 'not quite women' leave us vulnerable to manipulation by another great phallic patriarchal power, the big business. The more tension we feel, the more we consume in order to ease that tension and the better the market likes it. Our circle of self-destruction is their circle of assured markets and captive psyches. Keeping women in a state of dis-ease with their bodies may be good for the markets, but it is very bad for the women and girls. Naomi Wolf comments that the obsession with thinness is not about beauty at all but about female obedience. I wish to argue that this can be understood as both obedience to patriarchy, undermining female confidence and neutralizing women's power in society, and also obedience to the markets; the cult of thinness works on many different levels, and unsurprisingly none really advantages women. It may not be too great an exaggeration to say that for many women being a woman is about believing oneself to be too fat and spending time and energy to monitor that situation. This is certainly a great distraction from taking one's place as an equal in society!

Jesus diet for your sins

It was not really until the 1950s that the explicit link between size and religion once again raised its head, and this time it was well and truly a Protestant phenomenon with all the trade marks that one would expect. In 1957, Charlie Shedd wrote a book entitled *Pray Your Weight Away*, in which it is claimed that fatties are people who literally can weigh their sin.[20] Fat he argued is the embodiment of disobedience to God since it prohibits the Holy Spirit from penetrating one's heart – it can not get through the layers of fat. Shedd says that God did not ever imagine fat, and his justification for this statement is that the slender are those who succeed in the world. At this early stage the huge responsibility of women in this matter was emerging because Shedd dedicates six chapters of his book to explaining how women ruin other people's diets through their out-of-control gluttonous behaviour. Mothers are particularly to blame in his view since they set in place very sinful patterns in their children; they are the ruin of their children. Victor Kane some ten years later in his *Devotion for Dieters* was declaring that our birthright is to be firm, hard and godly, not flabby.[21] Here we see the phallic God of whom James Nelson speaks in *Body Theology* writ large on the bodies and in the psyches of believers.[22] What is quite striking amidst the rhetoric of food being of the devil is that there is no mention of the starving. It does not seem inconceivable to have a balancing rhetoric about sharing if one is to suggest that eating too much is a sin. However, there is absolutely no mention, and the purpose of restraint in eating is to overcome the devil in a very personal way with no social analysis at all. Among the books that appeared were the strangely named *Jesus Diet for your Sins* and *Heal Yourself for Christ's Sake*, both of which claimed that the dieter would be more use to God the slimmer they became because the path is narrow and one has to be able to get along it. As amusing as this may seem, there was no humour intended. Two books that appeared in the 1970s, Joan Cavanagh's *More of Jesus; Less of Me* and C. S. Lovett's *Help Lord, the Devil Wants Me Fat* both sold 100,000 copies,[23] each signalling in a rather worrying way that this strange theology had a following. Lovett tells us that diets do not work because they come at the problem from the

20 R. Marie Griffiths, *Born Again Bodies* (Berkeley: University of California Press, 2004), p. 166.

21 Griffiths, *Born Again Bodies*, p. 167.

22 James Nelson, *Body Theology* (Louisville: Westminster John Knox Press), 1992.

23 Griffiths, *Born Again Bodies*, p. 168.

outside when actually it is the devil holding us internally captive; a short fast rectifies this by breaking the hold of the devil, and then a diet will work because the Holy Spirit is now inhabiting where the devil once was. This is a perverse theology of food demons that it is hard to believe people accept in the twentieth and twenty-first centuries, but they do. This can be further attested by the fact that by 1981 there were 5,000 churches and 100,000 participants in the new 3D (Diet, Discipline, Discipleship) programme that replaced Weight Watchers for the religious. This was a programme set up by Carol Showalter in 1973 and was one of a number of such programmes aimed at overcoming the sin of fatness. So seriously was fat seen as sin that the Overeaters Victorious programme set up in Minnesota in 1977 had to close in shame when the founder Neva Coyle gained weight.[24] These groups could not be led by sinners. Other groups such as Step Forward and Jesus is the Weigh give a hint through the names of their theological underpinning: all one has to do is step up to Jesus and he becomes all in all for a person who no longer needs to eat excessively, the converse of this being that if one fails to lose weight then faith not metabolism is the issue. They do not exactly resort to knocking out people's front teeth as in days of old, but the guilt and shame are perhaps more crippling. One of the most successful groups has been First Place, which has a simple theology; put God first and the weight will drop off.

There is an even more worrying aspect to this diet industry, which is that the true Christian woman is not only becoming narrower but also has to be more beautiful if she is truly to reflect the heroic grandeur of her God. Along with the cookbooks, the devotional books and the fitness videos, there are also the beauty books. They tell us that God is beautiful, healthy and vital, and so the women who follow him also have to be; they must spend time each day making themselves as beautiful as they can as an advertisement for their God. Indeed, if they can provoke envy in other women this is a good thing, as it may bring them to Christ in the hope that they too can look this good in Christ.[25] To look good is Godly. Cynthia

---

24 Griffiths, *Born Again Bodies*, p. 170.
25 Griffiths, *Born Again Bodies*, p. 217.

Culp Allen and Charity Allen Winters have written a book for the beauty-conscious Christian called *The Beautiful Balance of Body and Soul*, in which they provide Bible passages with each beauty tip. Their justification for writing the book is that they believe you would not wrap a priceless gift in a dingy grocery bag, so 'Why represent Jesus to others without looking confident, put together and beautifully appealing inside and out?'[26] Neva Coyle and Marie Chapion have added to this aspect of the industry with their *Free to Be Thin* book (I assume this was before Neva gained weight and brought shame on herself and the project!), in which they castigate women for the eating problems of the entire family, seeing it as the fault of a lazy and selfish homemaker. However, they end their book quoting from the Song of Songs telling the readers that once they have overcome the wickedness of overeating, their reward will be to hear Jesus, who will be saying, 'Behold you are beautiful my love. Behold you are beautiful, I will hie me to the mountain of myrrh and frankincense. You are all fair my love, there is no flaw in you.'[27] The eroticism of these statements is never fully acknowledged, and certainly the passion of the text itself is almost expunged through a sweet and innocent approach to what the text is actually suggesting. These Jesus dieters could never face that much embodied passion – it is after all what they are fighting, through control of their appetites. There is however a bold message that just as God and Jesus are beautiful, so the good believer who has managed to overcome the demon in food will also be beautiful, and this beauty will be physical and the cause of great admiration by Jesus himself. There will be no flaw in the true believer, a worrying statement of theology.

The connection between Jesus and physical beauty, health and vitality has a sinister reverse side which is the way in which many of these fundamentalist Protestant groups view the matter of physical disability. In short, they see it as demonic, which we can understand from the way in which they represent health and fitness in their diet industries. As Christians have viewed God as perfect in every way, they have, to their eternal shame, viewed disability as imperfect and at times demonic.

26 Griffiths, *Born Again Bodies*, p. 223.
27 Griffiths, *Born Again Bodies*, p. 221.

Women with disabilities have carried an extra burden since they are viewed as doubly transgressive. Many of those burnt as witches had no greater deformity than a third nipple, the so-called 'devil's teat'. The conflation of sin and disability is a devastating error that Christianity would do well to repent, but many of the groups I have looked at do not seem anywhere near such a repentance. Indeed, they are vehement in their advocacy of the ideal, perfect, fit and healthy God who demands the same from his followers. What are his followers to do if they do not have it within their capacity to become the model of fully healthy and functioning people?

No examination of this multi-million-dollar industry would be complete without a serious look at Gwen Shamblin's Weigh Down programme, which has to be the most successful of its kind. Shamblin hit the headlines with her bold assertion that fat people do not go to heaven because grace does not go down to the pigpen.[28] In short then, Shamblin was offering slim hips and eternal salvation because of her contention that the fatness of Americans is due to a profound spiritual crisis. Her book *The Weigh Down Diet* has sold millions of copies, and the 12-week programme that she has developed is being used by over 30,000 groups throughout the USA. She asserts that people have to eat thin, which means picking at food and leaving most of it, but most importantly of all they have to acknowledge that they are truly suffering from a spiritual hunger which they are confusing with a physical hunger. Stop running to the fridge and turn to God instead. Of course, having examined from a feminist point of view in chapter 1 why women eat and how female size is viewed, it may be tempting to translate 'spiritual hunger' for 'hunger for justice and equality' and then conclude that Shamblin may have something valuable here. I think I will wait a while before I reach that conclusion. The first point that makes me stop in my tracks is the assertion by Shamblin that her programme can be used to overcome other forms of ungodly behaviour, not just eating, such as alcohol abuse, drug abuse, homosexuality and claims of wives to be on an equal footing with their

---

28 Griffiths, *Born Again Bodies*, p. 1.

husbands.[29] All these things show the depth to which people will go to change everything but themselves, she tells us, and all these sins can be overcome by turning to God alone. She and her followers do not believe that even the fundamentalist churches have been tough enough in their message, and so she started a church of her own called the Remnant Fellowship.

The advice Shamblin gives is very practical, even recommending the best way to eat food, for example sort through the pile of crisps you have on your plate looking for those with the most salt on, eat one or two as you go and leave the rest. She is not at all concerned about food wastage, quoting Exodus for her justification: God turned stored food into maggots. In the book she writes, 'If it rots or is wasted – so what. He has more for you.'[30] Perhaps this more than anything illustrates not God's abundant love but her American myopia and indeed arrogance. Shamblin does with her outspokenness allow us to see what is often at the heart of these religious diet programmes, and it appears to be a total lack of concern for anyone outside their own narrow world. Of course the 'have it and leave it' mentality is to show the strength of faith, but in my view it simply shows the worst form of consumerist anti-Christian religion it is possible to conceive of. However, to hear Shamblin speak is to hear a conversion experience, but one that took some time. God revealed the programme to her gradually, more in the manner of the Exodus from Egypt than the road to Damascus. She prayed for guidance at each step and slowly added more spirituality to a programme that had been to begin with a purely secular diet regime. Thus was born the Weigh Down Diet! Prayer has also allowed her to add jewellery products, bookmarks and CDs of her son Michael singing Christian pop to the Weigh Down industry.

Shamblin is very critical of the secular diet industry, seeing it as in the grip of Satan, because as she explains when one is in it there is no requirement to take the mind off food and direct it to God. Counting calories we are told is the work of the devil. The Bible on the other hand provides a

---

29 www.rebeccamead.com, p. 1.
30 www.rebeccamead.com, p. 3.

diet manual for us, the fatted calf proving that God approves of filet mignon, and low carbohydrate diets being in her view blasphemous because Jesus said 'I am the bread of life', so we too should eat bread and lots of it. Looking to Leviticus she notes that there is a grain offering made of oil, flour and salt and she declares with glee, 'My that grain offering is very similar to our present day Frito!'[31] Shamblin does suggest that people eat in moderation, which is good, and she also notes that the secular diet industry makes a great deal of money from diet foods. She has not yet branched out in this way, but she also says that the only exercise a person needs is getting on their knees to pray. Further, for Shamblin, her programme is a proof of the existence of God: people wish to lose weight, they believe they lose weight, therefore God exists. It really is as easy as that, except of course, she tells us, when they go to other churches they are encouraged to eat with all the bring-and-buy sales, and there is not a firm enough line about the evils of weight – this was what made her form her own church.

Shamblin also entices people into the programme with the promise of holy romance. She tells almost all female audiences that God is a handsome and charming, loving and rich husband; he is the hero they have all been dreaming of. As a feminist liberation theologian, there are a number of things here that worry me, not least the total buy-in to the hierarchy of rich, handsome, hero. I hear Audre Lorde declare that the master's tools will never dismantle the master's house, and here we see the master's tools set out before us; there is no questioning of social and economic hierarchies and the accepted assumption that women who become slender will have access to all these things – not just as a divine love affair but also in their lives. We have already seen that this appears to be true, with slender women having easier access to the trappings of patriarchal hierarchy, including the rich husband. There is something very disturbing for my Christian heart in this celebration of the divine consumer husband. Shamblin tells us that she has a crush on the Father, but on hearing these words I do not assume that we will be entering the world of

---

31 www.rebeccamead.com, p. 7.

Margery Kempe,[32] the medieval mystic who through her sexual relationship with Father and Son turned the reality of her gendered narrow world on its head. Margery entered into a sensual relationship with the Godhead that consumed her and actually turned her from a woman of vain glory into a passionate woman for justice and female empowerment. I do not see that happening with Shamblin's romance with God. Shamblin says she takes this rich husband of hers on shopping trips because she likes to dress for him but also because he has superb taste and is amazing at colour co-ordination. On her trips she asks if God likes her outfit, and then she buys – and these are designer clothes because as she says of God, 'He is fabulous, wonderfully good looking. He is so powerful, so rich, so famous. He has got on designer clothes.'[33] One must not let the side down and so must dress accordingly. This appeals to Shamblin's audience of mainly middle-class white women of a certain age who also find themselves swooning along with her over their heartthrob God. This may be dieting for Jesus, but it is doing so in a very classy way, with social advantage taken for granted in the rhetoric and assumed in the outcomes. The position of fashion accessory on the arm of God also extends to how Shamblin views the role of women; but there is a paradox here: Shamblin believes that women should not preach or carry a prophecy, and so she is sad that there were no men to carry her Weigh Down message; she can only make theological sense of this as a sign of the end time. She takes as her guide on this the book of Joel that says God will pour out his spirit on men and women alike in the last days.

Shamblin is not alone in her connecting the Jesus diet industry with the last days. On a website entitled *No fatties in heaven*[34] we are told that it was the Tribulation (the last days) that made this Christian and would-be thin person understand God's demands that we be thin. When the Tribulation comes will he/she really be able to go hungry and enable others to eat? The real answer seemed to be no, and so this called for preparation in this life in order to face what will come – what was needed

32 See Lisa Isherwood, *The Power of Erotic Celibacy* (London: T & T Clark, 2006).

33 www.rebeccamead.com

34 www.cust.idl.net/no fatties in heaven

was a faith that would work in the face of starvation.[35] The way to this was desperate prayer, prayer of the addict who would have everything destroyed by the devil because of a desire to eat. The biblical comfort for this believer was the verse, 'Woe unto you that are full for you shall hunger' (Luke 6.25), as it revealed that discipline was required now in order not to be left floundering at the Tribulation. In addition of course there are no fat people in heaven, and no forgiveness for them either it seems, because the fat have to remain fat for all eternity and watch the beautiful and the slim for that eternity, which would, it is assumed, be an eternal punishment. Weight loss also gives us a measuring stick by which to work out whether we are becoming disciplined people who deserve to survive the Tribulation at all. It is amazing that end-time thinking even affects the size of our hips! This form of thinking appears to be infecting the political Right in the USA with potentially devastating global consequences, as we know there is a push in certain corners to enable and speed up a bloodbath in the Middle East, since those of an end-time disposition understand the setting up of Israel to be the beginning of the end in a very positive way. We must not forget that those who hold an end-time view actually welcome it and will indeed work through politics and religion to hasten its coming. Such people in power depend on the votes of the masses, and as we know the electorate in the USA appears to be more concerned about candidates' moral positions on things than we appear to be in the UK. I do not really think it is too exaggerated to say that there are now thousands of women across the USA who are getting a diet of old-time/end-time religion along with their weigh-in, and they will slide their reduced bodies into voting booths for many years to come. Whether we like to admit it or not, President Bush has acted of late under the influence of end-time thinking, and so we do have an example of where that can take us. We also see that he has placed representatives in the United Nations and observers in the European Union who are actively attempting to subvert many of the gains of women and minority people; this too is end-time thinking. Religious fundamentalism is built on the backs of women who by divine decree are confined to the home to

---

35 Isherwood, *The Power of Erotic Celibacy*, p. 3.

rear children and serve men, an agenda that is also lurking in the Weigh Down programmes and others where women are seen as responsible for the size and shape of all their family. It is no wonder then that this religious/political Right is concerned about the United Nations and what it sees as its liberal policy-making,[36] which is to say its concern for the rights of women and children. The Christian Right believes that children's rights undermine parental authority and, for example, that the 'Convention for the Elimination of Discrimination Against Women' undermines and even destroys family life; they of course also wish to overturn any equality laws to do with homosexuality. We do not have to go very far to see this divisive thinking: we can see it in Shamblin's claim that her programme can be extended to other devil-inspired realities, such as women seeking equality, and homosexuality. There are links here that may make us uncomfortable but that we would be unwise to ignore. End-time thinking, as unbiblical as so much of it is in the finer detail, is becoming a big political threat, and if we are to ingest it along with a consumer-driven crush on God then we need to ask some hard questions.

It is difficult not to totally dismiss Shamblin as a lunatic, because the way in which she speaks of the Bible, faith, the Trinity and the body are nothing short of laughable. What stops me laughing is the message of advanced capitalism that lurks beneath this holy foolery, and of course as always keeping that in place, the gendered message of inequality. This is no laughing matter and really does deserve some theological response. Shamblin is not a theologian, but it seems increasingly these days that does not matter, she has a received message and strangely for a counter-cultural gospel, the message fits the dominant paradigm perfectly with the occasional religious curio thrown in such as Bible eating habits. I have for some time now been suggesting that the bodies of women within a counter-cultural incarnational religion are powerful sites of resistance to the worst excesses of patriarchy as practised through our

36 See Doris Buss and Didi Herman, *Globalising Family Values: The Christian Right in International Politics* (Minneapolis: University of Minnesota Press, 2003).

economic and social systems, and so such handing over of women as this programme makes possible fills me with horror as well as sadness. The radical gospel of equality that feminist theology has demonstrated to be close to the message of the early Jesus movement is nowhere to be seen here in gender, economics, class or, as we shall see, race. I almost dare to say Shamblin's Weigh Down group could be white supremacist simply because they are declaring a gospel of superior beauty and bearing which does exclude black people, whether deliberately or not. They would I think counter this claim by the few black women who appear on websites testifying to their transformed lives through surrender to Jesus and the Weigh Down Diet. As we know from years of postcolonial study, the discourse of whiteness goes deeper than this and even includes black people in its insidious projections.

Griffiths is among the first to point out to us that beneath the façade of the normal and natural beautiful body lurk some very concerning assumptions about beauty itself. She writes that Christian diet cultures have a central role in 'the reproduction and naturalization of a racialised ideal of whiteness purged of the excesses associated with non-white cultures'.[37] Right from the early days of the Christian diet literature, examples of the 'coloured' woman were used to show that indeed this was not 'for them', since they could not really understand what was being suggested. The 'otherness' of non-white and also non-middle-class women was used to illustrate the elect nature of those who could and should adopt the diet culture. It is spelt out very clearly by Anne Ortlund in her book *Disciplines of the Beautiful Woman*. In this classic work of white supremacy she states that 'primitives' are not expected to be slim, they are 'plump and dark', and she has witnessed it herself; she writes, 'I have bent down and stooped into a thatched hut deep in the jungles of South America and seen a cotton print dress hanging inside, the joy of that little primitive pudding-bag-shaped woman. Someone will have parted with it and through missionaries bearing the love of Jesus, it came to her.'[38] And what else came to her, I find myself yelling at the page! Just

37 Griffiths, *Born Again Bodies*, p. 225.
38 Quoted in Griffiths, *Born Again Bodies*, p. 227.

how embedded this toxic rhetoric of supremacy is within certain kinds of Christianity is I think made very clear by Ortlund's utterances, and although many of the Jesus dieters today would not be so obvious and indeed may be surprised when told they too were peddling a white supremacist agenda, it is still there to see. They may be tempted to defend themselves by saying they are writing for a white audience due to the historic African American lack of concern for matters of size – their community has not stigmatized the large in the same way that the white society has done. This however would in my view only be half a defence that fails to acknowledge the ideology of thinness that is linked to that of civilization and breeding.

The new Christian diets are meant to carry a truly democratic lifestyle that would appeal to American sensibilities and ideas deeply embedded about their country and its truly open mentality. We all have bodies, and with the right amount of will power we can all be thin. In reality of course we have seen that the Christian diet industry is profoundly class- and racially infected. Through its rhetoric fat people have become excluded, eroticized and made primitive, all of which symbolizes filth and ungodliness, which is all perfectly in keeping with a message that believes eternal salvation hinges on it. The Christian diet industry is dealing with the weight of a sinful world which appears to manifest as poor and black more often than anything else! The moral rhetoric about fat people has become embedded in fundamentalist theology which as we have seen in its Southern manifestations is already prone to racism because of its divisive dualistic underpinning that has never been tempered by liberal theological rhetoric. The so-called democratizing potential of the Christian diet industry is in reality another form of colonialism, it peddles an idea of beauty that is white all the way to its polished and manicured finger nails. Like so many good ides I believe we have to be careful before we ingest its rhetoric because we literally will be embodying our own oppression. There is no diversity in this model, as indeed there has not been in such ideas as the universal Christ who lives and breathes in metaphysical absolutes, and it is this Christ who has been overcome through calls for justice and equality. He may now be masquerading as a slim, white, affluent Christian woman but he still needs rooting out. It is also worth mentioning at this stage that this model is also heterosexual. Studies show that lesbians have to date been less affected by diet cultures than their heterosexual sisters, and whatever the positive reasons for this no doubt it will just be seen as another ungodly rebellion by those in the Jesus-diet camp. The Christian diet culture assumes and, one could even suggest, promotes a vanilla/girlie form of heterosexuality, and where it does deal with men there is a lord-and-master rhetoric. The men need to be slim in order to best discharge their manly duties of taking care of their families through hard work. Further their fasting can turn them into 'fortresses of flesh that protects the woman you love',[39] a reinstatement of the phallic God if ever I heard one. This is not at all surprising given the type of theology that underpins these programmes, and as we have seen Shamblin even believes that her diet programme can help correct other forms of deviance such as homosexuality and the desire of women to be equal with their husbands. The old binaries are in place in her system and they carry with them the hierarchical realities. Dangerously these are now linked with right-wing politics like never before, and the new control in the home is mirrored by a new desire for social control; the same men who fast to be fortresses at home also do so to aid George Bush with his new colonial enterprise.[40]

In the light of this, perhaps I should not find the consumer capitalism that is embedded in many of these programmes as truly disturbing as I do. After all, global markets are what the right wing are after. God is turned into an 'ultimate shopper' with great taste, so that he is a heavenly fashion consultant. His pockets are deep; he will provide you with the funds to be beautiful so that his name may be praised. What kind of Christ is emerging here, and should we be too surprised? Perhaps we should not, because this is really only an extension of the God who sees disability as sin and is therefore one of the beautiful people. We see before us the very God and Christ that liberation theology has unmasked as unjust and exploitative; it is as though the last forty years of experiential theology never existed. Although perhaps worryingly there is an

39 Griffiths, *Born Again Bodies*, p. 242.
40 Griffiths, *Born Again Bodies*, p. 243.

experiential element lurking here, but of the kind that never gets beyond what is good for the individual. The modern Christian diet rhetoric has moved on from notions of health based in good and bad food to the idea of prosperity: it is rare to read in the literature that one diets and gets healthy full stop. This health, and beauty, is not only the key to eternal salvation but also to a very good life here. The bodies of women, and some men, are being used in just the way Mary Douglas tells us they are used to create a bounded identity for a group, in this case the saved. But of course what is also happening is the creation of the body of Christ, and this Christ is being projected onto the world through the practices of the believers. In asking what this Christ looks like the modern-day theologian is not even asking if such a Christ actually ultimately exists, but rather what are the lived consequences of a Christ imaged in such a way? For feminist liberation theology Christ is always ethical rather than an abstract set of metaphysics. What world emerges if we lived 'as if' this diet Christ called us to do his will? A very narrow one devoid of the glorious rainbow of incarnational diversity and divine potential that is our birthright; a very politically aggressive one attempting to project the pale face of vanilla womanhood on a global screen for the economic advantages that such a projection ensures.

Sensuous revolutions

As Nelle Morton told us, then, the journey is home; but under the weight of a disempowering diet rhetoric this is a journey back to our bodies, to a place of once again inhabiting this vacant flesh that holds within it the divine incarnate. We are asked to once again touch and revel in our passions and desires, to touch, taste and see it is good, this invitation is laid out before us at the eucharistic table. A table that has become sterile and bounded but that in its inception was the radical space of sensuous engagement and commitment. It was here that the exchange model of a patriarchal society was challenged and the sharing of bread and politics ensured that patriarchy would always be challenged through this radical sharing. It is here that we are invited to refuse the assimilation of norms and to instead find counter-cultural ways of radical praxis, of living 'as if', that is to say as if the fullness of divine/human incarnation was enfleshed. It is through these repeated incarnational performances that the co-creation and co-redemption become lived realities.

Monica Hellwig has argued that the way in which we view the 'hunger of the world' should always be within the context of the Last Supper which was, as she sees it, the foundational meal of Christianity.[41] The context was one of oppression, and the act of communal eating a commitment of ultimate fellowship, the kind that would be embodied through these continued acts of eating and radical praxis. I would like to suggest that what one ingested was the passion of Christ understood not as a final sacrifice but as a radical way of living counter-cultural praxis through the skin. We are fed with incarnation possibilities and sustained to ever widen the boundaries of this contained patriarchal order that does nothing to embrace and allow for the flourishing of our divine/human reality. Hunger, Hellwig tells us, is a powerful experience that drives us to action, that is if it is not self-induced and prolonged, when as we have seen it brings with it inertia. A feminist Christ wants us to hunger and indeed shares that hunger with us. But this is not a desperate search for satisfaction, it is rather a continued commitment to expanding the edges through sharing and creative engagement with each other and with the resources of the planet. It is a traditional theological understanding among those from a high sacramental strand of Christianity to see connections between the feeding of the five thousand and the Last Supper. The former is seen to be a precursor to the latter, which is understood to be the ultimate food. I do not wish to spend time arguing the point, rather I wish to see the connection lying in a radical commitment to feeding the world when we eat from that eucharistic table. As we have seen, there is enough for each person on the planet to have 2,500 calories a day, in short enough that no one need die from lack of food. This commitment then is political rather than one that encourages us to starve ourselves: this does nothing. We are compelled to demand fairer production

---

41 Monica Hellwig, *The Eucharist and the Hunger of the World* (London: Sheed & Ward, 1992).

policies, better quality food, more equitable distribution and enough food on all tables, food that we eat with passion, with joy, with embodied pleasure, not praise God for his blessing and then bin it! The Fat Jesus then does not wish us to control our desire for food but rather to passionately engage with a desire for the world to eat and to celebrate the life that is enhanced through this abundance. Some years ago the theologian Tissa Balasuriya[42] urged Catholics to suspend the celebration of the Eucharist until such time as all were equal at the table. His argument was that around that table we proclaim the inclusion and equality of all in a world that in reality is unequal and excluding; his solution was then a suspension as a political act akin to individual hunger strikes in order to bring to the attention of global governments the need for radical change. I understand his motivation and indeed can see a place for such an action, but looking at the question from the perspective of women does rather put another light on it. Women around the world either through dieting cultures or because of the unequal distribution of food are every day the ones who do not get enough, and so asking that they get less, even in symbolic terms, does not seem the most radical praxis. Indeed, it is the power of the symbolic nature of food in the lives of women and by extension in patriarchal society that has been the focus of this book; women have carried much patriarchal cultural and psychic baggage, which has expressed itself in wanting less flesh on women's bones and demanding that women are less in society. Within this context then celebratory eating is a revolutionary step in itself, but of course when we realize what this may mean for women who will also be reconnecting with their desires and sense of power through this passionate eating, we begin to understand just how revolutionary this is.

We perhaps need to follow the example of Jesus of Nazareth and use food and drink in such a way that we too will be called gluttons! After all, he was proclaiming the kingdom of God through his eating and drinking with many of the outcasts of his day. Here then was a statement in itself about the nature of the world he asked us to commit to in sharing his

---

42 Tissa Balasuriya, *The Eucharist and Human Liberation* (London: SPCK, 1988).

table. However, I think this has other implications too, which are fundamental to who we are. We fail to see that our appetites can be an asset
since they reveal to us the centrality of desire in our full functioning as a
human person; desire is one of the deepest principles of life.[43] Carter
Heyward and I believe desire is the heart of our divine/human reality
because it most fully connects us with ourselves and also propels us outward into relationality, mutuality and vulnerability.[44] It is then something
to be embraced, and there has been a false and damaging distinction
between one's desire for God and one's desire for the 'things of the
world'. This desire is rooted in our *dunamis*, our erotic/divine natures,
and as such needs to be acknowledged and celebrated in a Christian life.
It is this attempt to control passion within Christian theology and religious practice that has actually badly backfired by cutting us off from our
deepest passions in order that we become disconnected from each other.
This has meant in the area of sexuality for example that the behaviours
that the churches meant to stop through a warning against passion have
simply increased and become even more meaningless because we are
not rooted in who we are. It is as though we are in a dream and simply
inhabiting our bodies rather than fully living in them. Of course, when we
are this disconnected we are also at the mercy of the manipulation of the
markets since we are adrift from our 'guts' (which is where the Gospels
tell us the true Christian life happens, *metanoia*, the word for conversion,
meaning a turning over of one's guts) and constantly in need of something to supply meaning. As we have seen, the markets are only too will-
ing to supply any range of meaning, all of which leave us craving more,
whether this is because of the addictive additions to food or simply
because of the superficiality of the meaning supplied.

Shannon Jung reminds us that eating and food have always been an
expression of humans' relationship with God, and he also argues that
they are an expression of our deepest values. He claims, 'eating is a spiritual practice that reminds us who we are'[45] not only in our own bodies

---

43 Shannon Jung, *Food for Life* (Minneapolis: Fortress Press, 2004), p. 14.

44 Carter Heyward, *The Redemption of God* (Washington: University of
America Press, 1986).

45 Jung, *Food for Life*, p. 6.

but also in relation to the world economy. Jung believes that we have forgotten the purpose behind the blessing of food and have been satisfied with an impoverished appreciation of eating. Once again we see how the Christian distrust of desires and appetites has led to a disconnection from an essential human/divine activity. For Jung there are very embodied consequences that stem from this impoverishment; two world views actually emerge, one that is holistic and revolves around relationships and sharing while the other is business-orientated and involves slicing life up into bits.[46] He argues that eating is an intimate act which signifies how the world enters in to us and how we become part of it; food can then be a source of grace and revelation or it can be simply fodder for management and control. In this way, then, food and eating are performative acts displaying the Christian life. We are familiar with Judith Butler's notion of performativity of gender, whereby things that have no substance and reality in themselves are given life and meaning through their repeated performance. Well, Christians too can give meaning through their repeated joyous embrace of what we may call '*dunamis* eating'. That is of their connection with the raw and passionate heart of their divine/human natures, which will propel them into greater connection and relationality in the world. This manner of engaging with food and eating will I believe counter what I have suggested earlier is an alarming manifestation of what I have called 'secular metaphysics'. This is a not entirely un-expected phenomenon in a secular world that has so entirely attempted to erase the religious that it has forgotten what its heritage is; this has meant that the damaging split of body and spirit so beloved by the Church Fathers has continued in our society as the erroneous belief that mind and body are not one and that mind can control the unruly passions of the body.

For an incarnational theologian this continuation signals the degree to which we continue to believe that the heavens have not been collapsed by incarnation: a residue remains of unresolved metaphysics. We are still not at home in our flesh and so we fail to live the radical co-creative and co-redemptive implications of that reality. We will not fully commit to flesh,

---

46 Jung, *Food for Life*, p. 8.

and so we live as though we inhabited somewhere else. Of course the Christian understanding of incarnation shows us to what extent that living somewhere else did not work for God either – he too had to finally commit to the risk and vulnerability of flesh. We are told that God abandoned himself to flesh, but we, who claim to follow, will never do the same, we always attempt to control it through various discourses of gender, race, class and size. The truly world-transforming power of incarnation will always be delayed as long as we continue to live as though Greek metaphysics had won the day rather than the full enfleshment of the fully human/divine God. There are of course cracks in this dualistic dialogue within the secular world as there always have been in the theological and religious worlds, but there is no serious attempt to incorporate the radical implications of a counter-understanding since the markets and advanced capitalism benefit from the rupture in the human condition just as the Church coffers did in days gone by. A marvellous counter to this way of thinking of course would be to side with the fully incarnate one and live with the flexible edges; edges that are not constantly policed by the guardians of improved selves and manicured lives. Signalling that vulnerability and not control, softness and not self-censure are central to a Christian life may throw light on the worst excesses of secular culture. As followers of Jesus we are 'sensuous revolutionaries' living our deepest passions and connections in order that our free and full embodiment may sing of abundant incarnation. The sensuous revolutionary Christ who calls to us is in a true sense himself a sensuous hedonist empowering revolution through the skin and enabling abundant embodied living that is the counter to the worst excesses of our genocidal and disconnected world.

Susie Orbach and others agree with Jung that bodies affect the environments they are in, and therefore the female body, entering what had previously been the male terrain of business, had to become harder, more muscular and angular in order to not pose a threat to the system itself rather than simply the men within it.[47] The systems that have been built on separation, independence and control can not have within them any

---

47 Susie Orbach, *Fat Is a Feminist Issue* (London: Hamlyn, 1979).

hint of the maternal because the fear of the alternative values this holds would be overwhelming. The fear that the patriarchal order would crumble in the face of the devouring maternal is a real fear for those patriarchs who have built empires through lives running away from the intimacy with the mother that they felt was removed, and from which trauma they have never recovered. Fat women then have to be removed from corporate life as they literally embody a set of conflicting values that threaten. There is not only room but an extreme need for the presence of the Fat Jesus and her sisters then in the public world of the patriarchs; they need to carry their threat and their alternative life proudly on their broad shoulders and rolling Amazon hips.

Of course we live in a much-policed world where the pressure is immense for us to conform to the ever limiting and reducing monologues of oppressive hierarchical patriarchy. As followers of an incarnational religion it is within that same skin, that same policed body that our revolution lies, since it is here that the God we claim to believe in situated the power to transform the world. Perhaps then this incarnational theologian does not have to totally despair in the face of the diet rhetoric that is bringing about the death and disempowerment of millions of women, because as Foucault tells us, where there is power there is also resistance. So, sisters, will you Slim for Him or bake cakes for the Queen of Heaven? There is a lot resting on your answer!

9

Why Women Need to be Ripped, Shredded and Sliced: Political, Philosophical and Thealogical Reflections

PAUL REID-BOWEN

Introduction

Briefly stated, the purpose of this paper is twofold. First, attention is directed towards a late twentieth- and early twenty-first-century body option that transgresses the hegemonic body politic of the western world, namely, women's bodybuilding. This is a form of embodiment and praxis that powerfully challenges the normative cultural vision of what is 'natural', and specifically what is permissible, in terms of gendered/sexed bodily identities, in the West.[1] Women's bodybuilding constitutes a material/visual act that is deeply subversive within the socio-cultural environs and institutions that have given rise to it; and it is also a physical and sporting activity that is often remarkably empowering to those women who practise it. The primary aim of the paper is to introduce a range of issues, questions and theoretical positions that may illuminate this phenomenon and the various ambiguities, complexities and contradictions that define it. Second, the aforementioned concerns and reflections serve to inform a prescriptive, political and, one should add, religious/spiritual argument that speaks to the value of women's

---

1 It is recognized that the 'West' is a somewhat artificial geo-political category; however, the author utilizes the term as shorthand for those first-world, post-industrial and late capitalist nations that are, arguably, the primary forces behind cultural and economic globalization at the beginning of the twenty-first century.

bodybuilding. While an influential paper in the feminist spirituality movement once argued 'Why Women Need the Goddess',[2] this paper proposes why, to borrow from the jargon of competitive bodybuilding, women may need to be ripped, shredded and sliced.[3]

Before engaging with any theorization, it may be valuable to raise some common responses to the form of embodiment under consideration and also reflect on one's personal reactions to it. Consider, for example, the fact that labels of 'freak', 'grotesque', 'gender benders', 'looking like a man', 'wanting to be a man', 'lesbians', 'unnatural' and far worse are regularly directed towards female bodybuilders; and these labels are also often deployed publicly and in a confrontational face-to-face manner. What is it that evokes and promotes such attributions and acts of discursive violence? There is certainly something disturbing, strange, or, in Judith Butler's terms, 'troubling' about the bodily presence of the female physique athlete in contemporary western culture. But what precisely is it that is troubling and how ought one respond to it? In my own case, my interest in women's bodybuilding intersected with the very beginnings of my engagement with feminism in the late 1980s and early 1990s. As a 'gym body' myself during that time, I was both familiar with and fascinated by the women's side of the sport, and certainly never experienced anything like revulsion. However, I was troubled. Although, as a man, I was emotionally motivated by my readings of feminist literature on such issues as abortion, pornography and male violence, it was women's bodybuilding that proved to be the issue that made me angry. Here was an arena of life where women's bodily freedoms were clearly, or so it

---

2 Carol Christ, 'Why Women Need the Goddess: Phenomenological, Psychological and Political Reflections', in C. Christ and J. Plaskow, eds, *Womanspirit Rising: A Feminist Reader in Religion* (San Francisco: HarperCollins, [1972] 1992), pp. 273–87.

3 Ripped, shredded and sliced are bodybuilding terms used to describe particularly high levels of muscular definition. 'Ripped: A condition of extremely low bodyfat with superior muscle separation and vascularity. Variations include sliced, cut, and cross-straited. . . . Shredded: To get ripped, to have extremely low bodyfat with superior muscle separation. Also, sliced, cut, and cross-straited' (http://www.getbig.com/glossary/jargon.htm).

seemed to me, being contested and fought over. Here was a discourse and practice where the cultural meanings of femaleness and femininity were revealed as constructed and also disputed. Here was a political field where patriarchal institutions – in this case those of professional body-building – were attempting to render their female membership safe and culturally acceptable. Women's bodybuilding was clearly something new and deeply unsettling for the patriarchal status quo in the West. Susie Orbach had argued persuasively, in her 1978 book of the same name, that *Fat is a Feminist Issue*. For me, muscle was obviously a feminist issue too. Problematically, though, feminist engagements with bodybuilding were – perhaps rather tellingly – largely absent from the academic and political arenas during that period of time. It was not until 1998 that two books appeared that charted the growth and possible feminist meaning of women's bodybuilding: Maria R. Lowe's *Women of Steel* and Leslie Heywood's *Bodymakers*.[4] In what follows some of the issues raised in these two books are summarized; however, it is the manner in which my own male feminist consciousness has reflected on these issues over the last twenty years that is prioritized. Women's body-building is, I suggest, troubling, in Butlerian and other senses, and this is, at least in certain feminist and religious terms, healthy and valuable. Precisely how this conclusion is arrived at, though, is, in part at least, the result of one's theoretical assumptions and overall methodological approach to the far broader subject of the body.

Feminism and the theorization of embodiment

Rather than attempt to provide an overview of the significant outpouring of research and theoretical approaches to the body that emerged in the late twentieth century, it will be sufficient for my purposes to summarize some of the ways by which feminists have theorized embodiment.

---

4 Leslie Heywood, *Bodymakers: A Cultural Anatomy of Women's Bodybuilding* (New Brunswick, NJ: Rutgers University Press, 1998) and Maria R. Lowe, *Women of Steel: Female Bodybuilders and the Struggle for Self-Definition* (New York: New York University Press, 1998).

Feminist theoretical approaches to the body can, I propose, be usefully divided into two broad and potentially incompatible tendencies or types. One can either focus upon the lived body, the body as it is experienced and reported, the inside. Or, one can direct one's methodological attention towards the body as it is changed, effected and inscribed by external forces, the outside. The theorization of the lived body relates very much to the apprehension or sensation of having or being a body, it is the awareness of embodiment and bodily existence. It encompasses the study of such aspects of identity as the internalization of a body image and the corporeal experience of possessing a particular sexual morphology. Freudian psychoanalysis, for example, is concerned with the construction of subjectivity according to anatomical differences between the sexes. The phenomenology of Merleau-Ponty attempts to anchor sentience and experience of the world in the sensations and perceptual capacities of the body. Both of these approaches can be understood to directly relate to the lived body. Current feminist understandings of the lived body tend to expand upon the insights of such theoretical positions as these. They note that the experience of the lived body is not historically or culturally fixed but is rather the result of the interaction between the givenness of corporeal existence and the contribution of the wider historical/cultural system of meaning that one inhabits. Inscriptive approaches to the body, in contrast, move away from corporeal experience and focus almost exclusively on the powers of the wider system.

The inscriptive model of embodiment in many respects posits the body as blank slate upon which the cultural and social becomes inscribed. The body is a cultural, historical artefact, it is changeable, malleable, and is produced through a complex array of power relations. That is, the model is, to cite Elizabeth Grosz, 'concerned with the processes by which the subject is marked, scarred, transformed, and written upon or constructed by the various regimes of institutional, discursive, and nondiscursive power as a particular type of body'.[5] This approach draws heavily on the works of the cultural historian/philosopher Michel Foucault and has proved particularly useful in supporting

---

5 Elizabeth Grosz, 'Introduction', *Hypatia* 6.3 (Fall 1991), p. 3.

feminist analyses of how bodies are politically acted upon. Indeed, for Foucault, bodies are the most fundamental level of political power relations; 'the body . . . is directly involved in a political field: power relations have a direct hold upon it; they invest it, mark it, train it, force it to carry out tasks, to perform ceremonies, to emit signs'.[6] Culture, history and politics can be understood to work directly through, and act directly upon, bodies. Cosmetics, diet, dress, fashion, posture, sport, surgery, work, all of these are cultural, historical and politicized constructs and products that participate in the formation of individual bodies. The body is theorized as a text that functions as the 'inscribed surface of events'.[7] For many feminists the model of text is a particularly useful theoretical tool as it side-steps the materiality of the body, a materiality which has so often been deployed against the interests of women. However, this materiality is rarely wholly denied; it is simply suggested, as Lois McNay notes, 'that it is impossible to know the materiality of the body outside of its cultural significations'.[8]

The inscriptive model, despite its strength in explaining and making sense of the place and function of power in the production of bodies, presents a couple of serious problems for feminists. First, the model can all too easily reduce people to the status of passive, 'docile' bodies. That is, agency, individuality and experience are elided and de-emphasized in the Foucauldian discourse of power relations; and feminism cannot afford to have women reduced once more to the level of passive victims. Second, by side-stepping the materiality of the body, the inscriptive model can be insensitive to sexual difference. The very corporeal givenness of sexual difference can, as many feminists have argued, entail widely different inscriptive regimes. Foucault's insights typically fail 'to explain how it is that men and women relate differently to the institutions

---

6 Michel Foucault, *Discipline and Punish: The Birth of the Prison*, trans. A. Sheridan (London: Penguin, 1982), p. 25.

7 Michel Foucault, 'Nietzsche, Genealogy, History' in P. Rabinow, ed., *The Foucault Reader* (London: Penguin, 1984), p. 83.

8 Lois McNay, 'The Foucauldian Body and the Exclusion of Experience', *Hypatia* 6.3 (Fall 1991), p. 131.

of modern life'.[9] How, then, can one make sense of women's body-building through these theoretical perspectives and positions?

Often when confronted with widely divergent theoretical positions (e.g. inner/lived vs. outer/inscribed), there is a desire for theoretical coherence and comprehensiveness followed by an attempt to reconcile the competing theories or postulates into a broader framework. Feminism is little different in this, and there have been various attempts to draw together the seemingly opposed approaches to theorizing and understanding embodiment. Elizabeth Grosz's *Volatile Bodies*, for example, is one approach which proposes that the relationship between inner and outer theorizations of the body can usefully be visualized and understood in terms of a moebius loop, wherein inner and outer positions are always already continuous with one another; inscribed bodies are lived bodies and vice-versa.[10] This suggestion is, I stress, vital for making sense of women's bodybuilding. While there are some excellent feminist analyses that highlight the inscriptive regimes and hegemonic forces that construct the embodiment of women bodybuilders, these rarely give due attention to the lived experiences of the bodybuilders themselves.[11] I propose that such an attempt at unification should be made. Although I advocate no single method or resolution to the feminist theorization of the body, as a principle of theoretical adequacy and applicability, the insights of both approaches – lived and inscribed – need to be considered. But what, though, precisely is bodybuilding?

---

9 McNay, 'The Foucauldian Body', p. 131.

10 Elizabeth Grosz, *Volatile Bodies: Toward a Corporeal Feminism* (Bloomington Ind.: Indiana University Press, 1994).

11 See Anne Bolin, 'Vandalized Vanity: Feminine Physiques Betrayed and Portrayed', in F. Mascia-Lees and P. Sharpe, eds, *Tattoo, Torture, Adornment and Disfigurement: The Denaturalization of the Body in Culture and Text* (Albany, NY: SUNY Press), pp. 79–99. Although Bolin's analysis is based on detailed ethnographic research it is the cultural construction/inscription of beauty and the feminine physique that she focuses on.

The corporeal and cultural practice of bodybuilding

Bodybuilding is a modern cultural activity concerned almost entirely with the pursuit of an ideal of physical embodiment. By regularly engaging in a systematic inscriptive regime of weight training, a ritual activity paralleling and exceeding most religious rites in its intensity, and by the critical and obsessive management of diet, the bodybuilder endeavours to shape the body into a model of muscular perfection. Although this activity is considered deeply narcissistic by many, and simply odd or outlandish by others, bodybuilding is coextensive with the mainstream health industry, possesses a competitive/sporting aspect, and is also supported by several international federations and organizations. Quite simply, bodybuilding is a part of the cultural world of meaning of the West; images of the professional bodybuilder are an integral part of western consciousness; and one may plausibly argue that bodybuilding possesses its own neo-tribal patterns of social organization.[12]

To begin to theorize this activity, though, one may note that bodybuilding is, first and foremost, concerned with the intentional production of a particular kind of embodiment; and this productive activity encompasses issues of boundary construction, the management of one's purity and the expression of physical identity/integrity. Thus, as Stephen Moore claims, 'bodybuilding is a purity system, arguably the most rigorous purity system to be found in western culture'.[13] Moreover, with reference to the theories of the anthropologist Mary Douglas, Moore further suggests that 'the competitive bodybuilder would be paradigmatic of the ritually pure subject, his or her symbolic universe being bound up, almost without remainder, with his or her physical person'.[14] Or, from a psychoanalytic perspective, one can argue that the male bodybuilder's complete focus on the regulation and mastery of the body can be associated with a desire, in Elizabeth Grosz's words, to 'render the whole of the male body

---

12 For an account of neo-tribal forms of association, see M. Maffesoli, *The Time of the Tribes: The Decline of Individualism in Mass Society* (London: Sage, 1996).

13 Stephen Moore, *God's Gym* (London and New York: Routledge, 1996), p. 76.

14 Moore, *God's Gym*, p. 82.

into the phallus, creating the whole male body as hard, impenetrable, pure muscle'.[15] However, as is so often true of psychoanalysis, the question of women is highly problematic. Where do women stand in relation to a psychoanalytic account of bodybuilding? Are women bodybuilders attempting to render their bodies man- or phallus-like for reasons that are explicable in terms of a narrative of unconscious forces and psychosexual development? Bodybuilding is, I would argue, of far more interest in so far as it raises important theoretical and practical questions about body politics, gendered identities and accounts of what it means to be human. Women bodybuilders problematize many accepted accounts of an essential human nature and/or fixed gendered and sexed bodily identities. They emphasize that, again in Grosz's words, 'there must already be a plastic and pliable body in order for it to be possible to mould and sculpt it according to the canons and dictates of bodybuilding protocols'.[16] The patriarchal cultural hegemony, in which we all live, endeavours to keep gendered identities, sexed embodiment and also sexuality under very strict control; it maintains that these things come together 'naturally' in discrete packages. Women bodybuilders, though, challenge and destabilize these ideas; they forcefully reveal that physical, gendered and sexed identities do not come, cohere or remain in such neat categories. Not surprisingly, a conflict arises; and this conflict – and the metaphor of the body as a battleground may be particularly apt – is one conducted between the normative vision of the cultural hegemony of the West and the lived bodies of individual women.

The first point at which hegemonic power exerts itself over the bodies of female bodybuilders is the institutional level, the level of competitive bodybuilding. The evaluation of competitive bodybuilding physiques is a process governed by a panel of seven to nine judges well-versed in bodybuilding aesthetics. Competitive success, in the case of the men's sport, is based on the evaluation of three physical criteria: muscular mass (size), definition (absence of fat) and symmetry (overall balance and proportion); and, within the sport of bodybuilding, these criteria form an

15 Grosz, *Volatile Bodies*, p. 224.
16 Grosz, *Volatile Bodies*, p. 143.

aesthetic code 'built up according to laws as unambiguous and as inflexible as those that once governed the construction of sonnets'.[17] However, in the case of the women's sport, things are rather more complex. That is, a remarkably treacherous fourth criterion must also be in evidence, namely, femininity. Within the canons of professional bodybuilding judging criteria, the female physique athlete must appear feminine or be judged and scored down accordingly. The governing federations of bodybuilding want 'muscularity with femininity', and the competitive world is littered with women who, while possessing superior mass, definition and symmetry, failed to balance this with femininity. The cultural message is clear: muscularity must be limited for the female. Muscularity is incompatible with feminine bodily identity. Muscularity is ultimately cognate with masculinity, and masculinity is the domain of the male alone.

Not surprisingly, the aforementioned judging criterion makes competitive women's bodybuilding a rather schizophrenic activity.[18] How does one maintain the masquerade? How does one satisfy the, largely male, gatekeepers and judges of the sport? As Maria Lowe observes, this state of affairs has given rise to what Jan Felshin defined as the 'feminine apologetic', a process by which female athletes 'may compensate for their participation in the traditionally masculine domain of sports by emphasizing their femininity'.[19] For the female bodybuilder, though, this apologetic does not arise out of any personal desire to emphasize their femininity, rather it is institutionally promulgated and reinforced. Some of the women who have evidenced the most muscular physiques, such as the powerlifter turned bodybuilder Bev Francis, have been told, quite explicitly in one judge's words, to 'get feminine or get out of competitive bodybuilding'.[20] Moreover, this feminization must often be taken to

---

17 Moore, *God's Gym*, p. 77.

18 Numerous critical and humorous analogies for this state of affairs were in circulation during the 1990s, including the examples of requesting a 100-metre sprinter to compete while wearing a dress and heels or demanding that a downhill skier restrict her speed lest she appear too masculine.

19 Lowe, *Women of Steel*, p. 121.

20 F. Coles, 'Feminine Charms and Outrageous Arms', *Trouble & Strife* 29/30 (Winter 1994/5), p. 68.

quite extreme lengths in order for women to 'prove' their femininity: bright, heavy make-up, glamorous or erotic clothing, abundant preferably bouffant hair and, increasingly, plastic surgery (notably breast implants, so that cleavage remains present during competition). At the institutional and competitive level of bodybuilding, women are constrained within a sphere of what is defined and perceived as culturally acceptable and 'natural'; and this containment is rigidly maintained and policed by a wide range of rules and sanctions.

In addition to the regimes of control exerted over women through competitive bodybuilding, it is also important to draw attention to a far broader cultural strategy of domination and management, namely the eroticization and sexualization of female bodybuilders. As Anne Balsamo notes, 'female bodybuilders who develop big muscles, and consequently greater strength, are considered transgressive of the "natural" order of things – an order that defines women as weak and frail'. But, she continues, 'their transgressive body displays (of female bodies that are also strong bodies) are neutralized in the mass media through the representations that eroticize their athletic bodies – their sexual attractiveness is asserted over their physical capabilities'.[21] This neutralization of the female bodybuilder became increasingly common in both the bodybuilding and mainstream media throughout the 1990s (and it is a trend that continues in the early twenty-first century). Not only were female bodybuilders featured less and less within the pages of popular bodybuilding magazines, when they did appear they tended to be eroticized. The cultural and patriarchal logic behind this process is seemingly quite simple: if a woman is erotic she is also feminine, safe, culturally desirable and, one may also argue, marketable. A regular feature in the bodybuilding magazine *Flex* during the 1990s was particularly revealing of this type of reasoning. This feature consisted of several pages of semi-naked, eroticized images of a female bodybuilder, accompanied by the following text:

21 Anne Balsamo, 'Forms of Technological Embodiment: Reading the Body in Contemporary Culture', in M. Featherstone and R. Burrows, eds, *Cyberspace, Cyberbodies, Cyberpunk: Cultures of Technological Embodiment* (London: Sage, 1996), p. 217.

Women bodybuilders are many things, among them symmetrical, strong, sensuous, and stunning. When photographed in competition shape, repping and grimacing or squeezing out shots, they appear shredded, vascular and hard, and *they can be perceived as threatening*. Offseason they carry more body fat, presenting themselves in a *much more naturally attractive fashion*. To exhibit this *real natural side* of women bodybuilders, FLEX has been presenting portrayals of female competitors in softer condition. *We hope this approach dispels the myth of female bodybuilder masculinity and proves what role models they really are.*[22]

A reference to nature is deployed twice in this extract and constitutes a modern use of essentialism to legitimate a particular (patriarchal/ hegemonic) state of affairs. The message is, I think, clear: the muscular, vascular and hard female bodybuilder is masculine and transgressive of the 'natural' order; muscularity is the privilege of the male; and, as Susan Butler succinctly notes, '[y]ou can only have permission to be this strong if you can also look this beautiful.'[23] Sex rather than athleticism becomes the focus in these cultural mediations of women's bodybuilding; female physical and sporting achievement is minimized by sexualizing it.[24] This is a highly successful patriarchal strategy for neutralizing women's body-building and other physical achievements. However, despite the presence of these mechanisms of patriarchal control, it is far from certain what value feminists may want to assign to women's participation in body-building.

Bodybuilding can, for a number of reasons, be deeply problematic for feminists. For example, the emphasis that the bodybuilder places upon cognitive control of the body may resonate rather worryingly with an anorexic's obsession with self-mastery and slenderness. The desire for mastery of the body can be understood to express a general dissatisfaction with life; the body being perceived as the last bastion of control in an

---

22 *Flex* 12.11 (January 1995), p. 126, emphasis mine.

23 Cited in S. Gilroy, 'The EmBodyment of Power: Gender and Physical Activity', *Leisure Studies* 8 (1989), p. 165.

24 See also, Heywood, *Bodymakers*, pp. 97–9.

increasingly complex and risk-laden world. Or, women's participation in bodybuilding may reflect another mistaken attempt to make oneself beautiful and please the male gaze; for example, posing in a bikini, seeking the affirmation of a panel of judges, closely parallels the ethic of a beauty pageant. Feminists may prefer instead to address the forces that induce people to feel out of control and unhappy with their bodies, rather than accepting that problems necessarily reside with or within bodies. They may observe, too, that those women who do participate in bodybuilding may be engaging, far too closely, with a masculine ideal, and may be adopting highly questionable masculinist values; that is, female bodies may be in danger of being assimilated into a phallocentric universal or the logic of the same. This is a proposal that may stray remarkably close to the aforementioned psychoanalytic view of bodybuilding being concerned with the transformation of the whole of the body into the phallus; although it may also simply be an expression of a general feminist worry about women becoming embroiled with masculine projects of physical achievement and perfectibility. None of these concerns, though, pays sufficient attention to the positive feminist value of women's participation in bodybuilding.

Women's bodybuilding as feminist activism

Feminist scholars have I contend significantly underestimated the merits of women's bodybuilding. Several arguments may be advanced in support of this contention. First, as Helen Lenskyj comments, 'developing one's full physical potential . . . [is] compatible with the greater general goal of self actualization, and thus with feminist principles'.[25] Taking control of one's life, desiring to be in control of one's body, cannot be simply condemned, in a knee-jerk manner, because of an apparent excess. Linkages with anorexia, for example, are probably misplaced given the actualities of the bodybuilder's relationship with food and their

---

25 Helen Lenskyj, *Out of Bounds: Women, Sport and Sexuality* (Toronto: Women's Press, 1986), p. 135.

bodyweight/mass; that is, the bodybuilder is typically concerned with gaining or maintaining muscular mass, and any sacrifices in strength and overall health can only be tolerated for short periods of time (i.e. during preparation for competitions). Furthermore, as Leslie Heywood argues, 'bodybuilding can function as a basic – if unnamed – form of activism in many women's lives'. Although the individualist focus of bodybuilding can render it problematic as a form of activism, a difficulty that is duplicated within the environs of post- or third-wave feminism, it does enable women to 'change how they see themselves and their position and relations to the larger world, and how they are seen by others'.[26] Moreover, this body practice, according to the testimonials and narratives of many of the women who do engage in it, is physically, psychologically and, one might add, spiritually empowering. To cite Heywood again, 'women's bodybuilding is about the ability of women to partake of some sense of sovereignty, too – and in a way that expresses it physically, visually'. It is 'an unequivocal self-expression, an indication of women's right to *be*, for themselves, not for children, partners, fellow activists, not for anyone else. In a culture that still defines women's purpose as service for others, no wonder female bodybuilding is so controversial.'[27] These points should not fall from view in any feminist analysis of women's bodybuilding, although I would argue that there are more persuasive reasons for conceiving this body praxis as a form of feminist activism.

Women's bodybuilding as a subversive act

More significant for feminism than the empowering aspect of women's bodybuilding is the degree to which it is very clearly a counter-cultural activity. Female bodybuilders regularly and repeatedly encounter considerable hostility and stigmatization for their physical difference from the cultural and patriarchal norm. If some feminists are worried about this form of female embodiment, the wider culture is openly antagonistic

---

26 Heywood, *Bodymakers*, p. 57.
27 Heywood, *Bodymakers*, p. 171.

towards it. The phenomenon of women's bodybuilding powerfully emphasizes the hold that patriarchal constructions of the gendered body and the natural have over the popular imagination, and it also highlights the lengths that the wider culture will go to, to maintain those constructs.

There is, I must stress, nothing inherently sexed about muscles or strength, there are only the genetic and sex-correlated limitations and potentials. As the Amazon-like, feminist icon Sojourner Truth asked in 1851, '[A]in't I a woman? Look at me! Look at my arm! I have ploughed and planted and gathered into barns, and no man could head me! And ain't I a woman?'[28] Some women have always been bigger, stronger and/or more muscular than many men. Is women's bodybuilding, then, a form of cultural embodiment that feminists should concern themselves with? Does it constitute a practice that requires feminist exploration? I am certainly not suggesting that all feminists ought to start bodybuilding, or pumping iron, as a matter of principle. But they ought to be interested in the empowering and potentially subversive value of this late twentieth- and early twenty-first-century body praxis. Female bodybuilders induce considerable discomfort in the majority of the population, male and female alike. Their bodies are not culturally desirable; they forcefully destabilize established patriarchal constructions of masculine and feminine bodily identity; and, in so doing, they open up a space for a critique and rethinking of those constructs. Judith Butler touches upon this possibility when she argues that subversive bodily acts, such as these, reveal, via parody, the culturally constructed nature of gendered bodies.[29] Susan Bordo, in turn, expands upon Butler's point and argues that subversion is less a process of parody than an encounter with ambiguity.[30] She continues,

28 Sojourner Truth, 'Ain't I a Woman?' in K. Conboy, N. Medina and S. Stanbury, eds, *Writing on the Body: Female Embodiment and Feminist Theory* (New York: Columbia University Press, 1997), p. 231.

29 Judith Butler, *Gender Trouble: Feminism and the Subversion of Identity* (London and New York: Routledge, 1990).

30 Susan Bordo, *Unbearable Weight: Feminism, Western Culture, and the Body* (Berkeley: University of California Press, 1993), pp. 292-3.

[s]ubversion is contextual, historical, and, above all, social. No matter how exciting the destabilising potential of texts, bodily or otherwise, whether those texts are subversive or recuperative or both or neither cannot be determined in abstraction from actual social practice.[31]

This passage is important in so far as most women bodybuilders do not aim to parody the gendered bodies of men, it is simply the case that within our cultural and historical context muscularity is a powerful signifier of both masculinity and male embodiment. Women's body-building effectively destabilizes and subverts earlier dualistic constructs of human nature and embodiment by creating ambiguity. The culturally ambiguous bodies of female physique athletes make us confront what Bordo terms 'an unclear and uncharted continuum'.[32] It is this continu-um that feminists – and indeed all of us – probably need to reflect upon if we are to begin to think and engender a post-patriarchal world.

Women's bodybuilding and spiritual empowerment

I conclude this paper by offering a positive religious interpretation of women's bodybuilding. This endeavour may seem somewhat unusual, given that it may be reasonably argued that most of the world's religious traditions have historically served to inform and legitimate patriarchal constructions of embodiment, gendered identities and the 'natural'. There may, therefore, seem to be little of feminist value that can be drawn from a religious analysis of women's bodybuilding, aside, that is, from commenting on its deviance from one or more prescribed religious gender norms. However, the late twentieth century was particularly significant, in religious terms, in so far as it witnessed the rise of a range of feminist and women's religious movements that actively sought to explore and theorize the meaning of women's religiosity in post-patriarchal – or at least post-traditional – terms. Many of these movements

---

31 Bordo, *Unbearable Weight*, p. 294.
32 Bordo, *Unbearable Weight*, p. 293.

have developed narratives that are capable of understanding women's bodybuilding as a positive phenomenon, and at least one part of the feminist spirituality movement actively valorizes the subversive qualities that female bodybuilders possess.

Thealogy (Goddess-talk, or the logos of thea) is a label for the religious discourse that arose, in a predominantly grassroots manner, among many women, and some men, who were searching for an alternative to God-centred religious language in the West during the 1970s, '80s and '90s. Predominantly linked today with the Goddess movement and, in a more politicized manner, what may be termed Goddess feminism, thealogy articulates and reflects on the meaning of female divinity and sacrality; it tends to be experientially grounded, not to mention a self-consciously body-centred and corporeal discourse, but is also increasingly open to systematic and abstract reflection on the nature of knowledge, reality/deity and value.[33] Of significance to this paper, though, is the fact that femaleness – understood in biological, ontological and spiritual terms – is conceived as, in some sense, beyond or outside the control of patriarchal hegemonic power. The radical feminist thealogian Mary Daly character-ized this state of affairs in terms of the patriarchal foreground, which is the cultural, institutional realm of patriarchal conditioning, inscriptive regimes and power, and the elemental Background, the realm of women's true selves and spiritual Be-ing.[34] Women who were not liberated, or rather accessing the Background, were often identified by Daly as fem-bots or Painted Birds, epithets that indicate their visual/material compli-ance with the norms of patriarchal beauty, behaviour and composure.[35]

---

33 See C. Christ, *Rebirth of the Goddess: Finding Meaning in Feminist Spiritu-ality* (New York: Addison Wesley, 1997); M. Raphael, *Introducing Thealogy: Discourse on the Goddess* (Cleveland, Ohio: Pilgrim Press, 2000) and *Thealogy and Embodiment: The Post-Patriarchal Reconstruction of Female Sacrality* (Sheffield: Sheffield Academic Press, 1996); P. Reid-Bowen, *Goddess as Nature: Towards a Philosophical Thealogy* (Aldershot: Ashgate, 2007).

34 See M. Daly, *Gyn/Ecology: The Metaethics of Radical Feminism* (London: Women's Press, 1991); *Outercourse: The Be-Dazzling Voyage* (London: Women's Press, 1993); *Pure Lust: Elemental Feminist Philosophy* (London: Women's Press, 1984).

35 Daly, *Gyn/Ecology*, pp. 333–7.

Only those women who were delving and moving in the Background were theorized to be sufficiently free to reject such outward markings of patriarchy. Other thealogians have, in turn, created, reclaimed and inter-woven countless narratives and myths of goddesses and female powers that they understand to oppose, precede or subvert the patriarchal status quo. It is these thealogical narratives that can usefully illuminate the practice and value of women's bodybuilding.

That which patriarchy has construed as 'dangerous', 'monstrous' or 'other' is repeatedly evoked and ritually engaged with by spiritual feminists and thealogians as of the highest religious value; such attributions serve, it is proposed, to reveal that which does not fit within and threatens the conceptual schemes of patriarchy. Moreover, those phenomena that are stigmatized in this manner are typically associated with some formation of femaleness. Thealogians note how mythical figures of Amazons, gorgons, crone-like witches, lamias and sphinxes, as well as various shapeshifting and theriomorphic goddesses, wolves and an array of other animals, have all been characterized as existing on the edges of patriarchal society and represent that which cannot be accommodated within the logic of patriarchal control. They are all models of a chaotic becoming that shocks and disrupts any patriarchal and metaphysical notions of fixed essences, firm ontological boundaries and linear evolution.

For thealogians it is the monstrous, gorgon-like or Amazonian figures of myth that represent the diversity and power of a femaleness, and a nature, that patriarchy cannot control; they represent the failures of patri-archal political, scientific and social structures to confine reality within its oppressive frameworks and inscriptive regimes. Nature is thealogically conceived and valued as chaotic, open and wild; moreover, the fixed bodily, gender and ontological categories of patriarchy are viewed as a terrible mistake. Mythic figures, such as gorgons and goddesses such as Kali, are thealogical models of untamed female power, the metaphysical openness of nature and, more importantly, the capacity of femaleness to escape patriarchally imposed limits. Female bodybuilders, with their visual and corporeal transgression of what is patriarchally acceptable, are, I suggest, a powerful modern embodiment of the female myths and powers that thealogians seek to evoke. The spiritual feminist Emily

Culpepper relates a particularly powerful story of how she once scared away an assailant in her home by manifesting a terrible rage and countenance that she could only describe as gorgon-like, an appearance that initially petrified her assailant. She then argues that it is crucial that women 'learn how to manifest a visage that will repel men when necessary' and adds that '[t]he Gorgon has much vital, literally life-saving information to teach women about anger, rage, power and the release of the determined aggressiveness sometimes needed for survival'.[36] It would, I admit, be problematic, and indeed unwelcome, to suggest that women bodybuilders either do, want to or ought to embody the rage or aggressiveness that Culpepper speaks of, and this is not my intent. The point I wish to make is that bodybuilding possesses a spiritual and mythic capacity to both empower women and also cause 'gender trouble' that requires some serious feminist exploration. To draw upon a recommendation from the spiritual feminist Jane Caputi, 'we might conjure up images of the ontologically strange – of the anomie, of the dark that patriarchy has trained us to fear. We might visualize "monsters" – those female Powers that have been stigmatized as alien, inhuman, freakish, turbulent, and chaotic – not to fight them, but to become them.'[37] There might, I propose, be a feminist need, or at minimum a political and spiritual feminist rationale, for some women to become that which patriarchy fears: muscular, strong and sliced.

References

Balsamo, A., 'Forms of Technological Embodiment: Reading the Body in Contemporary Culture', in M. Featherstone and R. Burrows, eds, *Cyberspace, Cyberbodies, Cyberpunk: Cultures of Technological Embodiment*, London: Sage, 1996, pp. 215–37.

---

36 Culpepper, cited in J. Caputi, 'On Psychic Activism: Feminist Mythmaking', in C. Larrington, ed., *The Feminist Companion to Mythology* (London: Pandora Press, 1992), p. 431.

37 Jane Caputi, *Gossips, Gorgons and Crones: The Fates of the Earth* (Santa Fe, New Mexico: Bear & Company, 1993), p. 287.

Bolin, A., 'Vandalized Vanity: Feminine Physiques Betrayed and Portrayed', in F. Mascia-Lees and P. Sharpe, eds, *Tattoo, Torture, Adornment and Disfigurement: The Denaturalization of the Body in Culture and Text*, Albany, NY: SUNY Press, pp. 79–99.

Bordo, S., *Unbearable Weight: Feminism, Western Culture, and the Body*, Berkeley: University of California Press, 1993.

Butler, J., *Gender Trouble: Feminism and the Subversion of Identity*, London and New York: Routledge, 1990.

Caputi, J., 'On Psychic Activism: Feminist Mythmaking', in C. Larrington, eds, *The Feminist Companion to Mythology*, London: Pandora Press, 1992, pp. 425–40.

Caputi, J., *Gossips, Gorgons and Crones: The Fates of the Earth*, Santa Fe, New Mexico: Bear & Company, 1993.

Christ, C., 'Why Women Need the Goddess: Phenomenological, Psychological and Political Reflections', in C. Christ and J. Plaskow, eds, *Womanspirit Rising: A Feminist Reader in Religion*, San Francisco: HarperCollins, [1972], 1992, pp. 273–87.

Christ, C., *Rebirth of the Goddess: Finding Meaning in Feminist Spirituality*, New York: Addison Wesley, 1997.

Coles, F., 'Feminine Charms and Outrageous Arms', *Trouble & Strife* 29/30 (Winter 1994/95).

Daly, M., *Gyn/Ecology: The Metaethics of Radical Feminism*, London: Women's Press, 1991.

Daly, M., *Outercourse: The Be-Dazzling Voyage*, London: Women's Press, 1993.

Daly, M., *Pure Lust: Elemental Feminist Philosophy*, London: Women's Press, 1984.

Foucault, M., 'Nietzsche, Genealogy, History', in P. Rabinow, ed., *The Foucault Reader*, London: Penguin, 1984, pp. 76–100.

Foucault, M., *Discipline and Punish: The Birth of the Prison*, trans. A. Sheridan, London: Penguin, 1982.

Gilroy, S., 'The EmBodyment of Power: Gender and Physical Activity', *Leisure Studies* 8 (1989), pp. 163–71.

Grosz, E., *Volatile Bodies: Toward a Corporeal Feminism*, Bloomington, Ind.: Indiana University Press, 1994.

Heywood, L., *Bodymakers: A Cultural Anatomy of Women's Bodybuilding*, New Brunswick, NJ: Rutgers University Press, 1998.

Lenskyj, H., *Out of Bounds: Women, Sport and Sexuality*, Toronto: Women's Press, 1986.

Lowe, M. R., *Women of Steel: Female Bodybuilders and the Struggle for Self-Definition*, New York: New York University Press, 1998.

Maffesoli, M., *The Time of the Tribes: The Decline of Individualism in Mass Society*, London: Sage, 1996.

McNay, L., 'The Foucauldian Body and the Exclusion of Experience', *Hypatia*, 6.3 (Fall 1991), pp. 126–39.

Moore, S., *God's Gym*, London and New York: Routledge, 1996.

Raphael, M., *Introducing Thealogy: Discourse on the Goddess*, Cleveland, Ohio: Pilgrim Press, 2000.

Raphael, M., *Thealogy and Embodiment: The Post-Patriarchal Reconstruction of Female Sacrality*, Sheffield: Sheffield Academic Press, 1996.

Reid-Bowen, P., *Goddess as Nature: Towards a Philosophical Thealogy*, Aldershot: Ashgate, 2007.

Truth, Sojourner, 'Ain't I a Woman?', in K. Conboy, N. Medina and S. Stanbury, eds, *Writing on the Body: Female Embodiment and Feminist Theory*, New York: Columbia Unviersity Press, 1997, pp. 231–2.

Bibliography

Airaksinen, T. (1995), *The Philosophy of the Marquis de Sade*, London: Routledge.

Althaus-Reid, M. (2003), *The Queer God*, London: Routledge.

Althaus-Reid, M. and L. Isherwood, eds (2004), *The Sexual Theologian: Essays on Sex, God and Politics*, London: T & T Clark.

Alves Pereira, O., 'Deus é Travesti' (Comunidad Asha, Goiânia, Brazil); http://brasil.indymedia.org/pt/red/2003/08/259943.shtml (accessed 7 July 2006).

Anselm of Canterbury (1958), *Proslogium; Monologium; An Appendix in Behalf of the Fool by Gaunilon; and Cur Deus Homo*, trans. Sidney Norton Deane, La Salle, Ill.: Open Court.

Ash, J. and E. Wilson (1992), *Chic Thrills: A Fashion Reader*, London: Pandora.

Bakhtin, M. (1984), *Rabelais and His World*, trans. Helen Iswolsky, Bloomington: Indiana University Press.

Balasuriya, T. (1988), *The Eucharist and Human Liberation*, London: SPCK.

Balsamo, A. (1996), 'Forms of Technological Embodiment: Reading the Body in Contemporary Culture', in M. Featherstone and R. Burrows, eds, *Cyberspace, Cyberbodies, Cyberpunk: Cultures of Technological Embodiment*, London: Sage, pp. 215–37.

Barthes, R. ([1967] 1990), *The Fashion System*, trans M. Ward and R. Howard, Berkeley: University of California Press.

Barthes, R. (1977), *Sade, Fourier, Loyola*, trans. R. Miller, London: Jonathan Cape.

Beauvoir, S. de ([1949] 1972), *The Second Sex*, trans. H. M. Parshley, Harmondsworth: Penguin.

Benthien, C. ([1999] 2002), *Skin: On the Cultural Border between Self and the World*, New York: Columbia University Press, chs 3–6.

Berkins, L. (2004), 'Eternamente Atrapadas por el Sexo', in J. Fernández, M. D'Uva and P. Viturro, eds, *Cuerpos Ineludibles: Un Dialogo a Partir de las Sexualidades en América Latina*, Buenos Aires: Ediciones Ají de Pollo, pp. 19–24.

'Body Fascism: Another Form of Discrimination?' *Sportsteacher*, 25 February 2005; http://www.sportsteacher.co.uk/news/editorial/01autF_bodyfascism. html (accessed 4 May 2006).

'Body Modification', in *Wikipedia: The Free Encyclopedia*; http://en.wikipedia. org/wiki/Body_modification (accessed 4 May 2006).

Boenke, M., ed. (2003), *Trans Forming Families: Real Stories About Transgendered Loved Ones*, 2nd edn, Hardy, Va.: Oak Knoll Press.

Bolin, A. (1992), 'Vandalized Vanity: Feminine Physiques Betrayed and Portrayed', in F. Mascia-Lees and P. Sharpe, eds, *Tattoo, Torture, Adornment and Disfigurement: The Denaturalization of the Body in Culture and Text*, Albany: SUNY Press, pp. 79–99.

Bordo, S. (1993), *Unbearable Weight: Feminism, Western Culture, and the Body*, Berkeley: University of California Press, 1993.

Bronfen, E. (1992), *Death, Femininity and the Aesthetic*, Manchester: Manchester University Press.

Brookes, R. (1992), 'Fashion Photography: The Double-Page Spread: Helmut Newton, Guy Bourdin and Deborah Turbeville', in J. Ash and E. Wilson, eds (1992), *Chic Thrills: A Fashion Reader*, London: Pandora, pp. 17–24.

Brown, P. (1988), *The Body and Society: Men, Women and Sexual Renunciation in Early Christianity*, New York: Columbia University Press.

Bulgakov, S. (1993), *Sophia, the Wisdom of God: An Outline of Sophiology*, Hudson, NY: Lindisfarne Press.

Buss, D. and D. Herman (2003), *Globalizing Family Values: The Christian Right in International Politics*, Minneapolis: University of Minnesota Press.

Butler, J. (1990), *Gender Trouble: Feminism and the Subversion of Identity*, London and New York: Routledge.

Butler, J. (1993), *Bodies that Matter: On the Discursive Limits of 'Sex'*, London: Routledge.

Cameron, D. and E. Frazer (1987), *The Lust to Kill*, New York: New York University Press.

Caputi, J. (1992), 'On Psychic Activism: Feminist Mythmaking', in C. Larrington, ed., *The Feminist Companion to Mythology*, London: Pandora Press, pp. 425–40.

Caputi, J. (1993), *Gossips, Gorgons and Crones: The Fates of the Earth*, Santa Fe, New Mexico: Bear & Company.

Carter, A. (1979), *The Sadeian Woman*, London: Virago.

Chasseguet-Smirgel, J. (1985), *Creativity and Perversion*, London: Free Association Books.

Chernin, K. (1983), *Womansize: The Tyranny of Slenderness*, London: The Woman's Press.

Chillier, G. (1998), 'La sanción de un código de convivencia urbana: Causas y efectos de la eliminación de las detenciones arbitrarias por parte de la Policía Federal', lecture presented at the seminar *The Police Reforms in Argentina*, Buenos Aires: Centro de Estudios Legales y Sociales (CELS), 1–2 December.

Christ, C. ([1972] 1992), 'Why Women Need the Goddess: Phenomenological, Psychological and Political Reflections', in C. Christ and J. Plaskow, eds, *Womanspirit Rising: A Feminist Reader in Religion*, San Francisco: HarperCollins, pp. 273–87.

Christ, C. (1997), *Rebirth of the Goddess: Finding Meaning in Feminist Spirituality*, New York: Addison Wesley.

Clack. B. (2001) 'Sade: Forgiveness and Truth in a Desacralised Universe', *Literature and Theology* 15.3, pp. 262–75.

Clack, B. (2002), *Sex and Death: A Reappraisal of Human Mortality*, Cambridge: Polity.

Colebrook, C., (2003), *Gender*, Basingstoke: Palgrave Macmillan.

Coles, F. (1994), 'Feminine Charms and Outrageous Arms', *Trouble & Strife* 29/30.

Craik, J. (1994), *The Face of Fashion*, London: Routledge.

Cross, F. L., ed. (1957), *The Oxford Dictionary of the Christian Church*, London: Oxford University Press.

Daly, M. (1984), *Pure Lust: Elemental Feminist Philosophy*, London: The Women's Press.

Daly, M. (1991), *Gyn/Ecology: The Metaethics of Radical Feminism*, London: The Women's Press.

Daly, M. (1993), *Outercourse: The Be-Dazzling Voyage*, London: The Women's Press.

Davis, K. (1995), *Reshaping the Female Body: The Dilemma of Cosmetic Surgery*, London: Methuen.

De la Haye, A. (1997), *The Cutting Edge: Fifty Years of British Fashion 1947–1997*, London: V&A.

Di Berardino, A., ed. (1998), *Diccionario Patrístico y de la Antigüedad Tardía*, Salamanca: Sígueme.

Douglas, M. (2002), *Purity and Danger: An Analysis of Concepts of Pollution and Taboo*, London: Routledge.

Dworkin, A. (1981), *Pornography: Men Possessing Women*, London: Women's Press.

Ebersole, L. and R. Peabody, eds, *Mondo Barbie: An Anthology of Fiction and Poetry*, New York: St Martin's Press.

Ensler, E. (2004), *The Good Body*, London: William Heinemann.

Epstein, J. and K. Straub, eds, (1991), *Body Guards: The Cultural Politics of Gender Ambiguity*, London: Routledge.

Erikson, E. (1968), *Identity: Youth in Crisis*, London: Faber & Faber.

Falk, P. (1994), *The Consuming Body*, London: Sage.

Feinberg, L. (1998), *Trans Liberation: Beyond Pink or Blue*, Boston: Beacon Press.

Fernández, J., M. D'Uva and P. Viturro, eds, (2004), *Cuerpos Ineludibles: Un Dialogo a Partir de las Sexualidades en América Latina*, Buenos Aires: Ediciones Ají de Pollo.

Fiedler, L. (1978), *Freaks: Myths and Images of the Secret Self*, New York: Simon & Schuster.

Foucault, M. (1982), *Discipline and Punish: The Birth of the Prison*, trans. A. Sheridan, London: Penguin.

Foucault, M. (1984), 'Nietzsche, Genealogy, History', in P. Rabinow, ed., *The Foucault Reader*, London: Penguin, pp. 76–100.

'Frequently Asked Questions: What is Intersex?' *Intersex Society of North America*; http://www.isna.org/faq/what_is_intersex (accessed 4 May 2006).

Freud, S. (1905), 'Three Essays on Sexuality', in *Standard Edition of the Works of Sigmund Freud* (hereafter, *SE*), vol. 7, trans. J. Strachey, London: Vintage, pp. 125–245.

Freud, S. (1911), 'Formulations on the Two Principles of Mental Functioning', *SE* 12, trans. J. Strachey, London: Vintage, pp. 213–38.

Freud, S. (1919), 'The "Uncanny"', *SE* 17, trans. J. Strachey, London: Vintage, pp. 218–56.

Freud, S. (1937), 'Analysis Terminable and Interminable', *SE* 23, pp. 216–53.

Gallop, J. (1982), *Feminism and Psychoanalysis*, Basingstoke: Macmillan.

Gallop, J. (1995), 'Sade, Mother and Other Women', in D. B. Allison, M. S. Roberts and A. S. Weiss, eds, *Sade and the Narrative of Transgression*, Cambridge: Cambridge University Press, pp. 122–41.

Gear, N. (1963), *The Divine Demon: A Portrait of the Marquis de Sade*, London: Frederick Muller.

Gerhardt, S. (2004), *Why Love Matters: How Affection Shapes a Baby's Brain*, London: Routledge.

Gilroy, S. (1989), 'The EmBodyment of Power: Gender and Physical Activity', *Leisure Studies* 8, pp. 163–71.

Glasser, M. (1979), 'Some Aspects of the Role of Aggression in the Perversions', in I. Rosen, ed. *Sexual Deviations*, Oxford: Oxford University Press, pp. 278–305.

Golding, S., ed. (1997), *The Eight Technologies of Otherness*, London: Routledge.

Gregory of Nazianzus (1862), *Epistle 101*, Migne, PG 37, pp. 181–4.

Greve, B. (2006), 'Transformation', sermon preached at the chapel of Starr King School for the Ministry (SKSM), The Graduate Theological Union (GTU), Berkeley, Calif., 2 May.

Greve, B. (2006), *Courage from Necessity*, sermon preached at Church for the Fellowship of All People, Unitarian Universalist Church, San Francisco, Calif., 3 June.

Griffiths, M. (2004), *Born Again Bodies: Flesh and Spirit in American Christianity*, Berkeley, Calif., University of California Press.

Grosz, E. (1994), *Volatile Bodies: Toward a Corporeal Feminism*, Bloomington, Ind.: Indiana University Press.

Hansen, G. (1997), 'La concepción trinitaria de Dios en los orígenes de la teología de la liberación: el aporte de Juan Luis Segundo', *Cuadernos de Teología* 16.1–2, pp. 43–67.

Heywood, L. (1998), *Bodymakers: A Cultural Anatomy of Women's Bodybuilding*, New Brunswick, NJ: Rutgers University Press.

Hollander, A. (1993), 'Accounting for Fashion', *Raritan* 13.2, pp. 121–32.

Holy Bible. New Revised Standard Version, Oxford: Oxford University Press, 1977.

Hume, D. ([1779] 1947), *Dialogues Concerning Natural Religion*, Indianapolis: Bobbs-Merrill.

Hurley, K. (1996), *The Gothic Body: Sexuality, Materialism and Degeneration at the Fin de Siècle*, Cambridge: Cambridge University Press.

Irenaeus of Lyon, (1996), *Adversus Haereses* 5.27.9, in *Ante-Nicene Fathers*, vol. 1, ed. A. Roberts and J. Donaldson, Grand Rapids: Eerdmans.

Isherwood, L. (2006), *The Power of Erotic Celibacy*, London: T & T Clark.

Isherwood, L. (2008), *The Fat Jesus*, London: Darton, Longman & Todd.

Isherwood, L. and E. Stuart, eds (1998), *Introducing Body Theology*, Sheffield: Sheffield Academic Press.

Jantzen, G. (1998), *Becoming Divine: Towards a Feminist Philosophy of Religion*, Manchester: Manchester University Press.

Johnson, E. (2000), *She Who Is: The Mystery of God in Feminist Theological Discourse*, New York: Crossroad.

Jung, S. (2004), *Food for Life: The Spirituality and Ethics of Eating*, Minneapolis, Fortress Press.

King, P. and R. Steiner, eds (1990), *The FreudBKlein Controversies 1941–45*, London: Routledge.

Klein, M. ([1921] 1975), 'The Development of a Child', in *The Writings of Melanie Klein*, vol. 1: *Love, Guilt and Reparation*, London: Hogarth Press, pp. 4–13.

Klein, M. (1926), 'Infant Analysis', *International Journal of Psycho-Analysis* 7, pp. 31–63.

Klein, M. ([1932] 1997), *The Psycho-Analysis of Children*, London: Vintage.

Klein, M. ([1935] 1975), 'A Contribution to the Psychogenesis of Manic-Depressive States', in *The Writings of Melanie Klein*, vol. 1: *Love, Guilt and Reparation*, London: Hogarth Press, pp. 236–89.

Klein, M. ([1936] 1975), 'Weaning', in *The Writings of Melanie Klein*, vol. 1: *Love, Guilt and Reparation*, London: Hogarth Press, pp. 290–305.

Klein, M. (1946), 'Notes on Some Schizoid Mechanisms', in *The Writings of Melanie Klein*, vol. 3: *Envy and Gratitude and Other Works*, London: Hogarth Press, pp. 292–320.

Kristeva, J. ([1977] 2002), 'Stabat Mater', in M. Joy, K. O'Grady and J. L. Poxon, eds, *French Feminists on Religion: A Reader*, London: Routledge, pp. 112–38.

Kristeva, J. (2001), *Melanie Klein*, trans. R. Guberman, New York: Columbia University Press.

Lacan, J. (1977), *Ecrits*, trans. A. Sheridan, New York: Norton.

Lacan, J. and the École Freudienne (1982), *Feminine Sexuality*, ed. J. Mitchell and J. Rose, trans. J. Rose, London: Macmillan.

LaCugna, C. M. (1991), *God for Us: The Trinity and Christian Life*, San Francisco: Harper San Francisco.

Laplanche, J. and J. B. Pontalis ([1964] 2003), 'Fantasy and the Origins of Sexuality', in R. Steiner, ed., *Unconscious Phantasy*, London: Karnac Books, pp. 107–43.

LeBesco, K. (2004), *Revolting Bodies? The Struggle to Redefine Fat Identity*, Boston, Mass.: University of Massachusetts Press.

Lenskyj, H. (1986), *Out of Bounds: Women, Sport and Sexuality*, Toronto: Women's Press.

Lowe, M. R. (1998), *Women of Steel: Female Bodybuilders and the Struggle for Self-Definition*, New York: New York University Press.

Ma Vie en Rose (1997), dir. Alain Berliner, DVD, Sony Pictures.

Ma Vie en Rose (official web page), http://www.sonyclassics.com/mavieenrose (accessed 5 May 2006).

Maffesoli, M. (1996), *The Time of the Tribes: The Decline of Individualism in Mass Society*, London: Sage.

McNay, L. (1991), 'The Foucauldian Body and the Exclusion of Experience', *Hypatia* 6.3, pp. 126–39.

Meerson, M. A., (1998), *The Trinity of Love in Modern Russian Theology: The Love Paradigm and the Retrieval of Western Medieval Love Mysticism in Modern Russian Trinitarian Thought from Solovyov to Bulgakov*, Quincy, Ill.: Franciscan Press.

Merleau-Ponty, M. (1964), *The Primacy of Perception*, ed. J. M. Edie, Evanston, Ill.: Northwestern University Press.

Meyendorff, J. (1975), *Christ in Eastern Christian Thought*, New York: St Vladimir's Seminary Press.

Milton, J., C. Polmear and J. Fabricius (2004), *A Short Introduction to Psychoanalysis*, London: Sage.

'Misa en Palermo contra la oferta de sexo en la calle', *Clarín*, 29 June 1998; http://www.clarin.com/diario/1998/06/29/e-03801d.htm (accessed 15 August 2006).

Mitchell, J. (2003), *Siblings*, Cambridge: Polity Press.

Mollenkott, V. R. (2001), *Omnigender: A Trans-Religious Approach*, Cleveland, Ohio: Pilgrim Press.

Moltmann, J. (1992), *The Spirit of Life: A Universal Affirmation*, Minneapolis: Fortress Press.

Moore, S. (1996), *God's Gym*, London and New York: Routledge.

Moore, T. (1990), *Dark Eros: The Imagination of Sadism*, Dallas, Tex.: Spring.

Nelson, W. M., ed. (1989), *Diccionario de Historia de la Iglesia*, Miami: Caribe.

Orbach, S. (1993), *Hunger Strike*, Harmondsworth: Penguin.

Origen (1965), *Contra Celsum*, trans. H. E. Chadwick, Cambridge: Cambridge University Press.

Origen (1968), *Commento al Vangelo di Giovanini. A cura di Eugenio Corsini*, Turin: Unione Tipografico-Editrice Torinese.

Paglia, C. (1991), *Sexual Personae*, Harmondsworth: Penguin.

Peterson, S. (1996), 'Freaking Feminism: *The Life and Loves of a She-Devil* and *Nights at the Circus* as Narrative Freak Shows', in R. G. Thomson, ed., *Freakery: Cultural Spectacles of the Extraordinary Body*, New York: New York University Press.

Phillips, J. and L. Stonebridge (1998), *Reading Melanie Klein*, London: Routledge.

Poovey, M. (1995), *Making a Social Body*, Chicago: University of Chicago Press.

Rahner, K. (1970), *The Trinity*, London: Burns & Oates.

Rakestraw, R. V. (1997), 'Becoming Like God: An Evangelical Doctrine of Theosis', *Journal of the Evangelical Theological Society* 40.2, pp. 257–69.

Raphael, M. (1996), *Thealogy and Embodiment: The Post-Patriarchal Reconstruction of Female Sacrality*, Sheffield: Sheffield Academic Press.

Raphael, M. (2000), *Introducing Thealogy: Discourse on the Goddess*, Cleveland, Ohio: Pilgrim Press.

Reid-Bowen, P. (2007), *Goddess as Nature: Towards a Philosophical Thealogy*, Aldershot: Ashgate.

Rich, A. (1977), *Of Woman Born*, London: Virago.

Ruether, R. R. (1983), *Sexism and God-Talk: Toward a Feminist Theology*, Boston: Beacon Press.

Russo, M. (1994), *The Female Grotesque: Risk, Excess, and Modernity*, London: Routledge.

Scarry, E. (1985), *The Body in Pain*, Oxford: Oxford University Press.

Schussler-Fiorenza, E. (1999), *Jesus: Miriam's Child, Sophia's Prophet: Critical Issues in Feminist Christology*, New York: Continuum.

Schussler-Fiorenza, E. (2000), *In Memory of Her: A Feminist Theological Reconstruction of Christian Origins*, New York: Crossroad.

Scott, J. M. (2003), 'A Question of Identity: Is Cephas the Same Person as Peter?' *Journal of Biblical Studies* 3.3, pp. 1–20.

Seid, R. (1994), 'Too Close to the Bone: The Historical Context For Women's Obsession with Slenderness', in P. Fallon, M. Katzman and S. Wooley, eds, *Feminist Perspectives on Eating Disorders*, New York: Guilford Press, pp. 3–16.

Shapiro, J. (1991), 'Transsexualism: Reflections on the Persistence of Gender and the Mutability of Sex', in J. Epstein and K. Straub, eds, *Body Guards: The Cultural Politics of Gender Ambiguity*, London: Routledge, pp. 248–79.

Showalter, E. (1990), *Sexual Anarchy: Gender and Culture at the Fin de Siècle*, London: Viking.

Shute, J. (1992), *Life-Size*, London: Minerva.

Silver, A. K. (2002), *Victorian Literature and the Anorexic Body*, Cambridge: Cambridge University Press.

Slesinski, R. (1984), *Pavel Florensky: A Metaphysics of Love*, New York: St Vladimir's Seminary Press.

Stewart, S. (1993), *On Longing: Narratives of the Miniature, the Gigantic, the Souvenir, the Collection*, Durham, NC: Duke University Press.

Tannen, D. (1994), *Gender and Discourse*, Oxford: Oxford University Press.

Tanner, L. (1994), *Intimate Violence: Reading Rape and Torture in Twentieth-Century Fiction*, Bloomington: Indiana University Press.

Thomson, R. G., ed. (1996), *Freakery: Cultural Spectacles of the Extra-ordinary Body*, New York: New York University Press.

Truth, Sojourner (1997), 'Ain't I a Woman?' in K. Conboy, N. Medina and S. Stanbury, eds, *Writing on the Body: Female Embodiment and Feminist Theory*, New York: Columbia University Press, pp. 231–2.

Ward, G. (2004), 'On the Politics of Embodiment and the Mystery of All Flesh', in M. Althaus-Reid and L. Isherwood, eds, *The Sexual Theologian: Essays on Sex, God and Politics*, London: T & T Clark, pp. 71–85.

Warner, M. (1994), *From the Beast to the Blonde: On Fairy Tales and their Tellers*, London: Chatto & Windus.

Weldon, F. (1983), *The Life and Loves of a She Devil*, London: Sceptre.

Welsh, L. (2002), *The Cutting Room*, Edinburgh: Canongate.

West, V. [Beth Westbrook] (2003), 'Secret Identity', in Mary Boenke, ed., *Trans Forming Families: Real Stories About Transgendered Loved Ones*, 2nd edn, Hardy, Va.: Oak Knoll Press, p. 20.

Wigley, M. (1992), 'Untitled: The Housing of Gender', in B. Colomina, ed., *Sexuality and Space*, New York: Princeton Architectural Press, pp. 327–89.

Wolf, N. (1991), *The Beauty Myth*, London: Vintage.

Wolf, N. (1994), 'Hunger', in P. Fallon, M. Katzman and S. Wooley, eds, *Feminist Perspectives on Eating Disorders*, New York: Guilford Press, pp. 94–111.

Wood, C. (1981), *The Pre-Raphaelites*, London: Weidenfeld & Nicolson.

Yarborough, M. '*Ma Vie En Rose*: Transgender, the Child and the Family', http://village.fortunecity.com/carnival/383/ludovic.htm (accessed 5 May 2006).

Zhang, S. 'Gender Rights are Human Rights', report on the *Discussion Panel on Trangender/Intersex Issues* at the 65th Session of the Commission on Human Rights of the United Nations (13 April 2005), http://www.ngochr.org/view/index.php?basic_entity'DOCUMENT&list_ids'545 (accessed 18 August 2006).

Index of Names and Subjects

Mollenkott, Virginia Ramey 81n. 4,
    82n. 4
Moltmann, Jürgen 107n. 35
Mondeville, Henri De 32
Monroe, Marilyn (film star) 183
Montreuil, Mme de (mother-in-law of
    Marquis de Sade) 15
Moore, Stephen 213
Moore, Thomas 16, 25
moral order, transcendency rejected
    in Sade's works 9
mother-child relationships 14, 15–16,
    17, 23–4
motherhood 23n. 24, 33
mothers
    abandonment as rite of passage
        64–5
    annihilating mothers 22–5
    self-sacrifice in the Shoah 149n. 92
    sufferings of, as depicted in Sade's
        writings 7–8, 9–10, 13–14, 16
    violence against, as depicted in
        Sade's writings 17–22
Mount Carmel 168
mouths, significance 179
Müllner, Ilsa 162
Musafar, Fakir 57, 59
muscularity, regarded as incompatible
    with femininity 215, 216–17, 221
mutilation, and restoration 4
mutilative hermeneutics 75
mystical Islamic healers, self-harming
    practices 49–50

Naboth, vineyard 169
Nature
    processes represented by the mother
        17
    Sade's views 9, 20
Nazis
    appropriation of the swastika 151
    attrocities in the Shoah depicted in
        drawings and paintings 137
    calculations of calorific intakes for
        sustenance of human functioning in
        concentration camps 186

cruelty 149n. 92
    patriarchal masculine norms and
        behaviours 135
    scapegoating of the Jews 141
Nelson, James 134, 188
Nestorius 105n. 30
'New Flesh' scene, self-harming 50
Nicaea, Council (AD 325) 104
Nicholson, Chris 62
No fatties in heaven (website) 194–5
Nonnus, Bishop 70, 71
normality, and psychopathology 16
norms, reiteration 113–14

obesity 181
object relations theory 14
Oedipus complex 19
Omri (king of Israel) 168, 170
Orbach, Susie 205, 209
Origen 106n. 32, 106n. 33
Ortlund, Annem 197
other/ing, discursive and material
    technologies of 90–1
out-of-body experiences 57
'outside', notion of 44–5
Overeaters Anonymous 184
Overeaters Victorious programme
    189

Paglia, Camille 11n. 6
Painted Birds 222
Palermo (Buenos Aires) 94
'passing' 99
Patchett, Ruth (Weldon, *Life and
    Loves of a She Devil*) 30, 33–8, 44,
    45
patriarchy
    attitudes to feminism 222–3
    Christianity's challenge to 200–1
    effects of women's entering into the
        male world 205–6
    ideologies sustained by dualism 2
    sanctions male violence against
        women 132, 133–4, 136, 138–9
    suppression of women 172–3
Paul, St (apostle) 85, 103, 106n. 32

depiction of the sufferings of
  mothers 7-8, 9-10, 13-14, 16,
  17-22
as guide to psychosexual
  development 25-6
Juliette 22
Misfortunes of Virtue, The 18-19
mother-child relationships 17
Philosophy in the Boudoir 19
portrayal of the maternal 4
psycho-sexual development 14-16
psychoanalysis of 10-12, 13-14
Sadeian universe 8-9
sadism 21
saints 49, 70-1
salvation 153
  as affected by Jesus Christ's
    maleness 110, 112
  Christian understanding of 179
Samaritans, self-harming statistics 50
Sartre, Jean-Paul 18
scar tissue 52-3
'secret selves' 30
Seid, Roberta 182
self 32
self-definition, through beauty rituals
  40
self-harming 4, 48, 83n. 6
  adolescents' use 50, 51-2, 62, 65
  atonement theories 53-4
  cutting in 58-60, 62, 64-5
  expressions of 54-6
  as inverted aggression 66
  religious evidence for 49-50
  as rite of passage 51-3, 56-7
  rituals 56, 57, 59-60
  statistics 50
  witnessing to 56-64, 66-7
sensuous enjoyment, Christian
  attitudes to 176-7
sexism, in the diet industry 199
sexual abuse 144-5, 145n. 67
  see also abused women
sexual difference, corporeal givenness
  211
sexual identities 4, 78

sexuality 12, 14, 15
sexualization, women's body-building
  216, 217
shamans, self-harming 50
Shamblin, Gwen 191-4, 196-7, 199
Shapiro, Judith 81n. 4, 99n. 24
Shekinah 107n. 35, 153n. 105
shelter, privation 83n. 6
Shengold, Leonard 59n. 14
Shillito, Edward, 'Jesus of the scars'
  63-4
Shiloh 164, 166
Shoah *see* Holocaust
Showalter, Carol 189
Showalter, Elaine 30
shredded, concept 208
Shute, Jenefer
  Life Size 29, 30-1, 32, 33, 36
    on Barbie dolls' cultural
      significance 41
    bodily perceptions in 45
    fashion in 37-8
    modelling in 39-40
    on perception of bodies 42-3, 44
sinfulness, and fatness 187-9, 191-4,
  206
skin 53
  penetration of 4
sliced, concept 208
'Slim for Him' programmes 5, 174,
  178
slimming industries, religious
  justification 174-6, 178
Snow White 43
soliciting, regulation of in Argentina
  93-4
Solomon (king of Judah), marriages
  167
soul, and body 35-6
'Soul Murder' 59n. 14
Soviet territories, Holocaust ignored
  141
spiritual empowerment, and women's
  bodybuilding 221-4
Sportsteacher 84n. 7

Index of Bible References